BJ Kr

C........ ..
the Natural
Environment

'Nature to be commanded must be obeyed'
Francis Bacon

Longman Group UK Limited,
Longman House, Burnt Mill, Harlow,
Essex CM20 2JE, England
and Associated companies throughout the world.

First published 1989
Second impression 1990

Set in 10/12 point Palatino
Produced by Longman Singapore Publishers Pte Ltd
Printed in Singapore

ISBN 0 582 35597 4

British Library Cataloguing in Publication Data

Knapp, Brian, 1946–
    The challenge of the natural environment.
    —(Longman advanced geography).
    1. Physical geography
    I. Title   II. Ross, S.R.J. (Simon R.J.)
    III. McCrae, Duncan
    910'.02

Contents

Preface

An earthquake in Mexico kills thousands and costs millions of pounds; a typhoon in Bangladesh costs thousands more lives and leaves hundreds of thousands homeless; drought hits the Sahel and tips the fragile land into a pit of misery and despair, destroying the culture and well-being of whole peoples....

This seemingly endless list of 'natural' disasters may be your first conscious encounter with the effects of the environment, the forces that shape the natural world. But people are dealing successfully with problems due to the environment every day; there are thousands of valuable reservoirs, millions of hectares of profitable farmland, and tens of millions of homes built with the assurance that they will remain secure. All this is achieved with the help of a store of knowledge from generations of scientists, engineers, farmers and many others.

Today in our ever more complex world, where technology seems capable of overcoming all, there is still a vital need to work with the environment and not against it. An increasing number of people find great personal satisfaction in understanding how the natural world evolves, while many find it an indispensable part of their work.

This book has two aims: (i) to show you how natural processes shape the environment that we live in; and (ii) to show you how this knowledge can be put into action for the benefit both of humankind and the survival of the natural environment. So, whether you want to be a researcher, an engineer, help an international aid agency, become a planner, a farmer, an architect or a judge, if you are intending to be an environmental protester or simply have a love of understanding how things work, this is a book that will help fulfil these aims. The knowledge that we have gained and the help that we have received have been generously given by many people in both the developed and the developing world. To all these people who have become our friends we would like to express our sincere appreciation.

Brian Knapp, Simon Ross and
Duncan McCrae 1989

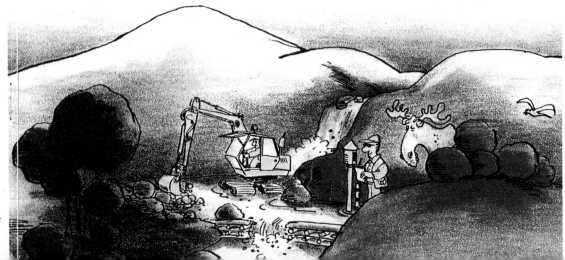

Theme: The geological challenge

'Civilisation exists by geological consent, subject to change without notice.'

Chapter 1
Plate tectonics

Introduction

'As solid as a rock' is a commonly used expression. But study of the earth's surface has shown that rock can be far from solid. This chapter focuses on crustal movements and their effects on people through the concept of **plate tectonics.**

Figure 1.1 shows the earth's surface as a patchwork of plates and their relative movements. Plate margins can be zones of great activity due to sliding, colliding and spreading effects. Earthquakes and volcanoes are frequent geological occurrences at plate margins (Fig. 1.1) and they frequently cause massive

Figure 1.1 *The global distribution of earthquakes, volcanoes and regions of high population density*

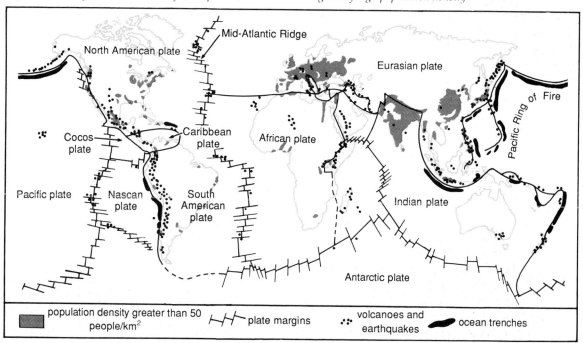

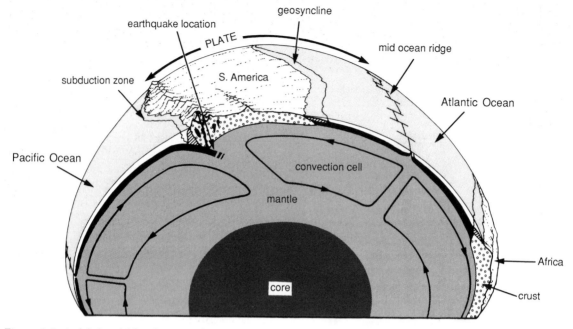

Figure 1.2 *A global model for plate tectonics*

and often instantaneous destruction of both the natural and the man-made environment. They trigger off a whole range of secondary effects such as tsunamis, landslides and even climatic alteration.

In places where plate margins coincidentally underlie areas of dense population, their intense and potentially catastrophic activity requires very careful study.

The structure of the earth

The earth is composed of concentric shells of rock-like materials (Fig. 1.2). The inner shells have little direct influence on activity at the surface except as the source region for magnetism. Of particular interest, however, is the upper part of the mantle. It contains only a small percentage of liquid, but this is sufficient to enable the layer to deform plastically under stress.

The upper mantle supports the thin surface crust and is most directly crucial to the nature and distribution of both earthquakes and volcanoes. The crust is cold, constantly losing heat to space, while the lower mantle is constantly

heated by internal nuclear activity (radioactive decay). Great temperature contrasts across the outer mantle initiate **convection currents** which cause the rock constantly to overturn. Where currents well up to the surface, hot mantle rock flows into the crust, bulging it up then splitting it apart. These upwellings are the sources of the **fissure volcanoes** that tear the great oceans asunder. They construct undersea volcanoes whose tips sometimes appear as islands of fire like Iceland. But such upwellings must be balanced by downturning currents, and the cells must be completed by vast horizontal flows. It is inconceivable that such lateral flows, involving immense movements of the upper mantle, could occur without a complementary movement of the thin crust. And indeed, such a conveyor belt effect has been identified in many oceans (Fig. 1.2).

The magma that flows out from the oceanic rifts quickly solidifies as **lava sheets** and **dykes**. While it is still thin it loses heat rapidly causing some of the underlying magma to solidify also. In this manner the crust thickens by **underplating**, much as ice thickens on a lake in winter. Soon, the oceanic crust is old, hard, thick and brittle. It is no longer subject to disruption,

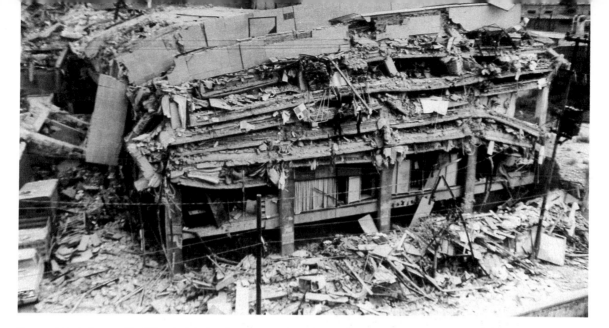

Figure 1.3 *A shattered building in Mexico City*

rather it moves quiescently on the unseen mantle conveyor.

Along the outer (trench) margins, where the ocean crust is no longer malleable, convection currents drag the crust back towards the mantle and begin the gradual process of remelting. The crust resists, foundering and scraping against the edge of the adjacent plate and creating friction in the collision region which is called a **subduction zone**.

These places of downturning mantle currents are clearly reflected in the crust. In their most dramatic form they occur as arcuate **trenches** marginal to the great oceans. The Pacific is ringed with such oceanic trenches, the deepest places on earth. They are also places where earthquake and volcanic activity are concentrated, hence the expression 'Pacific Ring of Fire' used to describe this circum-Pacific distribution (Fig. 1.1).

Geologists have used both earthquake and volcanic eruption data while formulating the theory of plate tectonics. Using fossil magnetism they have successfully traced the movement of the plates for over 500 million years and they are now able to predict plate movements – a crucial step in the process of earthquake and volcano prediction. Plate tectonic theory has therefore been an important stage in helping people cope with geological hazards.

Earthquakes

Earthquakes can last for several minutes, during which time the ground shakes violently and people become disoriented. On 20 September 1985 a magnitude 7.8 earthquake occurred in the Pacific Ocean 400 km from Mexico City as the Cocos plate slipped at a depth of 20 km, shifting a 200 km slab of crust 2 m eastward in two bursts some 26 seconds apart. It was early morning (Fig. 1.3).

> 'It was like the end of the world. As we were coming down the staircase (from the eighth floor of a hotel) it was swaying.'
>
> 'Buildings were swaying like ships' sails, firing out tiles and glass everywhere.'
>
> 'The building was weaving back and forth, and surely I thought it was coming down on us. We left the car with everything in it. Then we had to hold on to a tree because the ground was shaking so bad.'

In the devastation of Mexico City at least 4000 people died over 400 km away from the epicentre. It is especially notable that the modern 52 story Pemex building in central Mexico City, constructed to resist earthquake tremors, stood undamaged amidst a sea of destruction, but so did the centuries-old massive stone structure of the Metropolitan Cathedral (built before any

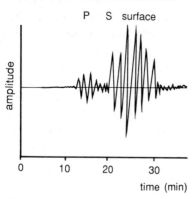

Figure 1.4a

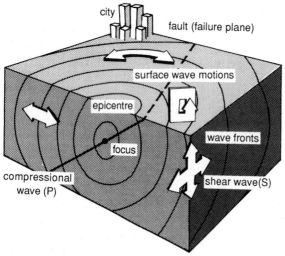

Figure 1.4b *The pattern of waves in an earthquake. Little warning is given by the arrival of P waves*

Why earthquakes cause damage

The immense frictional drag between plates in subduction zones causes movement to take place in a series of periodic jerks. Thus a long quiescent period, during which time the pressure builds to irresistible proportions, is followed by a sudden localised adjustment (an earthquake) as the pressure is released (Fig. 1.4a).

However, pressure may not be relieved by one simple movement as local slipping may impose excessive pressure elsewhere. In consequence an initial earthquake is commonly

Table 1.1 Modified Mercalli Intensity Scale of 1931

1 Not felt except by a very few under especially favourable circumstances.

2 Felt only by a few persons at rest, especially on upper floors of buildings. Delicately suspended objects may swing.

3 Felt quite noticeably indoors, especially on upper floors of buildings, but many people do not recognise it as an earthquake. Standing automobiles may rock slightly. Vibration like passing of truck. Duration estimated.

4 During the day felt indoors by many, outdoors by few. At night some awakened. Dishes, windows, doors disturbed; walls make cracking sound. Sensation like heavy truck striking building. Standing automobiles rocked noticeably.

5 Felt by nearly everyone, many awakened. Some dishes, windows, etc. broken; a few instances of cracked plaster; unstable objects overturned. Disturbances of trees, poles, and other tall objects sometimes noticed. Pendulum clocks may stop.

6 Felt by all, many frightened and run outdoors. Some heavy furniture moved; a few instances of fallen plaster or damaged chimneys. Damage slight.

7 Everybody runs outdoors. Damage negligible in buildings of good design and construction; slight to moderate in well-built ordinary structures; considerable in poorly built or badly designed structures; some chimneys broken. Noticed by persons driving automobiles.

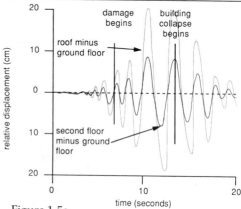

Figure 1.5a

Figure 1.5b (right) *Ground motion is amplified by tall buildings, even those designed to resist earthquake effects. The Imperial County Services building moved 18cm in one direction then 19cm in the opposite direction one second later. Similarly, up and down motions hammer the building into the ground causing buckling of supporting reinforced concrete columns*

thought of hazard mitigation) and most of the shanty structures put up by poor people.

8   Damage slight in specially designed structures; considerable in ordinary substantial buildings with partial collapse; great in poorly built structures. Panel walls thrown out of frame structures. Fall of chimneys, factory stacks, columns, monuments, walls. Heavy furniture overturned. Sand and mud ejected in small amounts. Changes in well water. Persons driving automobiles disturbed.

9   Damage considerable in specially designed structures; well-designed frame structures thrown out of plumb; great in substantial buildings, with partial collapse. Buildings shifted off foundations. Ground cracked conspicuously. Underground pipes broken.

10   Some well-built wooden structures destroyed; most masonry and frame structures destroyed with foundations; ground badly cracked. Rails bent. Landslides considerable from river banks and steep slopes. Shifted sand and mud. Water splashed (slopped) over banks.

11   Few, if any structures remain standing. Bridges destroyed. Broad fissures in ground. Underground pipelines completely out of service. Earth slumps and land slips in soft ground. Rails bent greatly.

12   Damage total. Practically all works of construction are damaged greatly or destroyed. Waves seen on ground surface. Lines of sight and level are distorted. Objects are thrown upward into the air.

(US Geological Survey)

followed by several **aftershocks** during the succeeding days, weeks and months, as the regional stresses are redistributed.

An earthquake begins as a rip in the earth's crust which, just like a pebble thrown into a pond, transfers the initial energy of motion into sets of travelling waves (Fig. 1.4b). The most important of these waves are those that reach the ground surface near to the earthquake **focus** (at a place called the **epicentre**) and then travel outward, shaking the ground violently until the energy has been dissipated. The waves are complex in nature and have up and down (vertical), side to side (transverse), and to and fro (horizontal) motions. As a result the ground moves violently in three dimensions.

Slippage normally starts from a well defined point (called the focus, usually located some tens of kilometres below the surface) and extends rapidly along the **failure plane** much like the rip that follows the snagging of a piece of cloth. The initial slip may be only a few kilometres or tens of kilometres long, but the direct **shock waves** (actual ground disturbance sufficient to cause a noticeable shaking) created by its movement may stretch for a radius of hundreds of kilometres. Sensitive detectors will pick up a major quake on the other side of the globe. The intensity of earthquake shocks is measured on the Richter scale (Fig. 1.8; Table 1.1). The Richter scale is a logarithmic scale, each increase of one unit of magnitude being a tenfold increase in intensity of effective vibration.

Damage by earthquakes results from the triggering off of four hazardous processes:
(a) ground shaking;
(b) liquefaction;
(c) landslides; and
(d) tsunamis.

(a) Ground shaking hazard

Ground shaking becomes a hazard when the earthquake shock waves are transmitted directly into man-made structures. Structures can pick up and even amplify all of the three types of transmitted vibration. For example, in the 1979 Imperial Valley California earthquake severe damage was caused to a six story building both because it shook from side to side by 37 cm in

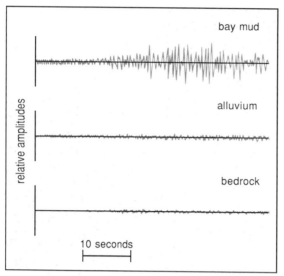

Figure 1.6 *Exaggerated ground shaking occurs with some unconsolidated materials, especially muds and other water-filled sediments*

Figure 1.7 (right) *A massive landslide caused by an earthquake blocks a road in California*

one second (dislodging the floors one from another) and also because it vibrated up and down (causing column failure) (Fig. 1.5).

It is important to note that direct **ground displacement** (i.e. a rip of the ground surface along the fault line) affects only a long narrow zone (perhaps less than 300 m wide) whose total area is small compared with the other effects. When ground shaking plays a major part in building collapse this is due to special characteristics of the deposits on which the structures are built. In particular, the intensity of shaking in certain frequency bands can be amplified by thick deposits of unconsolidated materials such as alluvial muds of rivers, old lake beds and coastal marshes (Fig. 1.6). The maximum amplitudes recorded at sites underlain by coastal mud are eight times larger than those recorded on nearby bedrock sites.

(b) Liquefaction

Liquefaction is common in saturated clay-free sediments such as sands and silts. During a tremor the shear waves shake the sediment and it begins to consolidate. If the water cannot get away during consolidation the water pressure increases dramatically and may become sufficient to balance the weight of the column of sediment. At this stage the saturated sediment behaves as a liquid. This 'quicksand' behaviour causes (i) **lateral spreading** of sediment, e.g. towards river channels or coasts; (ii) **flow failure** on slopes over about 3°; (iii) **loss of bearing strength** allowing buildings to founder and often tip over.

(c) Landslides

Landslides are discussed in detail in Chapter 5. However, slope stability can be upset by tremors. The result depends on the local circumstances.

(i) If the slope material is of weakly consolidated and saturated sands and silts it can cause liquefaction as described above. This initiates a mudslide or a mudflow.

(ii) Dry unconsolidated material can be shaken sufficiently for frictional contact to be lost. This can result in a rock fall or rock avalanche.

(iii) With soil over rock subject to vibration, shallow slides occur; with deeply weathered

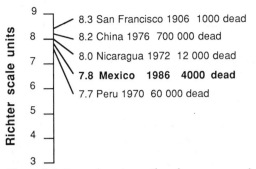

Figure 1.8 *Example major earthquakes as measured on the Richter scale*

Figure 1.9 *An ancient earthquake revealed as a fault in a road cutting*

materials, whole masses move as rotational slips (Fig. 1.7).

Landslides become a hazard in areas with many steep slopes. Buildings can be buried by slides or smashed to pieces by rock avalanches. Buildings on top of slopes can have their foundations undermined and then founder. In the San Francisco region of California, the greatest hazard is from landslides initiated by ground vibration.

(d) Tsunamis

A tsunami is a large simple ocean wave caused by a sudden movement of the sea bed as tremors reach the crustal surface during the earthquake. Tsunamis in the deep ocean are insignificant, usually no more than a few tens of centimetres in height. However, they have a long wavelength (often 100 km; see Waves, Chapter 6), and therefore they grow in amplitude as they reach shallow water. Typical tsunamis grow to 20 or 30m as they approach the coast. They are sometimes referred to as tidal waves. They have too long a wavelength to break up and lose energy as surf; instead they rush onshore, often penetrating over a kilometre inland.

Tsunamis can cause great loss of life. Their effects include structural damage to buildings, scouring of foundations, flooding, and inland transport of large quantities of debris.

Management in earthquake-prone areas

The toll from earthquakes can be horrendous (Fig. 1.8). A quake in Tangshan in China in 1976 cost the lives of perhaps 700 000 people and made millions more homeless. Such large earthquakes are not uncommon and many this century have even exceeded the strength of the earthquake which, in 1906, initiated the destruction of much of San Francisco.

Evidence of past quakes abounds: they are revealed by the myriad faults that crisscross every part of the world and are sometimes exposed at the shore or in road cuttings (Fig. 1.9). Almost all historic surface faulting has taken place along faults that have been recently (last 2 million years) active. So the prediction of risk areas is based on identifying these active

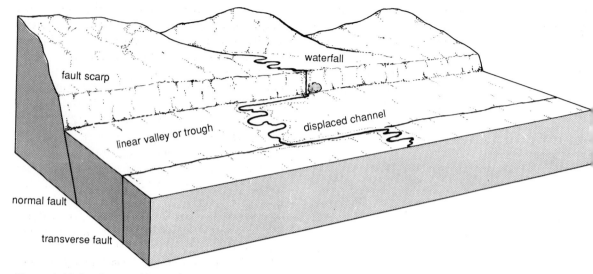

Figure 1.10 *Landscape evidence of active faults*

faults using both geology and landscape evidence (Fig. 1.10).

Although, within fairly broad limits, areas liable to suffer from earthquake damage can be identified, predicting the timing of an earthquake is far harder. It has recently been found that the decay pattern of waves produced by small tremors can give clues. A wave trace from a small tremor which is not going to be followed by a major slip fades slowly, like the sonorous fading of a church bell. But this coda (signature) changes when stresses within the rocks are high. In this case the trace rapidly dampens, much like a bell that has a crack. However, until further progress can be made people must rely on coping with earthquakes that occur without warning.

Buildings can now be designed to withstand a certain degree of motion but it is not economically possible to build a completely earthquake proof structure. The problem is that most building designs tend to amplify the ground motion (Fig. 1.11) However, the remedy is not as simple as restricting building heights, for tall buildings are prone to vibrations of one frequency while low buildings are prone to vibrations of a different frequency.

Old tall buildings that have not been built to earthquake resistant standards pose the biggest threat. The choices are (i) strengthen the struc-

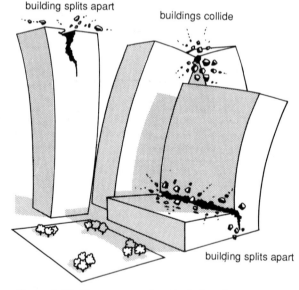

Figure 1.11 *The response of poorly designed structures to ground shaking*

ture; (ii) reduce the intensity of use (e.g. office to warehouse); (iii) demolish. All three solutions are expensive. For future buildings, planning can help (i) avoid areas of greatest risk from shaking or displacement; (ii) zone land for low density use in high risk areas; (iii) use earthquake resistant designs; and (iv) get insurance.

It is impractical to align services such as water pipes, electricity and gas cables to avoid fault lines. Ruptures of these services could be a major hazard, starting fires just as they did in San Francisco in 1906.

Planning to reduce the earthquake hazard

With the knowledge of processes gained above, let us reassess the nature of the Mexican earthquake and find out what were the main causes of the disaster. The long distance (400 km) that the waves travelled had a filtering effect. Mainly low frequency waves reached the city and these happened to correspond to the natural vibration frequency of many of the highrise buildings. As a result many of these were damaged, but low buildings (and even poorly constructed low buildings) remained mostly intact. Furthermore, because the city is set on what were once peats and silts of lakes and marshes, the unconsolidated material amplified the vibration. Shaking caused the wet ground to lose strength by liquefaction. Indeed, many of the buildings toppled over because of ground failure rather than direct shaking. With motion in three dimensions the effect was like shaking a bowl of jelly.

The extensive damage was caused by the unfortunate coincidence of all these factors (Fig. 1.12).

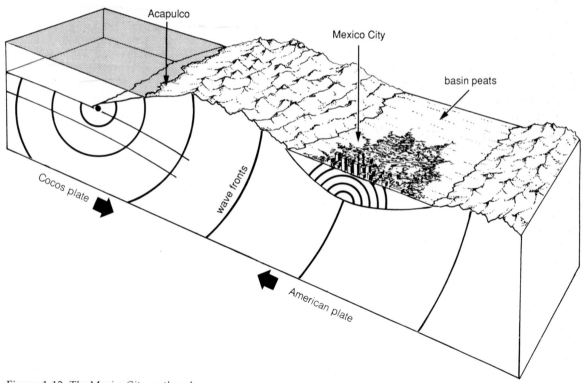

Figure 1.12 *The Mexico City earthquake*

> **Student enquiry 1A:
> Decision-making to alleviate the
> worst effects of the next earthquake
> in the San Francisco area**

The San Francisco Bay region lies astride one of the world's most famous and active faults: the San Andreas tear fault (Datafile 1). You will be asked to help in planning a strategy designed to alleviate a future disaster. For this you will need to study all the data sources given.

A1(a)

Datafile 1
Experience – what happened in 1906

On 19 April 1906 a magnitude 8.3 earthquake resulted in the loss of 700 lives and cost £400 milion (1906 value). The amount of the damage in each area of San Francisco was strongly dependent on ground geology. In the Telegraph Hill region, where rock is exposed to the surface, the effects of the earthquake were weak, with only the occasional fall of a chimney for example. But less than 0.5 km away, in an area underlain by artificial fill and water-saturated sediment, the effects were violent, with general collapse of buildings. However, the main impact was the generation of large numbers of landslides and the fracturing of many service lines. Gas lines ruptured and gas was ignited by sparks from broken electricity cables, while fractured water mains meant that the fire department was not able to cope with the consequent fires. Destroyed roads on the line of the ground rupture and extensive landslides across roads made access to areas difficult.

THE SAN FRANCISCO EARTHQUAKE.

THE TERRIBLE STORY OF DISASTER.

OAKLAND, CALIFORNIA, APRIL 19

The damage done at San Francisco by the fire which followed the earthquake renders the disaster one of the most serious in the history of the country. The first earthquake at 5.15 yesterday morning lasted about two minutes. It caused the collapse of many structures throughout the city and burst the water mains, and was followed by numerous outbreaks of fire. Five minutes later a slightly less violent shock was felt and after an interval of three hours there was still another. A final shock of brief duration was experienced shortly before 7 o'clock in the evening.

Every bulletin from the stricken city shows that the loss of life and damage to property were under-estimated in the earlier reports, which gave no real idea of the extent of the calamity. All day long dense smoke rose over the city, and spreading out in the shape of an immense funnel was visible for miles out to sea. Early this morning the flames were still raging uncontrolled and it looked as if the whole city was doomed.

During the night the fire spread into the residential districts, and the panic-stricken people rushed out of their homes carrying with them their portable valuables. Crowds took refuge in the parks and public squares, which were brilliantly lighted up by the glare in the sky. This was the only illuminant, there being no gas or electric light. Some of the refugees possessed tents, but the most of them had no shelter whatever, and huddled in frightened groups around their few household belongings. The business section suffered most severely during the day...

The Palace Hotel fell prey to flames, and the Claus Sprockel building was gutted. The Rialto building and dozens of other structures were also demolished. All the best playhouses, including the Majestic, the Columbia, and the Orpheus theatres, and the Grand Opera House collapsed, the debris in all cases catching fire. The Opera House contained the scenery of the Conried Opera Company and the private property of the players. In spite of the efforts of the firemen, the flames spread right across Market-street to the north side and swept up to Montgomery-Street almost as far as Washington-street. Along Montgomery-street are some of the richest banks and commercial houses in San Francisco. The famous Mills building and the Merchants Exchange, in which the Marine and Stock Exchanges are situated, are still standing, but the Mutual Life Assurance building and scores of other bank and office buildings are on fire. The earthquake partially wrecked the California Hotel, and its falling chimney and cornice crashed through the adjoining fire station, so severely injuring Mr. Sullivan the chief of the fire brigade, that he was unable to direct the work of fighting the flames, and had ultimately to be conveyed to hospital where he lies in a precarious condition.

The Fire Department, assisted by a detachment of the Oakland Brigade and many volunteers from outside, did yeoman service. Most of the mains having burst, the firemen were for the most part without water, except on the front, where supplies were pumped from the bay.

By 9 o'clock yesterday morning General Funston had 1,000 Federal troops guarding the streets and assisting the firemen in blowing up houses. The General recognised that stern measures were necessary, and he accordingly ordered the shooting of all looters. Four culprits were summarily shot before 3 o'clock in the afternoon. *The Times*

Clues emerge on quake damage to buildings

From Dan Williams in Mexico City

In the exposed skeletons of fallen buildings in the devastated areas of Mexico City, engineers are finding clues to a mystery: why did some seemingly sound buildings fall during the earthquakes and others, right alongside, remain standing?

Full answers could take weeks or even months, but important early signs are emerging, even while some of the evidence is being swept away as rubble.

In some cases, materials were used that were too weak for the size of structure, US engineers said. In others, supports between columns were missing or were too weak to absorb the lateral movement of the buildings caused by the earthquake and the aftershocks that followed. In such cases, the columns took the full burden of shifting weight and crumbled.

Still other buildings went up before advances were made in seismic-resistant construction techniques. Some engineers speculate that the already soft ground beneath many buildings — much of Mexico City rests on an ancient lake bed — was weakened by the construction of the city's extensive subway system.

Mr William Stone of the US Bureau of Standards said: "The damage depended a lot on what kind of ground the buildings were founded on. Of course, on soft ground precautions should have been taken about what kind of building to construct."

Many of the damaged buildings he had inspected were 25 to 40 years old and lacked advanced seismic-resistant design, he said. Many were taller than eight stories, and therefore tended to sway sharply in the tremor on September 19, which measured 8.1 on the Richter scale.

At the collapsed Bancomer bank building, an engineer pointed to a spaghetti-like tangle of steel rods that reinforce the concrete columns. "They're tiny," he said. "Much too weak for the size of the building, which is eight or nine floors."

Each floor of the Bancomer building collapsed like a stack of pancakes. This phenomenon was common.

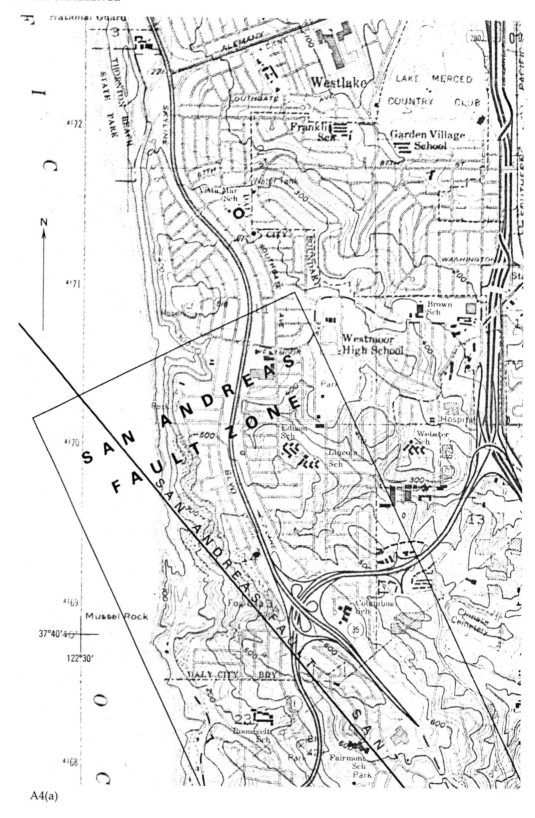

A4(a)

A4(b)

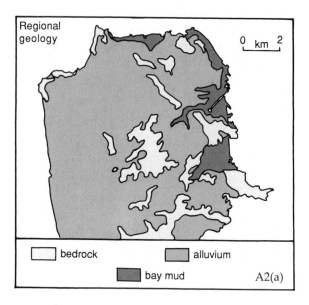

Regional geology

bedrock
bay mud
alluvium

A2(a)

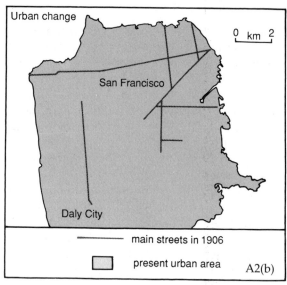

Urban change

San Francisco

Daly City

—— main streets in 1906
present urban area

A2(b)

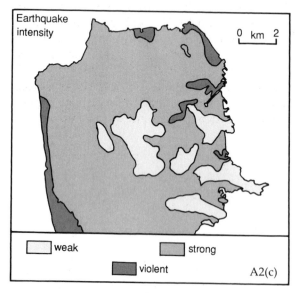

Earthquake intensity

weak
violent
strong

A2(c)

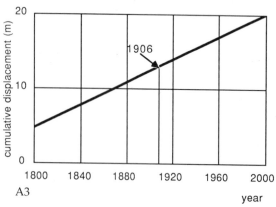

A3

Historic changes since 1906

The San Francisco Bay area contains a population of 5.4 million. More than half of the people have arrived since 1950. The inflow of newcomers and the migration of city dwellers to more pleasant neighbouring suburban counties, has imposed changing requirements for housing and public services. The demand has been met by new construction in existing towns and suburbs and by extensive development of nearby rural areas. Most of the established communities were originally located on gently sloping, well-drained alluvial plains. As development spread outward, however, the builders were faced with more difficult terrain and site conditions. As ridge crests, hillsides and marshes were converted to residential and commercial uses, an array of costly and unfamiliar problems harassed builders, homeowners and public officials alike.

Because the last major earthquake in the San Francisco region was in 1906 there has been reduced awareness of the hazard. Housing estates, schools and hospitals have been built over or near the three largest active faults. Along the same faults, dams and reservoirs loom over towns in the plains below. In the cities many tall buildings were designed to meet codes that seriously underestimated the intensity of earthquake effects and some buildings even pre-date the first building codes.

The planning problem

Enquiry 1A provides the sort of information that would be available to a planner. The object of the study is to produce the report detailed in question 7. The steps required to obtain the information for this report form the basis of questions 1–6. While you do not have to write down answers to all these questions, it is important that you have considered each one because they provide the structured approach needed to see this problem through.

1. Make a careful study of the description and photograph of the 1906 earthquake (A1) and also that in Mexico City given on page 15. Describe the effects of the earthquake, the damage caused, etc. Outline the aspects that you feel would be of value to planners responsible for the future growth of San Francisco.

2. Describe the physical growth of the San Francisco area since 1906 (A2).

3. With careful reference to the maps (A2), and using overlays if you wish, compare and comment on the earthquake intensity and its relationship with geology. Evaluate the extent to which the planners appear to have taken heed of this information in controlling the spread of urbanisation.

4. Refer to the graph which shows the fault displacements that have been measured for the San Andreas Fault to the south of San Francisco (A3), where earthquakes are more common. The last displacement at San Francisco was in 1906. How much catching up is required in the San Francisco region?

5. Comment on the land use in the San Francisco and Daly City areas, comparing it with the terrain, the type of geological foundation and the location of the active fault (A4).

6. In a group discussion, decide which are the most hazardous areas in the Daly City region. Using the maps of Daly City (A4) suggest what problems might arise if an earthquake struck (i) at 8.30 am; or (ii) at 11.00 am.

Enquiry objective

7. Produce, in report form suitable for non-experts, a summary of the hazards from earthquakes and the methods proposed to mitigate them. Use the planning process diagram (A5) to develop a suitable report structure. You will need to set the regional geological scene before you begin to focus on the San Francisco region. Be as thorough as possible in your report.

A5

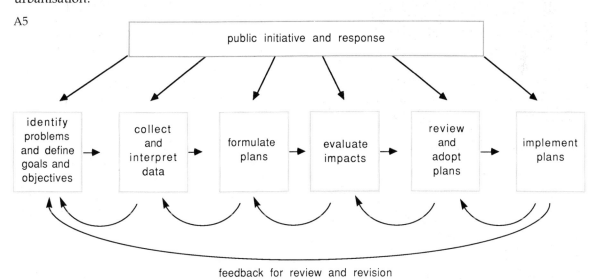

public initiative and response

identify problems and define goals and objectives → collect and interpret data → formulate plans → evaluate impacts → review and adopt plans → implement plans

feedback for review and revision

Ground ruptures due to human activity

There is not much that can be done about major earthquakes except plan to reduce the hazard produced. But it has proved possible for people to initiate earthquakes by their own activities. For example, on 14 December 1963, water burst through the foundation and earth dam of the Baldwin Hills reservoir, a hilltop water storage facility located in metropolitan Los Angeles, USA. The contents of the reservoir, some 950 million litres of treated water that had filled the 9 hectare reservoir to a depth of 20 m, spilled within hours on to the nearby communities, killing one person and damaging or destroying 277 homes.

When the water had subsided a crack could be traced from the dam wall, across the asphalt-lined floor of the reservoir and into the ground on the far side. What had happened was that a geological fault had been reactivated beneath the reservoir. This had slipped in a number of stages, but finally the cumulative displacement of .15 cm was sufficient to crack the dam wall (Fig. 1.13). As the report from the California water department later said, 'sitting on the flank of the sensitive Newport-Inglewood fault system with its associated tectonic restlessness, at the rim of a rapidly depressing subsidence basin, on a foundation that could be adversely influenced by water, this reservoir was called upon to do more than it was able to do'.

Two lawsuits filed in 1966 by the city and its insurers against the oil companies active in the Inglewood oil field at the time of the dam failure charged that the oil field operations had led to the events directly associated with the breaching of the dam. This was because, although the oil field had been exploited since 1924, the oil had begun to run out and, since 1954, the oil company had changed its strategy to one of pumping water into the oilfield in order to force the remaining oil out (a process known as secondary recovery). They charged that the water under pressure had allowed the friction on the fault lines to be relieved and the residual tension that builds up in all faults to be released.

The implications of this type of failure are considerable. Many people have suggested, for

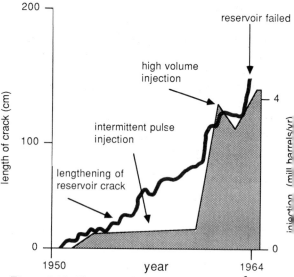

Figure 1.13 *Changes at the Baldwin Hills reservoir*

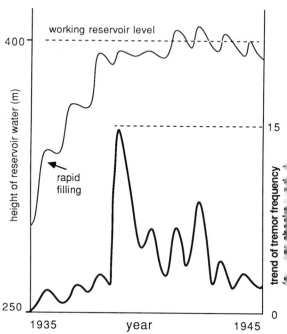

Figure 1.14 *Earthquake activity at the Hoover Dam*

example, that water can be pumped back into aquifers to recharge them during periods of water surplus. In this way they would hope to be able to recover more water for, say, irrigation during periods of peak demand. Similarly, people are contemplating using pressure injection at great depth to dispose of toxic and even radioactive wastes. All of these activities could have serious consequences if attempted in areas with faults. And it is important to notice that the faults do not have to be obviously 'active'.

The Baldwin Hills reservoir was sealed against drainage into the sandy material on which it was built. However, sealing the bed against leakage is totally impractical in any large reservoir. Thus it is possible for water to leak into a region of active faults. In many cases the pressure of this leakage water is insufficient to allow the release of any residual stresses in the fault zones. However, the world's deepest reservoirs do create water pressures sufficient to cause failure. There are many cases of earthquake swarms being generated as large reservoirs were filled. The closure of the Hoover Dam across the River Colorado in the USA and its subsequent rapid filling caused a pattern of earthquakes that began after a certain water depth had been reached and continued to get worse as the dam completed its filling. Earthquake activity only decreased after the reservoir had been filled (Fig. 1.14). Earthquakes with Richter values above 4.2 were recorded. Elsewhere dam failures in India and Italy have all been produced by earthquake activity that only started after the reservoirs began to fill. Tremors are most severe when the reservoir fills quickly and stresses can be relieved rapidly. Clearly the strategy here must be to fill deep reservoirs slowly and allow time for the stresses to be relieved slowly and through minor tremors.

The challenge of geology it not just a catalogue of disasters because people learn from the pattern of mistakes and improve their understanding of the workings of the natural environment. For example, the effects of fluid injection could be put to good use if it were possible slowly to release the stresses building up under San Francisco. If this should prove technically feasible before the inevitable natural adjustment takes place then many lives and much property will have been saved. Unfortunately short term economic advantage is often an overriding feature, as the pattern of San Francisco's expansion and the cartoon at the start of this chapter indicate.

Chapter 2
Volcanoes and volcanic hazards

Introduction

Volcanoes, like earthquakes, are mostly restricted to broad belts following the plate margins (Fig. 1.1). Volcanoes present serious management problems, especially in areas of high density settlement. In developing countries the flanks of volcanoes are often especially attractive because of the fertile soils that form on newly weathered material.

Volcanoes are of two contrasting types:
(a) the lava-dominated types where basalt flows almost like water from extensive fissures at spreading plate boundaries. These occur mostly in the oceans and create islands such as Iceland; and
(b) the ash-dominated explosive volcanoes like Mt St Helens (USA) and El Chichon (Mexico) that throw great clouds of incandescent pyroclastic materials from central vents associated with subduction zones. These explosive volcanoes construct cones mostly on land or on the arcuate strings of islands that parallel the great ocean trenches (e.g. Fuji Yama on the Japanese arc).

Each type of volcano has characteristic chemistry. Fissure volcanoes, dominated by mobile basalt lava flows, contain as little as 45 per cent silica. By contrast, explosive volcanoes tend to eject (andesitic) ash which is light in colour and contains over 60 per cent silica. They eject comparatively little lava.

People sometimes compare the eruption of a volcano with taking the cap off a bottle of fizzy drink. Shake the bottle, open the cap quickly and stand clear. A fountain of gas bubbles and spray immediately bursts out, followed by a stream of cascading froth – the lava in a volcanic eruption rising up from the magma chamber (bottle) deep below.

Volcanoes come in all shapes and sizes, and are built of a variety of materials (Fig. 2.1).

Their size, shape and composition reflect their formative environment and, incidentally, thereby also give clues to the nature of subcrustal activity. Some volcanoes, usually those associated with spreading plate boundaries, don't have cones because their extremely mobile lava issues from long **fissures** and spreads out in sheets. This has been the case with most of Iceland's volcanic features. Occasionally, if the fissure is short, cones build up. Thus, Mauna Loa rises 10 km from the sea bed to form Hawaii (Fig. 2.2). Called a **shield volcano**, it is over 100 km in diameter. Iceland, too, has a few cones amongst its lava sheets.

Volcanoes associated with subduction zones punch holes through the crust and issue as **central vent volcanoes**. Most of the material ejected is actually **pyroclastics** (ash, cinders and other semi-solid material) rather than lava. These explosive eruptions produce the awesome and spectacular events that capture the

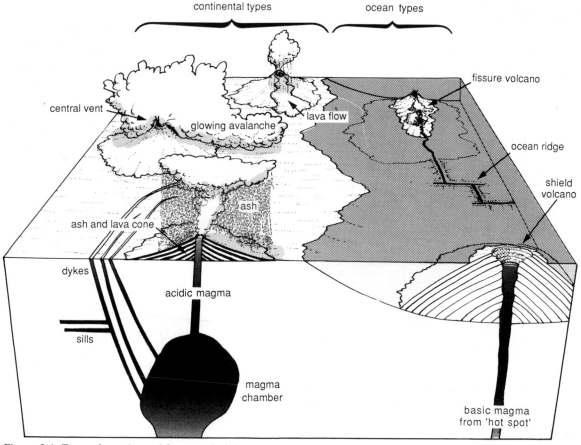

Figure 2.1 *Types of eruption and features of solid magma*

imagination and tell of the immense power that lies beneath an otherwise quiescent crust.

Many volcanoes give notice of intent to erupt. Advance warning signs include:

(a) local streams becoming warmer and having a higher sulphur content;

(b) shallow earthquakes increasing in frequency and beginning to be focused beneath the volcano's route to the surface;

(c) melting of snow and ice;

(d) uncharacteristic animal behaviour; and

(e) in some cases rising magma even forces the cone to **dilate** (bulge out) as was the case for Mt St Helens in 1980 (Fig. 2.3). In this unusual case the dilation on the flanks increased visibly, but more commonly, less spectacular dilation has to be measured by instruments called tiltmeters.

An eruption often tears the top off a central vent volcano, as old solidified lava is ejected

from the vent by the initial explosive escape of magma. In the case of Mt St Helens, over 400 m (measured by subsequent altitude) was blown away. Towards the end of the eruption lava and tephra falling within the area of the vent commonly reforms the cone. The previous time Mt St Helens erupted was 1831, and then it took 26 years of intermittent eruptions to reform an almost perfect cone.

Subduction zone magma probably rises to large balloon-shaped reservoirs which form within the continental crust (and which finally cool to give **plutons** called **batholiths**, the source of granitic materials). From these deep-seated reservoirs columns of acidic magma rise further to form the magma reservoirs that lie at shallow depths in the continental crust and which directly feed continental volcanoes and a multitude of intrusive volcanic forms (Fig. 2.1). When the silica-rich lava eventually reaches

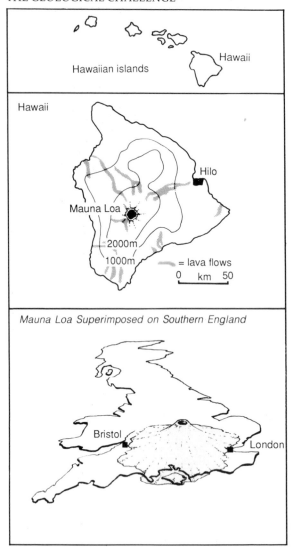

Figure 2.2 *Hawaii, an island tip of a vast submarine volcano. The whole Hawaiian chain of islands is believed to have been formed as the Pacific plate drifted over a stationary hot spot of rising magma. This has produced a succession of holes through the crust*

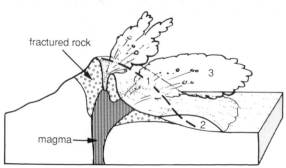

Figure 2.3 *The lateral outrush of hot gas and ash in a nuée ardente*

the surface it is much cooler than basalt (800°C). Both high silica content and low temperature are responsible for the high viscosity. Central vent lavas rarely travel far but instead help to construct the familiar steep-sided cone.

The main product of a central vent volcano is pyroclastic materials. The coarsest, such as cinders, quickly fall back to earth, building at the threshold angle of stability into a steep-sided cone. Only occasionally are they interspersed with significant lava flows. The remaining material drifts away in the troposphere, spreading out as a plume and carried in the direction of the prevailing wind. Ash rains down from this plume, often enveloping a large area.

Parasitic side vents that are forced open when the central vent becomes blocked allow material to be emitted laterally. Under such circumstances a large part of the thrust of the initial explosive eruption sends out a heavy mixture of fine rock, hot gas and steam which rushes down the cone flanks. This event is called a **glowing avalanche** (nuée ardente) and it can travel for several kilometres at speeds of several hundred kilometres an hour. When part of the cone of Mt St Helens collapsed it allowed the eruption from a side vent to produce a glowing avalanche (Fig. 2.3).

Figure 2.4 *The satellite picture shows the way high cloud spread out from Mt St Helens even though its main blast was lateral*

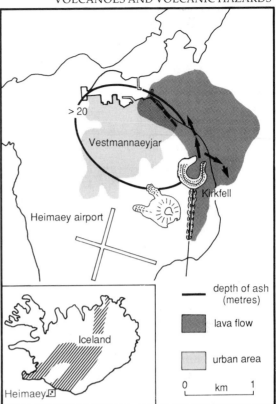

Figure 2.5 *The map of Heimaey has changed considerably with its new peninsula built into the sea*

An initial explosion from the central vent often punches material high into the atmosphere, commonly beyond the troposphere (p. 40) where rain-making processes would gradually wash it out, and into the stratosphere, where it may remain for years, helping to reduce levels of incoming solar radiation (Fig. 2.4). There is historic evidence of poor harvests in the two years following large volcanic eruptions. Thus, although the landscape impact of eruptions is small in terms of area, the climatic implications of an eruption may be of global proportions. Indeed, when El Chichon erupted in Mexico in 1982 its fine ash rapidly spread as globally enveloping high level dust.

Volcanoes as hazard

Explosive volcanic eruptions are rather rare, if spectacular, events. Because of the infrequency of eruption and their grandeur, volcanoes often attract rather than repel people. Tourists like to stand on the rim of a volcanic crater and gaze into the awesome pit; or ski on the snow-clad flanks. Farmers treasure the fertile soils that follow an eruption after a few decades of weathering, and nations see the potential use of hot rock as a source of geothermal energy.

Because the character of eruptions depends on the nature of the lava, volcanic hazard problems are very diverse. Even one volcano can eject a variety of materials. Usually if a volcano erupts frequently it ejects low silica materials that flow down the flanks of the cone. But when there is a longer gap than usual between eruptions the distillation process seems to become more pronounced and the material finally ejected is higher in silica and the volcano much more explosive in character. Keeping close tabs on a volcano, and tracing its eruption history back over the centuries is thus a critical part of hazard planning.

Figures 2.5, 2.6 and 2.7 show some of the results of the eruptions of Heimaey (Iceland), Nevado del Ruiz (Colombia) and Etna (Italy) and give an indication of the major hazards and their causes. Clearly the local authorities have taken contrasting steps prior to and subsequent to the eruptions. This is because they have different cultural, religious and economic circum-

Colombia landslide worst since Krakatoa

20,000 feared dead after volcano erupts

From Tony Jenkins in Bogota

As many as 20,000 people may have died in western Colombia after a long-dormant volcano in the Andes erupted and sent torrents of mud and water flooding the town of Armero.

Dismembered bodies were washed downstream in flood waters stained with sulphur as rescuers struggled to reach the scene. Colombian civil defence units reported that seven villages had also been destroyed.

The busy riverside town of Armero, with a population of 28,000, was devastated before dawn while its inhabitants were sleeping. If early estimates are confirmed the death toll will be the highest from a volcanic eruption since the eruption in Martinique in 1902.

Nevado del Ruiz stands nearly 18,000 feet high in the northern Andes, and its eruption caused an icecap and snow on the peak to melt. Together with torrential rainfall, the water burst the banks of the river La Lagunilla. Two hours after the eruption, the melting snow also sparked an avalanche.

The mud, rocks, and water flooded through Armero and swept away 85 per cent of the town. Captain Fernando Cervera, a Colombian airline pilot who flew over Armero yesterday, said: "It's Dantesque. It looks like a beach at low tide, just mud and driftwood. Trees, houses, and cars were all carried off".

The captain said that a few houses were still standing, and that the roofs were crowded with people waiting to be rescued.

Captain Cervera said that the volcano threw smoke 26,000 feet into the air, and filled the cabin of his plane with smoke.

"I had to ask the passengers to use their oxygen masks," he told Radio Caracol, after diverting his plane from a scheduled landing at Bogota to Cali. He said that visibility was so bad "we did not know it was an eruption."

Local radio crews struggled for 12 hours to get through to Armero — which is only 150 miles from the capital, Bogota — because a half-dozen bridges had been swept away and the road is covered in mud. After being there for only an hour they were obliged to withdraw, as the landslides continued to advance on what was left of the road.

The Times, 14 November 1985

stances. In the case of Colombia the financial resources, especially for education, monitoring, rapid hazard warning, and rescue communications are a major limiting factor.

Table 2.1 was produced by the US Geological Survey. It gives a description of volcanic hazards. Figure 2.8 shows the hazard map compiled by the USGS two years before the fateful eruption at Mt St Helens in 1980. The evidence available for this compilation included past geological deposits (Fig. 2.9) and the topography. This allowed them to guess at the areas of damage that might be expected from the various outpourings and secondary problems such as flooding after the summit ice cap melted. Clearly the map would have influenced public preparedness when the eruption became inevitable in 1980. However, it is clear that this advance information has severe limitations because the actual character of the eruption is so variable. Datafile 2A shows what actually happened.

Figure 2.7a

How Rolf turned the tide of history

by Dalbert Hallenstein

AT nine minutes past four yesterday morning, to the sound of a military trumpet, Mount Etna was attacked with rockets and bombs. The immense effort, to alter the course of a lava torrent, was a qualified failure.

The huge explosion, the world's first example of volcanic engineering, caused only a partial deviation of the fast flow: Scientists said it may take days to determine whether the plan to divert the lava into a man-made canal and away from inhabited areas has worked.

Some eminent Italians are not only disappointed in the result, but admit that the villages the explosion was expected to save had been in no real danger, anyway.

However, Rolf Lennart, the Swedish explosives expert in charge of the blasting, said he considered the operation "a complete success, considering the circumstances"

Lennart said the constant flux in the depth of the lava forced him and his team to change plans continually. He said the lava kept splashing over a restraining wall, damaging metal tubes that were to hold the dynamite and doubling the wall's thickness in two days to nearly 19 ft.

Renato Cristofolini, professor of vulcanology at Catania university, who helped prepare the attempted diversion, said: "We were asked by the Ministry of Civil Protection for our opinion. The original request for the project came from the Etna villagers. We agreed to help, but I admit the decision to go ahead was partly political."

What he meant was that there will be elections on June 26 and the local mayors saw a successful onslaught on the volcano as a useful campaign weapon.

The explosives technicians took terrible risks placing the charges in the lava wall. There was the constant peril of a lava slip burning them to death. But they also had to worry about a spontaneous explosion resulting from a temperature of 50 degC in the wall itself.

At 4am yesterday, the hundreds of technicians and journalists on the erupting volcano were ordered to lie down in sand-bagged bunkers, which had also been designed as grandstands. This was followed by the sound of the trumpet as a warning of the coming explosion.

At first it seemed that the explosion had completely failed. But as the dust and smoke cleared, glowing lava could be seen bursting out of the breach. The original lava flow began to slow down but then suddenly speeded up again to its former 10 miles an hour, and after more than three hours, the new flow had reached only 350 yards.

Lava has been pouring out of a crater from the summit of the 10,700 ft volcano nearly five miles down the south-eastern slope.

Cristofolini said the aim of the attempted diversion was to "buy time because the diverted lava will eventually rejoin the natural stream further downhill". The project was to slow the natural course by two weeks or so.

He said three nearby towns including Ragalna, nearly a mile away were in no danger even if the canal was not built, because the lava was slowing.

The Sunday Times, 15 May 1983

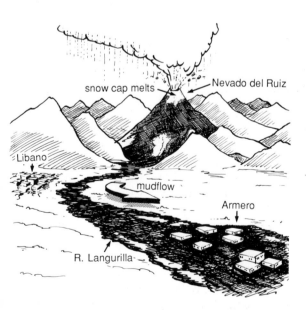

Figure 2.6b *The eruption at Nevado del Ruiz*

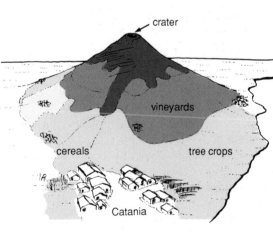

Figure 2.7b *Land use on Mt Etna*

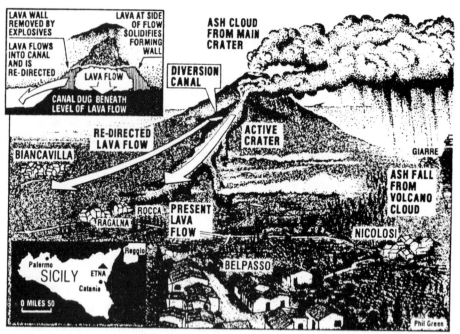

Etna's path of destruction and the course the engineers plan for the lava

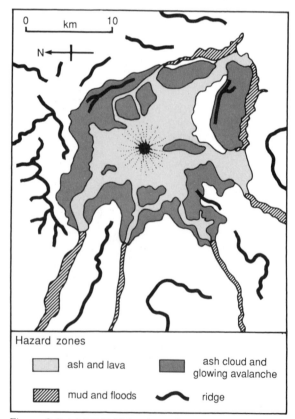

Figure 2.8 (a) *Mt St Helens hazard zones*

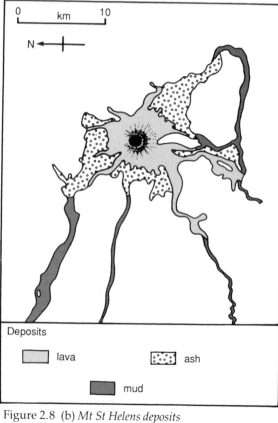

Figure 2.8 (b) *Mt St Helens deposits*

Table 2.1 *Description of volcanic hazards*

	Lava flows	Hot avalanches, mudflows and floods	Volcanic ash (tephra), gases and glowing avalanches
Origin and characteristics	Result from non-explosive eruptions of molten lava. Flows are erupted slowly and move relatively slowly; usually no faster than a person can walk.	Hot avalanches can be caused directly by eruption of fragments of molten or hot solid rock; mudflows and floods commonly result from eruption of hot material on to snow and ice and eruptive displacement of crater lakes. Mudflows also commonly caused by avalanches of unstable rock from volcano. Hot avalanches and mudflows commonly occur suddenly and move rapidly, at tens of kilometres per hour.	Produced by explosion or high-speed expulsion of vertical to low-angle columns or lateral blasts of fragments and gas into the air; materials can then be carried great distances by wind. Gases alone may issue non-explosively from vents. Commonly produced suddenly and move away from vents at speeds of tens of kilometres per hour.
Location	Flows are restricted to areas downslope from vents; most reach distances of less than 10 kilometres. Distribution is controlled by topography. Flows occur repeatedly at central-vent volcanoes, but successive eruptions may affect different flanks. Elsewhere, flows occur at widely scattered sites, mostly within volcanic 'fields'.	Distribution nearly completely controlled by topography. Beyond volcano flanks, effects of these events are confined mostly to floors of valleys and basins that head on volcanoes. Large snow-covered volcanoes and those that erupt explosively are principal sources of these hazards.	Distribution controlled by wind directions and speeds, and all areas toward which wind blows from potentially active volcanoes are susceptible. Zones around volcanoes are defined in terms of whether they have been repeatedly and explosively active in the last 10 000 years.
Size of area affected by single event	Most lava flows cover no more than a few square kilometres. Relatively large and rare flows probably would cover only hundreds of square kilometres.	Deposits generally cover a few square kilometres to a few hundreds of square kilometres. Mudflows and floods may extend down-valley from volcanoes many tens of kilometres.	An eruption of 'very large' volume could affect tens of thousands of square kilometres, spread over several states. Even an eruption of 'moderate' volume could significantly affect thousands of square kilometres.
Effects	Land and objects in affected areas subject to burial, and generally they cause total destruction of areas they cover. Those that extend into areas of snow may melt it and cause potentially dangerous and destructive floods and mudflows. May start fires.	Land and objects subject to burning, burial, dislodgement, impact damage, and inundation by water.	Land and objects near an erupting vent subject to blast effects, burial, and infiltration by abrasive rock particles, accompanied by corrosive gases, into structures and equipment. Blanketing and infiltration effects can reach hundreds of kilometres downwind. Odour, 'haze', and acid effects may reach even farther.
Predictability of location of areas endangered by future eruptions	Relatively predictable near large, central-vent volcanoes. Elsewhere, only general locations predictable.	Relatively predictable, because most originate at central-vent volcanoes and are restricted to flanks of volcanoes and valleys leading from them.	Moderately predictable. Voluminous ash originates mostly at central-vent volcanoes; its distribution depends mainly on winds. Can be carried in any direction; probability of dispersal in various directions can be judged from wind records.
Frequency, in conterminous United States as a whole	Probably one to several small flows per century that individually cover less than 15 square kilometres. Flows that cover tens to hundreds of square kilometres probably occur at an average rate of about one every 1000 years. (In Hawaii, eruption of many flows per decade would be expected.)	Probably one to several events per century caused directly by eruptions. Probably only about one event per 1000 years caused directly by eruption at 'relatively inactive' volcanoes.	Probably one to a few eruptions of 'small' volume every 100 years. Eruption of 'large' volume may occur about once every 1000 to 5000 years. Eruption of 'very large' volume, probably no more than once every 10 000 years.
Degree of risk in affected area	To people, low. To property, high.	Moderate to high for both people and property near erupting volcano. Risk relatively high to people because of possible sudden origin and high speeds. Risk decreases gradually downvalley and more abruptly with increasing height above valley floor.	Moderate risk to both people and property near erupting volcano; decreases gradually downwind to very low.

29

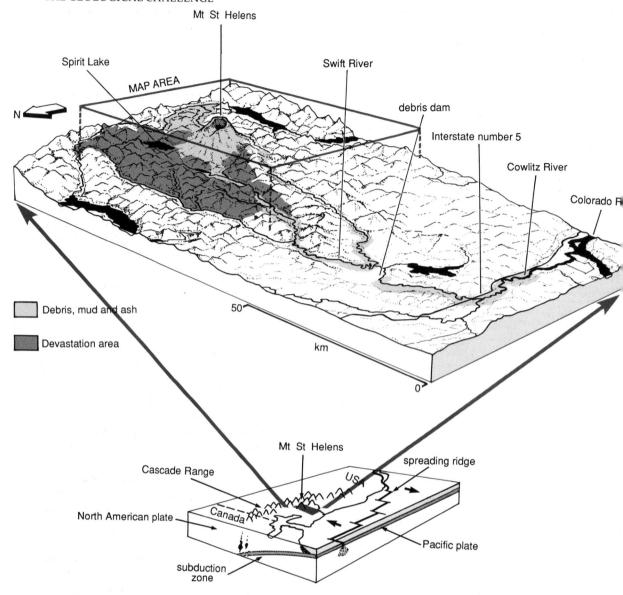

Figure 2.9 *The Mt St Helens eruption of 1980*

Student enquiry 2 A: Towards the comprehensive management of Mt St Helens

Before 18 May 1980 very few people outside Washington State had ever heard of Mt St Helens. Then, when the volcano erupted, the area became world famous overnight. For many months after the first eruption the whole area was closed to outside visitors because of the potential hazard from new eruptive events, but gradually, as the volcano quietened down, the pressure to reopen the area to the public became overwhelming.

Reopening was not a simple matter. Many roads had been destroyed and access was poor (A1). Furthermore, it was clearly going to be necessary to stop visitors inadvertently endangering themselves or ruining what had become a unique geological and ecological resource for many generations to come. Therefore to provide a framework in which government officials could act, the US Congress designated the region immediately surrounding the volcano as Mt St Helens National Volcanic Monument.

The way the balance between traditional uses and new uses has shaped up is indicated by the pattern of 1985 visits. Whereas before the eruption 78 per cent of visitors were from Washington State, only 23 per cent are now from the state, and 11 per cent are from outside the US altogether. About 1.1 million visits were made to the area, of which just under 0.3 million were for the traditional recreational pursuits of hunting, fishing and hiking in the forest; the remainder were generated by outside visitors whose main purpose was to see the volcano. These 'outsiders' have different needs from the local residents, not only in what they have come to see and do, but also in accommodation and transport.

A satisfactory operating system for the area was urgently needed. As well as protecting the geological and ecological resources this would help the local economy and cater for research, public enjoyment and visitor safety. Below you will find some of the data that were collected for two of the eight alternative strategies that were developed. One of the strategies presented here (A2) is representative of what may be regarded as minimum development (MIN) while the other (A3) typifies maximum development (MAX). The visitor map of Mt St Helens as given to the public in 1986 before any of the strategies was finally adopted is A1.

The quality of recreation experience depends on how successful a visitor is in achieving a satisfying experience. The key factors are:
(a) achieving the desired crater view (A4);
(b) not experiencing traffic congestion;
(c) receiving some form of interpretative information;
(d) creating easy access to the main features;
(e) providing some form of creature comfort such as toilets, food and drink shops and possibly motels;
(f) making the trip to all the features as convenient as possible;
(g) achieving a diversity of experiences;
(h) viewing the key features across an unmodified landscape.

Note that achieving aims a, b, d, e and f often presents a conflict with achieving aims g and h. Park strategy must achieve a balance between all these aims as well as conserving the natural resources.

The objective of this activity is to prepare the tourist broadsheet as set out in question 4. Questions 1–3 should be studied because they provide a structured approach to the way you should complete the final objective. However, the information gathered need not all be written down formally.

1. From an atlas or road map of western USA locate Mt St Helens, the main urban centres and access roads.
2. Study all the information for MIN and MAX (A2/3) and consider how MIN and MAX strategies differ.
3. Consider the present way the park is organised as shown by A1. How far does this meet the objectives of visitor enjoyment, research

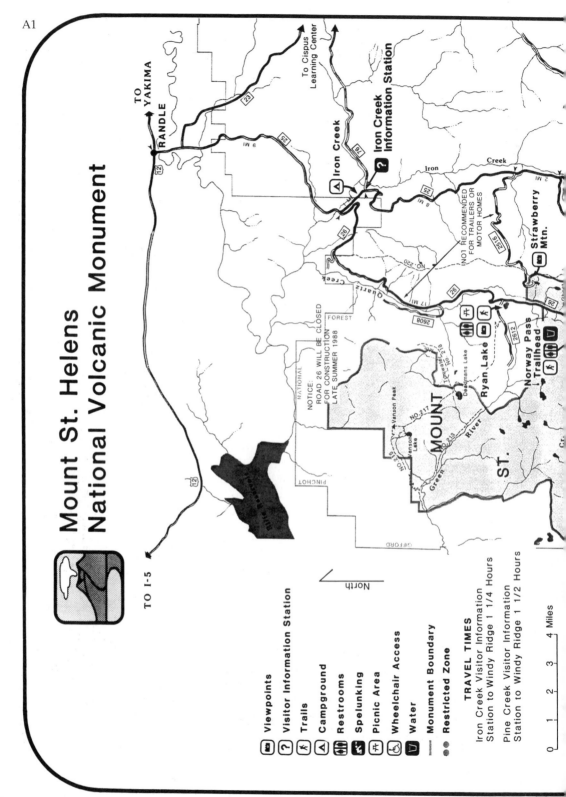

Mount St. Helens National Volcanic Monument

Viewpoints

? Visitor Information Station

Trails

Campground

Restrooms

Spelunking

Picnic Area

Wheelchair Access

Water

Monument Boundary

Restricted Zone

TRAVEL TIMES

Iron Creek Visitor Information
Station to Windy Ridge 1 1/4 Hours

Pine Creek Visitor Information
Station to Windy Ridge 1 1/2 Hours

North

0   1   2   3   4 Miles

REVISED 5/88

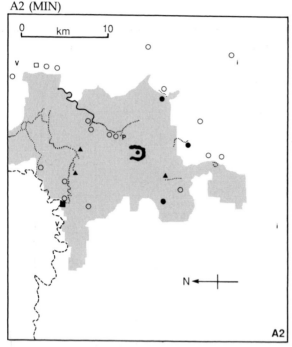

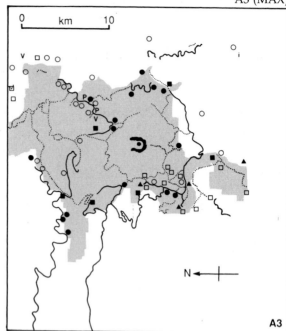

and protection? Remembering the objectives of the monument now try to suggest a compromise between MIN and MAX that may be more effective. Draw out and justify such a compromise on a copy of the visitor map. Be careful to identify the areas that are most hazardous or most fragile and therefore need greatest protection. You must also try to provide the greatest quality of recreation experience.

Enquiry objective

4. One of the main objectives of the Mt St Helens Volcanic National Monument will be to interpret the area for the benefit of visitors. Most of the visitors will not have any biological, geological or geographical background. They will therefore need interpretation to be simple but accurate. Diagrammatic help should be given top priority. Above all it must not talk down to the visitors, but leave them with the feeling they have learned something valuable.

Your broadsheet should feature the map prepared in Q3.

Make up the following themes into a double page spread suitable to be given out to visitors as a free issue as they enter the monument. the monument.

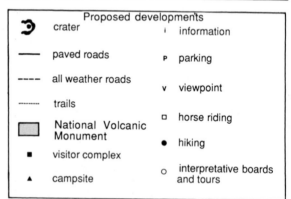

Key to A2 and A3

A5 *Key differences between alternatives*

	Minimum	Maximum
Area occupied by trails, roads and facilities	130 ha (of 44 500 ha)	245 ha
Research protection	None	10 925 ha
Key features made easy to view/visit	None	4
Road improvement	Double gravel road to Windy Ridge	Double tarmac road to Spirit Lake and windy Ridge
Overall ecological disturbance compared with present	130 ha	245 ha
Number of impacts on geological resources due to trails, roads, etc.	20	42
Quality of visitor experience		
a view of crater and dome	partial	full view
b traffic congestion	slightly improved	relieved
c interpretation	fair	good
d convenience to road visitor	low	high
e diversity of experience gained	limited	moderate
f research area	permit access	permit access
g approach access to monument	Build local type road from west to Coldwater Lake – improved road to Windy Ridge	Build to major road standard. From main west coast Highway 5 build main roads to Windy Ridge and Spirit Lake
h campgrounds	5	14
i motels/hotels	none	none
j total jobs estimated created in monument area	3500	4600

A4 *The visual focal point of the Monument is the north face of the mountain*

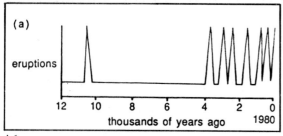

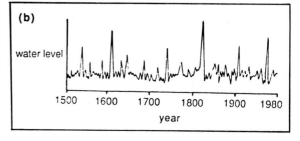

A6

The main interpretative theme would be:

'How and why Mt St Helens erupted so violently after a repose of more than a century'.

For this it will be useful to compare the eruptive cycle with cycles more commonly experienced in nature, for example, floods (A6). Explain why much of the landscape that visitors interpret as 'destruction' geologists regard as 'construction'.

Secondary theme:

People soon forget, but foreknowledge is still vital to prevent a natural hazard from becoming a place of human tragedy.

Tertiary theme:

Volcanic change may be sudden but ecological change is gradual.

Explain that it will take decades for the forest and wildlife destroyed in an instant to return to pre-eruptive conditions. People should be helped to interpret the ways recovery is expected to occur.

Attempt this section now, then re-evaluate (and upgrade) your material when you have completed studies on ecosystems, such as those in Chapter 12.

Additional resources: You may care to refer to the *National Geographic* magazine for 1980 and 1986 in this connection.

Grasping the geological challenge

Harnessing heat from the earth

The potential of geothermal energy seems vast. The heat flow from the earth's crust is about 3×10^{10}KW, and the heat stored in the top ten kilometres of the crust is equivalent to 2000 times the heat output from burning all the world's coal reserves. Yet most of the heat is unavailable at present levels of technology because it is at too low a temperature. Thus potentially exploitable resources are mostly confined to regions where there is a rapid transfer of heat to the surface (Fig. 2.10). Such places mostly occur at spreading boundaries, where magma rises on the continental side of subduction zones, or areas of major rifting (crustal extension) such as the East African Rift Valley.

Despite the restricted locations of geothermal sources, amounts of potential electricity generation are substantial and certainly economic against a background of increasingly scarce and expensive fossil fuel reserves. There are estimated to be about 14×10^7KW available over 30 years in the US alone. This is equivalent to about 150 large thermal power stations. Much more energy is available through lower temperature sources which could be channelled for space heating of homes, offices, greenhouses, and so forth. Even water at 40°C can be used to heat homes. Thinking on these lines offers more scope for global exploitation.

Geothermal power is presently obtained by using steam captured directly from the rock, or by capturing superheated water at depth and allowing it to expand to create steam in boilers on the surface. The steam is then used in the conventional manner to drive turbines.

Many countries have regions of high heat

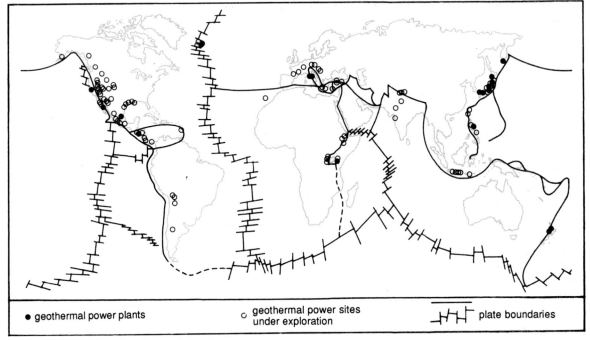

● geothermal power plants ○ geothermal power sites under exploration ⊣⊢⊣⊢ plate boundaries

Figure 2.10 *The Earth's major crustal plates*

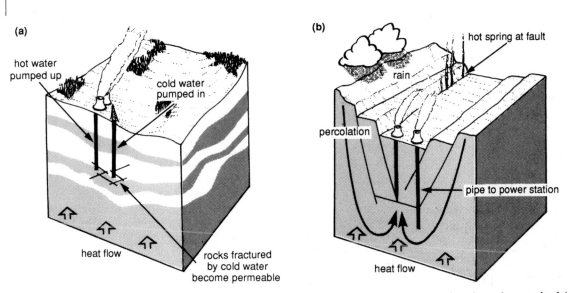

Figure 2.11 (a) *Recovery of geothermal energy from artificially fractured rock;* (b) *Recovery of geothermal energy by driving pipes into naturally fractured rock*

flow but these are not connected with permeable rocks. Even Britain (which is nowhere near an active plate boundary) has two residual regions of high heat flow where subterranean granite masses are still cooling. Here the technique under experiment is to force cold water down a well or to set off an underground explosion, causing the heated rock to fracture. The fractured rock would thus be made permeable and, once heated, the water could then be recovered from a separate well (Fig. 2.11).

Geothermal power in this form must not be thought of as a truly renewable power supply. Under normal exploitation at commercial levels it is mined and steadily depleted. A drawdown cone quickly develops around each well head and the water pressure declines. The first field to be commercially exploited was in Tuscany, Italy. This plant continues to maintain a power output of 400MW, but only by drilling more wells over an ever increasing area.

There are environmental disadvantages too, as large volumes of water extracted from the ground cause subsidence (over 5 m in areas of New Zealand), and groundwater often contains large amounts of poisonous trace elements such as boron and arsenic. Effluent cannot therefore be put into rivers or on to fields. Indeed, water disposal (even reinjection into nearby boreholes) can often be too great a cost to make a site economic.

One of the major advantages of geothermal energy is the small economy of scale: relatively small units, such as may be needed by developing world countries, can be operated nearly as economically as the 2000MW giant planned for the Geysers area of California. Iceland contains many of the conditions for successful exploitation of geothermal energy: there is high heat flow and a small population and therefore small demand. Reykjavik (itself Icelandic for 'smoking bay'), Iceland's capital, is surrounded by steaming springs; Geysir itself is just to the north. Nevertheless, much of the water is below 150°C and is thus unsuitable for direct steam generation. Instead the community makes use of the hot water directly to heat property. In the north of Iceland they do generate power at the Krafla station, but conditions there are quite hazardous.

Key terms

Crust: the outermost shell of the earth; granitic composition in continents; basaltic composition below oceans.

Glowing avalanche: a mixture of hot gas and rock fragments ejected by a volcano that cascades down the sides of the cone at great speed.

Igneous rocks: rocks derived directly from molten material of the mantle. Granite is an igneous rock with large crystals that cooled slowly when deep within newly forming mountains; basalt is a finely crystalline rock which has cooled quickly at or near the earth's surface.

Isostacy: the concept of floating when applied to plates. It assumes that the crust floats on the mantle and that, in equilibrium, the total thickness of the crust, both visible and buried in the mantle, is proportional to the observed height of the land.

Mantle: sub-crustal shell whose outermost regions are plastic and deform under the weight of the crust. The outer mantle contains very slow moving convection currents that are responsible for much of plate tectonics.

Metamorphic rocks: rocks that have been partially melted and reformed under heat or pressure. Most show banding and fine crystalline form.

Plate: a large irregular segment of the earth's crust and upper mantle containing both elements of ocean floor and continent and capable of moving over the earth's surface as a coherent body.

Plate tectonics: the theory to explain the movements of the earth's crust both at a local level (as faulting) or on the grand scale of continental drift. The theory explains the features and location of the continents and oceans, their past movements and (as predictions) future events.

Pyroclastic rocks: pieces of molten or near molten material thrown out of a volcano during explosive eruptions (includes cinders and ash).

Sedimentary rocks: rocks formed at the earth's surface by consolidation or cementing of sediment eroded from pre-existing rocks.

Subduction zones: elongated regions at destructive plate margins where one plate dives below another into the mantle. They are normally marked by geosynclines or ocean trenches and island arcs, earthquakes and explosive volcanoes.

Theme: Living with the weather

Chapter 3
Global weather

EPA

Introduction

You will have seen many photographs similar to Fig. 3.1 over the last few years as drought has raged across the African continent. Droughts, floods, hurricanes and tornadoes are just some of the ways in which the weather can have an adverse effect on our lives. But, as the article 'Shrugging off winter's cold' shows, even more

'I can practically tell you, within 100 miles, where you live by asking you four or five questions about acid rain . . . that's not like the normal pollution problem.'

Figure 3.1a *Some of the tragic effects of the Sahel drought*

Shrugging off winter's cold

A SUSTAINED spell of exceptional cold in northern Europe is demonstrating how even advanced economies can be driven to relying on one single artefact of modern technology for survival.

In this case, the lifeline is provided by about 30 icebreakers defying this winter's complete freeze up of the Baltic Sea. Finland, normally the only one among the seven littoral states to be completely besieged by ice, deploys nine breakers of its own; Sweden eight; the USSR six; and Denmark four. The Poles and East Germans make do with one apiece and the West Germans have the Hanse, frequently on loan to Finland, and a flotilla of ice-strengthened tugs.

The Soviet Union endeavours to keep three Baltic commercial ports open whatever the weather — Riga, Tallinn and Leningrad— and Sweden manages a dozen. The Finns emulate their skills in building most of the world's icebreakers — no-

tably for the Soviet Arctic — by giving ships continuous access to 22 designated winter harbours. Careful measures of cost effectiveness, bearing in mind the circumstances of each hinterland, have determined the number.

Eighty five per cent of Finland's visible trade, totalling 50 million tons in 1984, is conveyed by sea. If no icebreakers existed, the coast would be effectively blockaded for a third of the year.

About 15 million tons of merchandise would have to be routed by rail or road through Sweden — and the cost of shifting much of it would be prohibitive.

"Our icebreaker fleet, operated by 600 men, costs us about £14 million a year," says Mr Jan-Erik Jansson, director general of the Finnish Board of Navigation. "Its quite a price, but if you weigh up all the options is not all that high."

With 4.9 million people, Finland provides Europe's

best example of how to shrug off the cold. The high share of imports in energy consumption — 70 per cent — has given a fillip to the most sophisticated energy saving techniques. So has the energy intensiveness of the industrial mainstay, pulp and paper, forming 40 per cent of exports while absorbing 60 per cent of electricity and fuel.

Back pressure power stations providing district heating are 85 per cent efficient, against 35 per cent efficiency for conventional condensing plants. Skilful insulation and ingenious glazing provide big savings in heating homes and offices.

This winter, however, has been rather too much of a good thing. Officials estimate that the national fuel bill totals £945 million a year, about three quarters of outlays go in the more wintry half of the year, with January and February respectively accounting a little over and slightly under 15

per cent. But this year the bill soared by somewhere between 20 and 40 per cent above normal and February is following suit.

Delays in Soviet crude oil supplies to Finland — presumably caused by an upsurge in domestic needs and production and distribution difficulties in the Russian and Siberian cold — has not led to panic. The strategic 200 day stock pile of petroleum and coal is far from being eaten into.

Linking calculations made in the 1970's to inflation, it appears that for every degree Centigrade the annual temperature falls below the mean, the Finns must pay an extra £32 million in district heating costs.

Amazingly, everything functions smoothly, however bad the winter becomes. Streets are efficiently cleared of snow and ice, and delays to transport are exceptional.

Donald Fields

The *Guardian*, 21 Febuary 1985

Figure 3.1b *Areas affected by the Sahel drought*

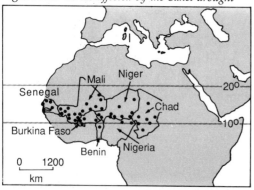

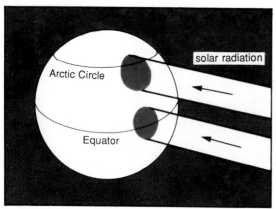

Figure 3.2a

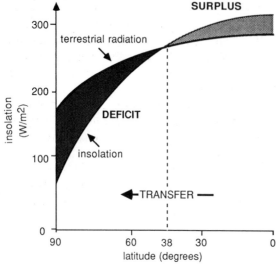

Figure 3.2b

Figure 3.2 *Equatorwards of 38° latitude the Earth receives more heat than it radiates; the reverse obtains at poleward latitudes. Atmospheric-ocean circulations operate in response to the temperature gradients*

predictable and less dramatic events can affect our pockets and our lifestyle directly.

In order to live with the weather and minimise its adverse effects we need to understand the workings of the atmosphere through the study of meteorology. This chapter will consider the influence of the atmosphere upon us, and our potential influence upon it. To start with, we need to set the scene by studying the global weather machine.

The global weather machine

The general atmospheric circulation is produced by the influence of:

(a) variations in solar heating; and

(b) the effect of the earth's rotation.

The driving force behind the weather is the heat energy received from the sun. The radiation received from the sun (**insolation**) is not evenly distributed over the earth (Fig. 3.2a) and there is a net surplus of insolation equatorwards of 38° latitude and a net deficit polewards of this (Fig. 3.2b).

The earth is encapsulated within a 'shell' of air. The entire shell is called the **atmosphere**, although most of the 'weather' is produced by air flows in the innermost part of the atmosphere known as the **troposphere**. The troposphere is largely transparent to insolation and thus the sun's energy is principally absorbed by the earth's surface. Because the sun's radiation is most concentrated when it is overhead, the tropical land and ocean receive a much greater heat input than land or ocean at higher latitudes. There are several ways in which heat is then transferred from the surface to the air (Fig. 3.3):

(a) by conduction;

(b) by convection;

(c) by evaporation from oceans and condensation of water vapour within the troposphere as cloud; and

(d) by direct radiation and subsequent absorption by atmospheric gases such as carbon dioxide and water vapour.

Tropical air is much warmer and thinner than cold polar air. These contrasts cause air to flow from the tropics to the poles and 'power' the **global circulation**. All parts of the earth are

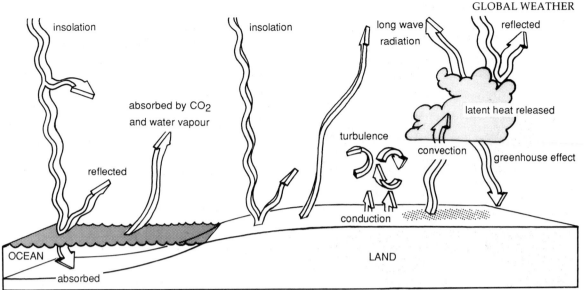

Figure 3.3 *Heat transfer processes between the atmosphere and the ground. Note the important re-radiating 'blanket' effect of clouds. This causes the so called 'greenhouse effect'*

broadly interconnected by this global air flow.

Two forms of air movement occur in the atmosphere as it moves:

(a) vertical flows (called **convection**) which are dominant near the tropics and poles; and
(b) horizontal flows (called **advection**) which primarily dominate the mid-latitudes.

The major components of the circulation

The Hadley cell in the tropics

Energy (heat) transfer by convection in tropical latitudes produces a circulation called the **Hadley cell** (Fig. 3.4). This cell extends the whole way round the tropical part of the globe and is by far the largest and most important part of the global circulation. At its equatorward side air rises (in a region called the inter-tropical convergence zone, **ITCZ**). It is in this region that the powerful tropical thunderstorms occur. At the poleward end of the cell air subsides and gives the great areas of calm, dry weather below which lie the world's major deserts. This region of subsiding air is called the **sub-tropical high pressure zone** and it is from here that warm air flows to the mid-latitudes.

The Rossby waves in the mid-latitudes

In the mid-latitudes the troposphere is not thick enough to allow large convective cells. Heat energy is now transferred poleward by advection (Fig. 3.4). This process allows hot air from the tropics to penetrate to the poles, and also allows a return flow of cold air, giving rise to the strings of depressions and anticyclones that are such a typical part of North American and European weather. Some people liken the pattern of horizontal transfers of energy to a set of 'gear wheels', whose function is to transfer the surplus energy of the tropical 'engine' to the polar regions. The surface gear wheels are seen as **depressions** and **anticyclones**. At higher levels these rotary air flows fade out and a different system of transferring energy occurs. The wave-like flow of air at high altitudes is known as the **Rossby wave** whose fast-moving core (with winds up to 200 or 300 knots) is called the **jet stream** (Fig. 3.4).

Figure 3.4 *A profile of global circulation. The satellite photograph reveals the general circulation in patterns of cloud. Notice how the model is a very simplified version of reality*

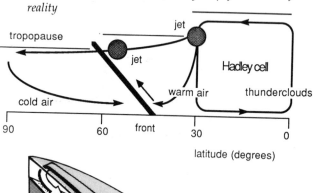

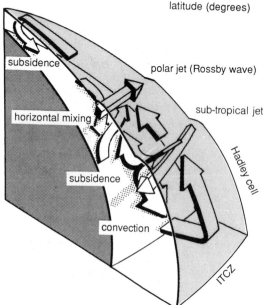

Coriolis force

Air moving between the tropics and the poles is affected by the earth's rotation. The deflecting force produced by rotation is called the Coriolis force and its effect is to deflect air to the right in the northern hemisphere and to the left in the southern hemisphere. It is most severe at the poles and gradually lessens towards the equator. Thus its effect on the Hadley cell is small, but it is extremely significant in the mid-latitudes where it creates a westerly air flow – the 'westerly winds'.

Jet streams

If we now look more closely at the general circulation we find there are two key regions where the Coriolis force has a particularly marked effect:

(a) at about 15° air sinks as some tropical air is returned to the equator to complete the Hadley cell. Here lies the **sub-tropical jet stream**.

(b) Between 40 and 60° a further rapid change occurs where cold and warm air flows meet at the **polar front**. Here a large thermal wind develops, reinforcing the general westerly airflow and causing the central fast-moving high level **polar jet**. The polar jet is also at the core of the Rossby waves.

The polar jet is connected with the mid-latitude Rossby waves and plays a highly significant role in steering mid-latitude depressions, while the sub-tropical jet is associated with the onset of the monsoons.

Air pressure, height and stability

Air is primarily heated from below but this does not automatically result in convectional overturning. There are physical laws governing the relationship between pressure, temperature and volume for rising air. Think of a body of air about a kilometre across and a kilometre or two thick, such as might eventually make a

Figure 3.5 (a) *cumulus clouds*

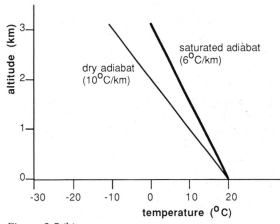

Figure 3.5 (b)

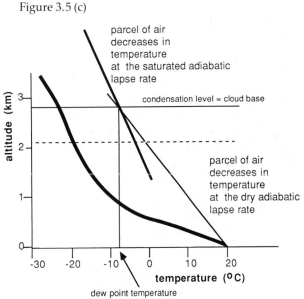

Figure 3.5 (c)

Figure 3.5 (d)

small cumulus (pillow cloud) (Fig. 3.5a). Air is a good insulator and when such a body of air rises from the ground quickly it neither gains nor loses a significant amount of heat to the surrounding environment. Changes that take place without heat exchange are said to be **adiabatic**. The **gas laws** state that under these conditions several complementary changes occur. First the pressure goes down because there is less weight of air above. This allows the air to expand (it becomes less dense), and as it does so its temperature falls. All these things take place at standard rates, such that a rising body of unsaturated (dry) air always decreases in temperature at 1°C/100m of ascent. This rate of change is called the **lapse rate**, so the rising dry air cools at the **D**ry **A**diabatic **L**apse **R**ate (abbreviated to **DALR**. It is *always* 1°C/100m of ascent.

Because air can only hold a certain amount of water vapour at a given temperature, as the air cools, the amount of water it can hold decreases and the air approaches saturation. This is measured as an increase in the **relative humidity**. At a certain height (which varies with the initial temperature and moisture of the air) the air has cooled to a temperature (the **dew point** temperature) at which it can no longer hold all the moisture as vapour. At this stage **condensation** occurs. This releases **latent heat** which, in turn, stops the air cooling as fast as at the DALR. The lesser rate is called the **S**aturated **A**diabatic **L**apse **R**ate (**SALR**) and is variable, but commonly around 0.6°C/100m of ascent.

The gas laws hold the key to the reason why air does not always rise. Figure 3.5(b) shows the temperature profile of the lower atmosphere. If a parcel of air is pushed bodily from the ground (as marked by the thin line), it changes temperature according to the gas laws. Notice that by the time it has reached 2 km it is cooler than the environment surrounding it. Thus the air parcel is more dense than the rest of the air at this height and, if the pushing stops, it will sink back to the ground. Indeed, although the air near the ground is warmest, it does not automatically result in convectional overturning. Cloud will only form in such air if it is forced up by, say, flowing over a mountain range or rising over cold air in a depression. This yields the cloud layers called **stratus** or **cirrus**.

Contrast Fig. 3.5(b) with Fig. 3.5(c) which shows environmental air with a very different temperature profile. When this air is pushed from the ground it still cools according to the gas laws, but it remains warmer, and therefore less dense than the atmosphere at every height. This air is unstable and will continue to rise, eventually cooling to its dew point and then producing cloud (Fig. 3.5(d)). The air will only stop rising when it reaches a great height. The depth of air that is saturated would be seen to an observer as **cumulus** cloud.

Global circulation and climate

The satellite photograph on page 42 shows the major implications of the circulation on the weather. Areas of rising air (called regions of instability) commonly experience cloud and rain; areas of subsiding air, however, are areas of **stability** with little cloud and rain. Notice

again that the main deserts of the world, for example, coincide with areas of subsiding air.

There are many inter-relationships between areas of rising and subsiding air. Although we have so far described them in an almost static manner, it is important to realise that the whole troposphere is constantly in turbulent motion. This is why so much of the weather, and even the climate, is unpredictable. The following example illustrates well the way in which the global circulation works as a complex set of inter-relationships.

Case study: El Nino

El Nino is the name given to a gentle warm breeze that sometimes wafts over the west coast of equatorial South America about Christmas time (El Nino is Spanish for 'child'). El Nino is one part of a major global disturbance that occurs on average once every five or six years.

Normally in December the South Pacific is **dominated by SE (trade) winds. These are caused by air flowing from the intense high pressure system over the cool ocean towards the intensely heated low pressure region over Indonesia** (Fig. 3.6a). The winds cause the ocean waters to pile up the West Pacific. During El Nino the pressure systems become disturbed as the low moves from Indonesia out over the Pacific (Fig. 3.6b). This is matched by the development of a high stretching from Australia northwards to Indonesia.

Clearly there has been a dramatic change in pressure in the South Pacific and the knock-on effects are both widespread and substantial. For example, there is no longer a SE trade wind, but a westerly wind that pushes water eastward across the Pacific to pile up against the Americas. This surge of water – known as the Kelvin wave – may take two months to complete, but eventually the warm water reaches America and displaces the cold ocean currents that normally well up at the shores. Winds blowing over these warm waters create the balmy breeze called El Nino.

The results of this southern oscillation in pressure systems stretch beyond the South Pacific and are truly world-wide (Fig. 3.7). In

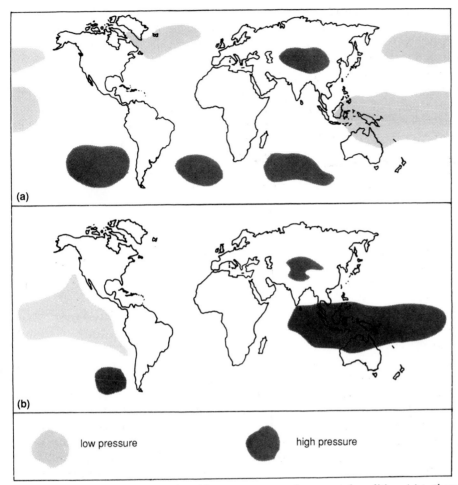

Figure 3.6 *The global shifts in high and low pressure zones from normal conditions* (a) *to those when El Nino occurs* (b)

1982 it caused drought, bush fire and famine in places as widely scattered as India, Australia and South Africa by deflecting or cutting off the vital monsoon rains (Fig. 3.8); it brought typhoons to Tahiti and floods and landslides to Ecuador. Flooding in the streets of the shanty towns made the incidence of water-borne diseases soar to epidemic proportions.

The warm waters displaced the normal cold ocean currents that well up from the ocean floor off South America and are vital to marine life because they bring with them the nutrient supply that is the basis of the complex coastal food web. With no nutrients rising to the surface, the plankton did not bloom and the fish no longer fed in their traditional grounds. Fishermen went bankrupt and sea bird flocks were decimated as their food supply was cut

off. In the same areas 'freak' storms wracked the coasts and many people lost homes and livelihood.

The air flows that drove the water east and created El Nino faded in the spring of 1983. But the pattern of southern oscillations that causes El Nino is very unpredictable: in 1976 warm water spread up the west coast of America which was associated with a high pressure system. This deflected the high level jet stream into a new path. In turn this brought the coldest weather and highest heating bills for decades to the eastern seaboard of the USA. The knock-on effects also sent temperatures in Europe plummeting. In Birmingham it fell to minus 28°C, making the city colder than Siberia, while the sea began to freeze off the coast of East Anglia.

45

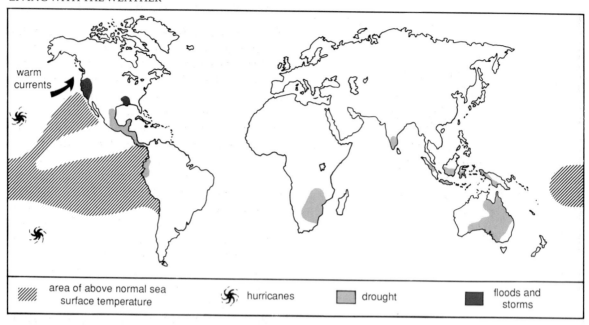

Figure 3.7 *The results of El Nino*

Figure 3.8 *El Nino at work* (a) *hurricane damage, USA* (b) *bushfire in Australia*

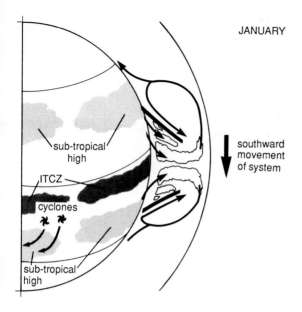

JANUARY

sub-tropical high

ITCZ

cyclones

sub-tropical high

southward movement of system

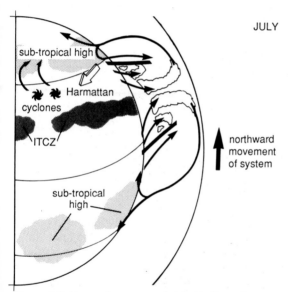

JULY

sub-tropical high

Harmattan

cyclones

ITCZ

sub-tropical high

northward movement of system

Figure 3.9 *Seasonal movements of the Hadley call*

Low latitude weather

Except when El Nino occurs, the low latitudes experience patterns of weather that are extremely predictable. They are under the influence of the Hadley cell and the seasonal movement of the overhead sun (Fig. 3.9). In the low latitudes changes in the attitude of the sun are small and thus there is no great variation in seasonal temperature. Rather the contrasts between seasons are produced by patterns of rainfall. For many areas in the low latitudes, the movement of the overhead sun and the consequent change in position of the Hadley cell means that convectional instability dominates for one part of the year, while dynamic subsidence dominates for the other.

Some islands and coastal zones near the equator remain under the influence of the tropical low throughout the year and you can almost set your watch by the time the rain begins and ends each day. By contrast, in deserts years may pass without a rainstorm and many children simply do not understand what is meant by 'rain'.

Although the rainforest and desert regions are vastly different in their rainfall, people in both these types of regions are able to adapt to the climate readily because it is predictable. By contrast, in those regions that experience a dry season and a wet season the climate is often much more difficult to cope with. To understand this, we must look at the interface between the dry, hot subsiding air flowing out from the sub-tropical highs and the moist, warm equatorial air that ascends near the intertropical convergence zone.

In West Africa about June the sun is overhead at the most northerly point and the ITCZ has been drawn northward to lie at about 10–15°N. Hot dry air (bringing the infamous desiccating **Harmattan** wind) blows over the Sahara and down across West Africa. Warm air, which has gained moisture by being pulled across the Atlantic Ocean, flows in over the coast. In the Sahara no rain falls; at the coast rain now falls every day from huge convective thunder clouds. But over the latitude that includes the northern region of Nigeria and Ghana the hot air meets the warm moist air. Because the warm moist air is more dense (it is

47

Figure 3.10 *Clouds that do not spell rain. These cumulus clouds in Sahelian Africa will not develop sufficient depth to produce rain*

cooler and has more moisture) it flows *under* the Harmattan air forming a wedge. The hot air rides up over this, acting like a lid. Convection is only possible in the moist air, but clouds will not produce rain until they are sufficiently tall. Thus in the angle of the wedge many clouds will not grow sufficiently big and no rain will fall (Figs 3.9, 3.10).

Both the amount and the timing of the rain over this wedge area, which we may now call the **Sahel**, depends on two factors: (a) the latitude reached by the wedge; and (b) the ability of the hot air to keep the lid in place. Both these factors are variable and unpredictable, thus giving this region its unpredictable rainfall. In this region 'normal' rainfall – i.e. the statistical average from 35 years of rainfall records – must be treated with caution.

We shall now consider two further aspects of low latitude weather – monsoons and hurricanes.

Monsoons

Many places within the tropics experience a pattern of seasonal rainfall, but when local circumstances come together to produce a sharp start to the rainy season, this is called a **monsoon** (from an old Arabic word meaning 'season'). Monsoon seasons do not consist of a period with rain falling continuously. Rather they have a pattern of a few days with torrential rain followed by a respite with sunshine, only to be followed in turn by a further period of torrential rain. The rainfall is torrential because it falls from tall convection clouds that are a feature of tropical and near tropical regions. Most monsoon rain falls in the months of June to August in the northern hemisphere and December to February in the southern hemisphere. However, the hottest part of the year is not near January or July because at these times rainfall and cloud keep temperatures down. Instead the hottest time of the year immediately precedes the onset of the monsoon.

Each monsoon region has its own particular character. Most famous, and at the same time most difficult to explain, is the monsoon that affects the Indian subcontinent. Here the monsoon results from a combination of three factors:

(a) the presence of a large land mass that heats

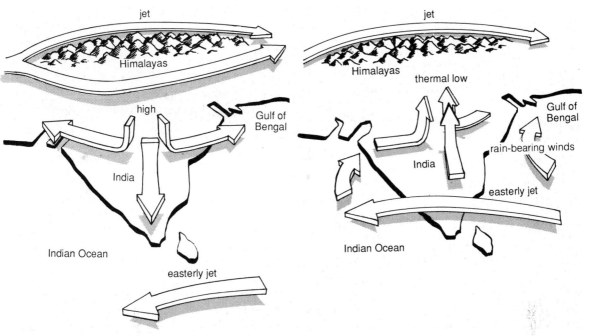

Figure 3.11 *The seasonal change in circulation that results in the Indian monsoon*

up rapidly with the approach of the overhead sun;

(b) a large mountain range (the Himalayas) that prevents the normal smooth shift of the pressure belts with the seasons;

(c) the presence of both a westerly jet stream near the Himalayas and an easterly jet stream off the southern coast of India. Both are capable of transferring large amounts of air and thus changing the local troposphere very quickly.

Perhaps without the mountain barrier the pattern of seasonal rainfall would be far less abrupt.

We can begin by imagining the continent cooling down in winter as the sun moves into the southern hemisphere. As high pressure develops over the subcontinent, air subsides and flows outward, giving dry conditions (Fig. 3.11). In spring, as the overhead sun heats the ground it creates a thermal low and replaces the high by a rising convective airflow. It is as though the continent breathes out in winter and breathes in during summer. As the Indian subcontinent is adjoined by the Indian Ocean and the Gulf of Bengal, inflowing warm air will have a large moisture content and thus will be

capable of producing a large amount of rainfall.

This simple pattern of seasonal changes in the pressure system will not, however, explain the abrupt start to the monsoon. For this we have to look at the effect of the Himalayas. This vast mountain barrier stops the seasonal shift of the pressure belts towards the pole, and the jet stream that flows in this latitude is trapped on the equatorward side of the mountains, feeding air into India and maintaining the high pressure well into late spring. At some stage the system becomes unstable and the jet stream flips to a new, more northerly position. Thus the high level air flow is abruptly cut off from India and the thermal low is able to form because the hot air can now rise rapidly. This brings air rushing in from the oceans and begins the monsoon.

The pattern of rainfall is, however, not uniformly distributed around the coast. Air does not flow in from all directions, but is controlled by the easterly jet stream that quickly moves over the southern part of the subcontinent. It is this that controls the location of rain-bearing winds.

People living in areas of seasonal rainfall

Figure 3.12 *Drains two metres deep are needed in Singapore to cope with torrential rain*

Figure 3.13 *Monsoon flooding in Bangladesh is worsened by deforestation in the Himalayas*

have many problems to cope with. To prevent flooding they must install large drains in the towns and cities (Fig. 3. 12) and design buildings to withstand torrential rain; or they must prepare for flooding (Fig. 3.13). Soil erosion is also a considerable problem in areas receiving torrential rainfall after a dry season in which no crops can be grown to protect the soil. In many cases, moreover, the potential flooding has been made far worse by deforestation, especially in the foothills of the Himalayas. Coastal regions are thus much more vulnerable to flooding than they once were.

Hurricanes

Tropical cyclones (called **hurricanes** in the Atlantic and **typhoons** in the Pacific) are a special feature of some parts of the low latitude

weather regime. They have a particularly severe impact: during a few days, sufficient energy to power Europe or the US for years is dissipated through frictional contact with the ground.

Tropical cyclones differ from mid-latitude depressions because they are are not closely steered and fed with energy by a jet stream. Instead they are eddies on the loose, detached parcels of air drifting in the SE trades and occasionally influenced by semi-permanent features of the circulation such as the Bermuda High off the coast of the Gulf of Mexico (Fig. 3.14).

When the ITCZ reaches its farthest poleward latitude the Coriolis force is at its greatest and a parcel of hot moist air that comes adrift will soon develp a spinning motion. Energy for development comes by feeding on the ocean's

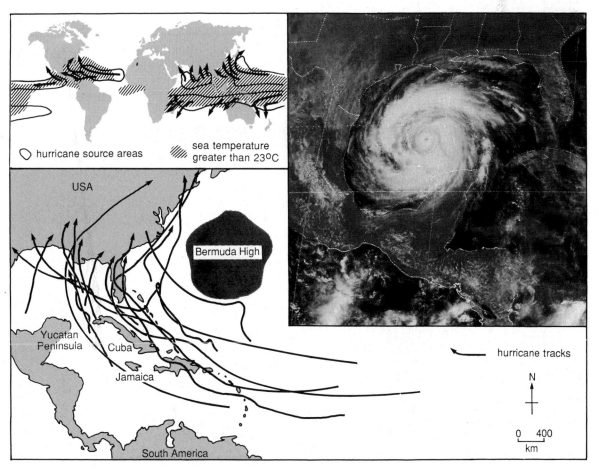

Figure 3.14 *Common hurricane tracks in the Gulf of Mexico.*

warmth. The spinning cyclone builds into a hurricane (wind speeds over 120 km/hr) by gulping in vast quantities of warm water as vapour evaporated from the ocean surface and carrying it aloft. In the upper air condensation produces giant rain-bearing thunder clouds which release enormous amounts of latent heat (Fig. 3.15). It is this energy that intensifies the instability and generates an ever deepening low pressure.

While it is over warm water the system becomes self-reinforcing (experiences positive feedback) sucking in more moist air, carrying it aloft and releasing latent heat on cloud formation. In this way a hurricane intensifies further. Hurricanes typically have a life cycle of up to two weeks, during which time they track from the warm tropical oceans to the mid-latitudes, curving as a result of the Coriolis force (Fig.

3.14). A hurricane decreases in intensity when its source of warm water is cut off – either because it moves over land or because it tracks into the cooler waters of the mid-latitudes.

Hurricanes bring fearsome winds that rip at houses and smash then like matchwood. They also whip up seas and drive them onshore creating a storm surge. If the winds drive water into progressively narrowing estuaries a surge may cause the height of the water to rise up to 10m higher than normal high tide. They have become a particularly important hazard as more and more people move to the coastal lowlands of hurricane-prone regions, either due to pressure on land (in developing countries), or to enjoy the benefits of a normally pleasant environment (in developed countries).

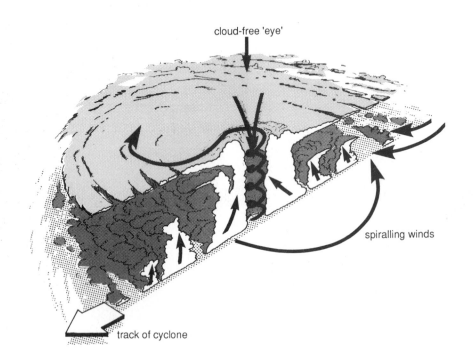

Figure 3.15 *The anatomy of a hurricane*

Student enquiry 3A:
Meeting the challenge of hurricanes

Some well-defined regions are prone to hurricanes, but the irregular and unpredictable track of each event means that, at any one location, the risk of damage from a hurricane is uncertain.

A1 *Home development along the southern US Atlantic coast*

A2

A3

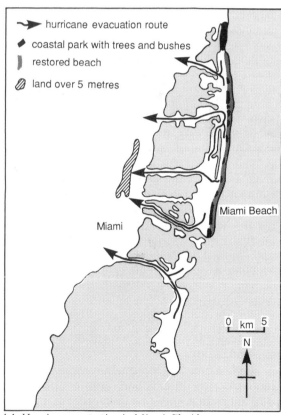

hurricane evacuation route
coastal park with trees and bushes
restored beach
land over 5 metres

Miami

Miami Beach

0 km 5

N

A4 *Hurricane protection in Miami, Florida*

Urirchar Island, Bangladesh

Four days after the cyclone virtually swept this island clean of human habitation the smell of death is unpleasantly obtrusive. The standard dwelling in these parts is the bari, a group of huts of bamboo and thatch, almost under one roof, around a courtyard. Not one has been left standing.

Wandering around the remains of the bari is a desolating experience. Brilliant blue cushions are scattered in the mud. The carcases of cattle, swelling outrageous size in the heat, point their legs like sextants at the sun. Tumbled among the ruins of their homes the bodies of the woman inhabitants remain grimacing at the sky. Their skins are tight and black, the bangles on their arms showing that though they may have been poor they were not destitute. A child's body lies alone, eyes wide open staring at the mud where his parents dug a living. A batch of chillies is laid out to dry in the sun, drying still, but ownerless.

All along the muddy coast the scene is repeated. Most of the bodies have now been buried, but many will lie face down where the tidal bore abandoned them. The corpses of the cattle have not been dealt with, and lie like jetsam at the water's edge.

According to the authorities more than 6,000 people lived on this island, so flat that it is little more than a mud bank – and which was nothing more than that a few years ago. But thanks to the vagaries of the currents, and of the whims of the rivers Ganges and Brahmaputra whose oozing delta is Bangladesh,

Urirchar grew, and grew grass. People on the nearby island of Sandwip (the name itself means "New Island") lost their land when the rivers eroded it, and moved here instead.

Men like Abdus Sattar brought their families across five years ago to take advantage of the new rich silt piling up, to graze his cattle and grow paddy. It was a hazardous existence, as the island did not really exist on maps or even in the eyes of the government at the time, and there was a constant risk of inundation by high tides.

Then came the night of the storm. Storms are frequent at this time of the year in the Bay of Bengal. Depressions form ahead of the monsoon and roar into Bangladesh, Burma or India, but a bad cyclone had not struck Bangladesh for 15 years. Warnings were issued by the authorities who had seen the depression form on Thursday, but 10 warnings had been issued in the past 15 years and each time the storm either dwindled or veered off to some other coast, so not much notice was taken.

Abdus Sattar does not own a radio and so did not hear the warnings. Even if he had there is not much he could have done. There is no high ground on the island and a long journey faces anyone taking an open boat to get away. So he sat and listened to the wind rising, and worried whether his house would stand it.

Fortunately the pole had been well rooted, and held while everything else was swept away. Abdus Sattar saw a bed made of planks bobbing

in the tide. He grabbed it. Bibbi Mahfuza was constantly ducked as she grasped the pole – and felt her grasp inch by inch being weakened. She let go and also grabbed the bed.

Together Abdus and his daughter survived. His three sons and his wife are lost." What will I do?" he asked. "I have lost everything."

Of the 6,000 or so inhabitants of Urirchar a thousand are now refugees on nearby Sandwip, including Nurul Islam. The sub-district executive officer reckons that perhaps 2,000 people remain on the island and somewhere between three and four thousand are unaccounted for, swept, like the families of the Sattars, the Islams and the Amins, into the Bay of Bengal.

Those that remain are remarkably phlegmatic, although a number of them have been encouraged into scenes of emotion by photographers. They regard what happened as God's will, and are content to see their rescue as still another demonstration of that will. They would be glad to find, however, that it was also God's will that they should get sufficient relief material to survive for long enough to plant and grow another crop, and to start raising their cattle again.

The most heartening sight on the islands, as we flew away from the scenes of horror, was that of tiny shelters built out of the salvaged ruins being put up again where the old baris had stood. It may be many months before the salt flood water will be leeched out of the soil, but survivors are determined to rebuild their lives as best they can.

The Times

Enquiry objective

Compare and contrast:

(a) the reasons for hurricane hazard; and

(b) the way people can best respond to the challenge both in the developed and the developing world.

To develop a structured way of tackling this problem it may be useful to answer the questions below.

1. Suggest a high technology system for tracking and predicting the almost random path of each hurricane.

2. Explain how any information obtained could be translated into action and consider the difficulties that might be involved.

3. Comment on the effectiveness of each of the

following strategies for the developed and developing world (notice that emergency relief is only required **if** a hurricane strikes; the other measures are required **in case** a hurricane strikes):

(a) emergency relief provision;

(b) warning systems;

(c) evacuation;

(d) provision of hurricane-proof shelters;

(e) building sea defences; and

(f) do nothing.

4. Comment on the likely course of action if you were a planner for Bangladesh (with a largely rural population) and Florida, USA (with a largely coastal urban population), bearing in mind the contrasts in GNP/head.

Keeping a weather eye . . .

In recent years, millions of people have been attracted to the gulf states of the USA (the sunbelt) for retirement. On the sunbelt coasts the houses used to be simple wood slat cottages on stilts which were boarded up and abandoned at the slightest hint of a hurricane. Today these have been replaced by brick-built homes and mobile home parks (A1). Thousands of homes have been built on low-lying sandspits and barrier beaches using material dredged from the seabed. With the deepened bays there is less seabed to act as a buffer for the approaching waves (see Chapter 6). Many people have already experienced disaster (A2 and A3). In 1967, for example, Hurricane Beulah washed away much of the 180 km Padre Island in Texas, dividing it into 31 islets. But since then the pressure on development land has caused the beaches to be filled in and vast new housing schemes have been constructed.

People increase the hazard in these barrier islands in several ways. Coastal counties in the US get more taxes by releasing new building land. The wave-absorbing sand dunes are bulldozed flat to enable development of roads and buildings. As the beach is reduced in size so each hurricane poses a greater threat to coastal communities.

Today 40 million Americans live in areas vulnerable to hurricanes. There seems little possibility of reducing the hazard by enforcing land use limitations. Planning for disaster mitigation is the only solution. But even the difficulty of evacuation could be immense, so warning as far ahead as possible is vital. . . .

Mid-latitude weather

Unlike the low latitudes, the mid-latitudes have highly irregular weather patterns. This is because the mid-latitudes form a battleground between horizontal air flows with contrasting properties (Fig. 3.4). For example, in winter there is a sharp temperature gradient between the snow-covered land and warm offshore ocean currents off the coast of eastern Asia and eastern North America (Fig. 3.16). Air originating over land is cold and dry, whereas air from the ocean is warmer and very moist. Rossby

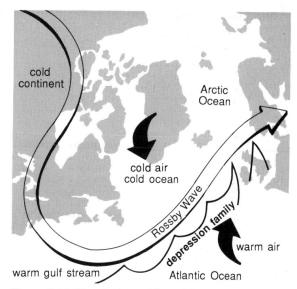

Figure 3.16 *The relative positions of the jet stream and fronts*

waves are primarily responsible for bringing different air types together along the poleward arm of a wave. Here a combination of low pressure, Coriolis deflection and air contrasts produces the familiar depressions with their swirling Catherine wheels of cloud and pronounced rain belts (Fig. 3.17).

Depressions bring together air masses from a variety of different sources (Fig. 3.18). This gives each depression a unique set of characteristics. Each type of air (known as an **air mass**), with its particular characteristics of temperature and humidity acquired by travelling over land or sea (source region) becomes **modified** at its base as it is drawn towards the 'battle zone'. This has the effect of making cold air moving over warm sea very unstable, and warm air moving over cold land increasingly stable (Fig. 3.19). For example, the clear, dry, cold air that lies over the snow-covered tundra of Canada during winter often flows south over the warm ocean currents of the Gulf Stream in the western Atlantic (Fig. 3.16). Heat is transferred into the lower air layers and once overwarmed they become unstable, start to rise and form cumulus clouds (see p. 43).

In contrast, warm air moving over a cold surface can be stabilised. For instance, in winter warm, moist air from tropical ocean sources moves up from the Gulf of Mexico and is drawn across America. The subsequent cooling and

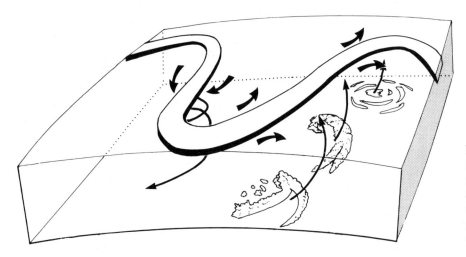

Figure 3.17
Relationship between upper air convergence and divergence along the jetstream and ground level features on a synoptic level

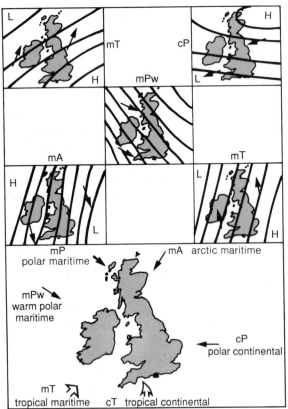

Figure 3.18 *Britain receives five major air mass types*

Figure 3.19 *Temperature/height modifications produced when air masses move (a) equatorwards; (b) polewards*

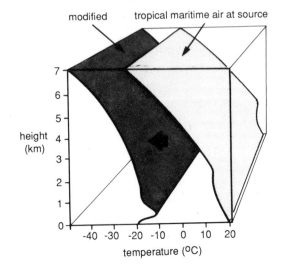

drying of the lower layers decreases the temperature contrast between upper and lower air, there is no chance of convection, and only thin stratus cloud occurs.

In a depression the warm, less dense air flow overrides the colder air ahead and is undercut

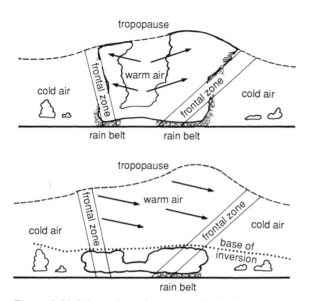

Figure 3.20 *Warm air can be sent rapidly aloft near the centre of a depression. This gives well defined cloud (a) near the margins of a depression; or, where the air is not actively being drawn out of the centre of the depression, cloud formation is suppressed (b)*

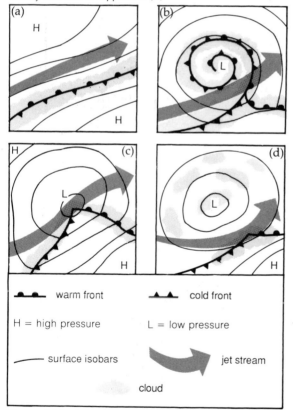

Figure 3.21 *A life cycle model of a mobile, frontal northern hemispheric depression, produced from satellite photograph analysis*

by the cold air behind. The classic depression has extensive uplift along two fronts (Fig. 3.20(a)) and an intervening region of thin strato-cumulus cloud in the warm sector caused by turbulent mixing of air near the ground. Sometimes the uplift of warm air is suppressed and the cloud severely restricted (Fig. 3.20(b)).

As the cold front moves faster than the warm front, it gradually catches up, undercutting or overriding it to form an **occlusion**. At this final stage the warm air is lifted completely off the ground and is transferred polewards.

Satellite images reveal clearly how complex the pattern of depressions is (Fig. 3.21). There is usually no simple 'low' centre as indicated in the previous diagrammatic models, but complex almost 'amoeboid' forms that writhe along the waves in the jet stream. In cloud patterns the depression is first seen as a comma cloud associated with the jet stream, developing through a convex bulge towards the colder air, to a spiral pattern rather like a Catherine wheel (Fig. 3.21(d)).

Where air is pushed down on the equator-ward arm of a Rossby wave this frequently produces anticyclones. Because anticyclones are regions of subsiding air they are rarely associated with rain. In summer they are frequently associated with fine sunny weather. By contrast, in winter, the anticyclones allow great heat loss from the earth's surface. Especially when air is subsiding sluggishly, such heat loss may cool the air in an anticyclone down to its dew point through great thicknesses of the atmosphere. This produces substantial stratus type cloud and the common experience of 'anti-cyclonic gloom', because the sun may not be seen for days on end.

Student enquiry 3B:
The pattern of mid-latitude weather

1. Using tracing sheets placed over the photograph series on page 59, draw on the major features of the circulation (fronts, depressions, anticyclones, polar air, tropical air, jet stream, etc.) by comparing the patterns with the diagrams in the previous section.

2. Describe the pattern of change that took place over the week and the likely change in weather for (a) New York; and (b) Cambridge. Use the newspaper extracts to help with this task. Use the headings (i) pressure; (ii) movement of fronts; (iii) winds; (iv) weather.

'Thaw today' after snow battering

By CHARLES NEVIN

Forecast: *Less cold with rain and sleet showers in the South. Wintry showers or some longer outbreaks of snow elsewhere.*

Gales whipped driving blizzards across much of Britain yesterday, leaving power failures, floods and deep drifts in their wake. Last night weathermen were cautiously predicting the start of a thaw today.

The entire West Country and pockets up as far as Gloucestershire and Surrey were without electricity for much of yesterday as ice and winds of up to 100 mph sweeping eastwards played havoc with ice-laden power lines.

The winds also caused flooding along the East Kent, Hampshire and Sussex coast, and at Christchurch,

Dorset, the rivers Avon and Stour burst their banks, leaving some streets under 18 inches of water.

The worst is over however - and that's official. A thaw is on its way to southern counties, and the rest of Britain will find it less cold and snowy, the London Weather Centre said last night.

Heavy snow still falling over the Midlands and East Anglia, Northern England and Southern Scotland, will die out from the northwest after continuing for much of the night.

Meanwhile, much warmer weather is already crossing the country in the wake of the blizzard from the south-west.

Despite the forecast thaw, commuters still face dreadful conditions on their way into work this morning.

Losing battle

The RAC said gritting lorries were fighting a losing battle, with

snow covering the grit soon after it had been laid.

"Countless roads are blocked, there have been hundreds of accidents and numerous stranded motorists. It's a giant disaster area," said an RAC spokesman.

British Rail warned that the snow fall and drifts were bound to have a serious and widespread effect on its service today.

The snow swept into the South West yesterday morning and travelled across the country all day as the warmer Atlantic rain clouds clashed with the Arctic air that had ben lying still and freezing over past days.

Within hours all major roads in Devon, Cornwall and Somerset were impassable, a picture steadily repeated over farther eastwards as the day continued.

All over the country motorists were forced to abandon their cars in mounting drifts.

The *Daily Telegraph*, 14 December 1981

'No end in sight yet'

By CON COUGHLIN

As winds sweeping down from the Arctic covered roads in ice and dumped snow over wide areas of Britain the London Weather Centre reported last night: "There is no end in sight at the moment."

In the Cotswolds and the Forest of Dean, police reported snow was two feet deep in places.

In London, where snow made Big Ben's clock run an hour slow during the early afternoon, meteorologists said high pressure over Greenland was forcing northerly winds over much of Britain and had contributed

to the coldest pre-Christmas weather since 1950.

Glasgow reported its coldest December night since records began in 1888 with temperatures down to 9F (-13C) at the city's airport.

The forecast is for more snow and hard frosts throughout most of England and Wales and parts of Scotland during the weekend. A spokesman for the London Weather Centre said: "We can only make forecasts for a few days ahead, and what we see at the moment is more cold weather and snow."

Airports closed

Heathrow airport was brought to a standstill by six inches of snow. Incoming flights were diverted to air-

ports throughout Europe and out-going services were delayed indefinitely.

Most airports in England, including Manchester, Liverpool and East Midlands, were closed for periods.

The British Airports Authority said problems at Heathrow had been compounded by freezing fog on Thursday. Some passengers had been waiting for up to 36 hours for their flights before yesterday's snow caused further disruption.

Heathrow's Terminal Three was worst affected by the disruption. Thousands of passengers were sleeping rough. One said: "It looks like a refugee camp."

The *Daily Telegraph*, 12 December 1981

B2 *12 December 1981*

13 December 1981

14 December 1981

Tracing the pattern of mid-latitude atmospheric pollution

Pollution is an example of humankind's capability to score own goals. In Scandinavia the countryside has a new hazard: helicopters jetting white powder out into the lakes (Fig. 3.22). It looks like a new form of pollution, but in fact it is designed to achieve just the opposite effect: to balance the growing menace of air pollution called **acid rain**.

Trout in the lakes and rivers die when the pH falls to below 5.0. Other creatures, such as pike and frogs, are more resistant, but they, too, die when the pH falls to 4.0. Now still, silent and dark these lakes are dead, killed by the release of toxic aluminium leached from soils by acid rainwater. The Scandinavians accuse the countries to the west of causing the acid rain by uncontrolled releases of sulphur and nitrogen gases from Europe's great fossil fuel-burning power stations (Fig. 3.23). In Britain, for example, of the 3 million tonnes of sulphur released to the air each year only a third lands on the country itself. But the question is complicated and depends very much on the pattern of winds.

The central issue of the whole debate about acid rain concerns 'linearity', i.e. how far is the amount of acid emitted into the atmosphere over Europe linked to the amount of acid rain that falls on Europe? Acidity data from the lakes near Pitlochry, Scotland reveals a close correspondence between total British emissions of sulphur dioxide, the sulphate content of rain, and the pH as reflected in the diatom content of the lake sediments at Pitlochry (Fig. 3.24).

With an established argument for linearity, the evidence of the track of depressions provided by meteorological studies shows that pollution carried up in the warm sector of depressions will gradually become fallout over southern Scandinavia. This meteorological knowledge will result in hundreds of millions of pounds being spent on cleaning up power stations and exhaust fumes throughout Britain. And the same knowledge will ensure that thousands of billions are spent worldwide over the next decades.

Figure 3.22 *Attempts to combat acid rain by spreading lime*

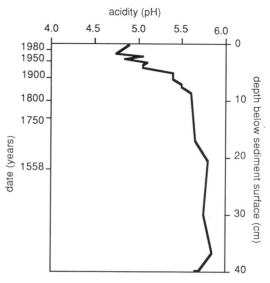

Figure 3.24 *The profile of lake acidity at Pitlochry*

A model of the atmospheric sulphur balance
Oxidisation of SO_2 to SO_4

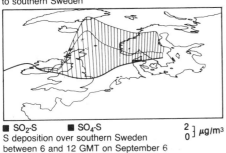

Emission of SO_2

SO_2 in the atmosphere

SO_4 in the atmosphere

5 % of the SO_2 emitted is directly converted to SO_4

15 % of the SO_2 is directly deposited near the emission sources

Dry and wet fallout of SO_2

Dry and wet fallout of SO_4

◄ By means of a simple model it can be seen how quickly the emitted sulphur dioxide is converted to acidifying sulphate and how soon the elements fall to the ground. In combination with the data on emissions and precipitation, the model can further be used to determine the concentrations of sulphur in the air along the length of the trajectory.

SO_2-S and SO_4-S concentrations along the trajectory to southern Sweden

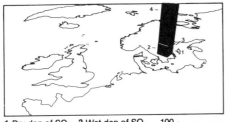

■ SO_2-S   ■ SO_4-S $\begin{smallmatrix}2\\0\end{smallmatrix}$] $\mu g/m^3$

S deposition over southern Sweden between 6 and 12 GMT on September 6

◄ At the start the sulphur content is assumed to be nil, but on passing over the British Isles the air picks up considerable amounts of sulphur dioxide. Some of this is converted to sulphate and deposited over the North Sea — thus reducing the sulphur content to some extent. But then there will be new additions of sulphur as the air passes over Denmark.

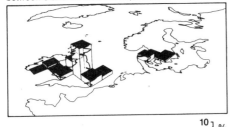

1 Dry dep of SO_2 3 Wet dep of SO_2 $\begin{smallmatrix}100\\0\end{smallmatrix}$] $\mu g/S\ m^2\ hr$
2 Dry dep of SO_4 4 Wet dep of SO_4

◄ It is raining in southern Sweden. When the air reaches the precipitation front, sulphate ions are deposited with the rain-drops over land and water — and thus the air again loses some of its sulphur.

It is now known how much sulphur the air held when it arrived over southern Sweden, and the extent to which the sulphur is converted and falls to the ground has also been assessed. On account of the rain it will be the sulphate in particular that is deposited. It can then be calculated how much sulphur per hour then fell over southern Sweden.

Origin of S deposited over southern Sweden between 6 and 12 GMT on September 6

$\begin{smallmatrix}10\\0\end{smallmatrix}$] %

◄ It has now been seen how much sulphur was added to the air at various stages along its trajectory, as well as the extent to which sulphur pollutants were deposited en route — and from this the source of the sulphur can be determined.

Prevailing winds

Northern Europe lies in the windbelt where westerlies predominate, especially in the layers at a height of 5 to 10 kilometres. The winds are however also mostly westerly at heights up to 2000 metres (2 km) at which pollutants are transported — although their directions are more variable.

The air reaching Sweden has thus mostly come via the British Isles and the northern fringe of the European continent. Samples taken in Scandinavia also show a higher concentration of pollutants when the winds come from the west than from any other direction. The contrast is especially striking when one compares polluted air from the west with that in a clean northerly air current.

Mean winds in January
◄ The approximately average wind directions over northern Europe in winter — at a few hundred metres above sea level, the height at which a great part of the pollutants is usually transported.

Figure 3.23 Major power stations are seen as an important cause of pollution

Student enquiry 3C:
Tracking the Chernobyl cloud

How the computer model works

THE MODEL we have used at the Imperial College of Science and Technology to study the release from Chernobyl was developed under contracts from CEA/Euratom and the EEC. We have applied the model statistically in the past to study how hypothetical accidents might spread radioactivity into neighbouring countries.

To simulate the dispersal of a radioactive cloud, we divide the release into 3-hour periods. We then track, in detail, puffs of

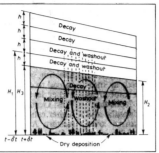

New Scientist 17 July 1986

Rain causes 'wet deposition', but gravity also brings the radioactivity to Earth

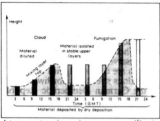

A temperature inversion acts as a ceiling to upward mixing of the plume

material released at the beginning and end of each 3-hour period, across the map according to the evolving meteorological situation. We assume that material released in between fans out between these trajectories, contaminating the area in between. We deduce the trajectories from analysed observations of surface pressure taken at 3-hourly intervals. This analysis is similar in principle to deducing the pattern and strength of the winds from isobars on a meteorological chart.

The model uses routine data from weather stations in the international network. Along each trajectory, the way that the radioactivity spreads and is depleted depends on how meteorological conditions vary, including the effects of the diurnal cycle of heating by the sun during the day, followed by cooling at night. Deposition on surfaces, from contaminated air and by the scavenging effect of rain on the radioactive cloud, depends on the chemical and physical form of the radionuclides.

We deduce rainfall from routine reports of 'present weather' that indicate the type of precipitation. The model smoothes out the occurrence of rainfall over grid cells with an area of 10 000 square kilometres. In practice, however, rainfall will sometimes be extremely patchy, on a scale of a few kilometres. In the case of Chernobyl, local hotspots of higher contamination are closely associated with cells of intense rain during the passage of the radioactive cloud, which we can deduce in England from the radar operated by the Meteorological Office. □

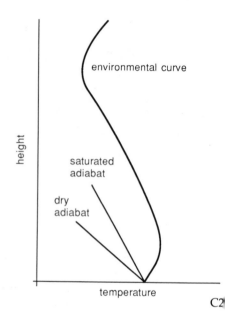

C2

C1

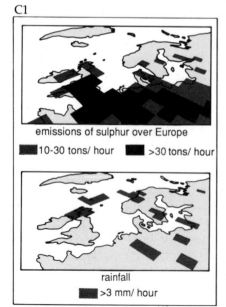

emissions of sulphur over Europe

■ 10-30 tons/ hour   ■ >30 tons/ hour

rainfall

■ >3 mm/ hour

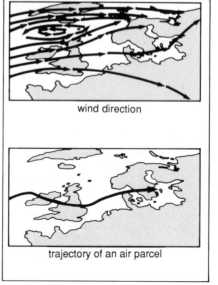

wind direction

trajectory of an air parcel

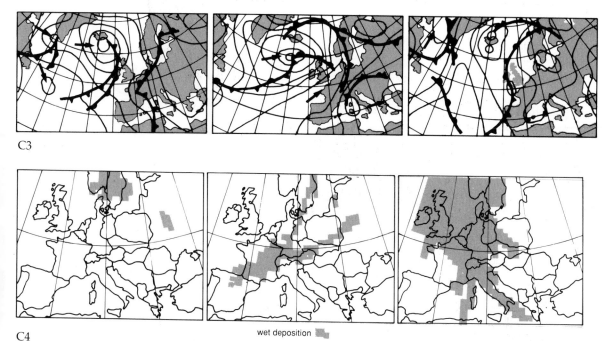

C3

C4

wet deposition

One of the most disturbing events in recent history is the release of radioactive gases from the failed nuclear reactor at Chernobyl near Kiev in the USSR in 1986. It has become vitally important to be able to trace the path of pollutants within the atmosphere so that people can be given adequate warning and precautions taken in the event of another accident.

The objective of this activity is to explain the meteorological conditions that affected the path of the radioactive fallout after the Chernobyl accident and to consider how meteorological information was vital to predicting those places which were at greatest risk.

C1 shows the model for the dispersal of pollutants. There are two major effects to notice:

(a) that a temperature inversion such as that associated with an anticyclone causes the pollutants to be confined to a region close to the ground and the concentration therefore remains high, although the spread is limited;

(b) rainfall releases radioactivity out of the cloud, causing enhanced contamination of the ground. Crops and animals that eat crops will thus concentrate radioactivity. With this scenario, it may become unsafe for people to eat either crops or animals for a considerable period.

The accident at Chernobyl occurred at 0100 hours on 26 April with the bulk of the radioactive emissions (gases and particulates) occurring between then and 30 April. The heat from the core would have helped the particles to be lofted high into the troposphere in just the same way as smoke is lofted from a chimney.

1. There was a high pressure over the area at the time. Study C2 which shows the temperature/height diagram typical of a high pressure region. What would the impact of such a high pressure have been on pollution lofting? Would it have been good or bad for the people in nearby Chernobyl town?

2. At the start of the release material would have flowed northward, parallel to the 1024 isobar and towards Finland. Use the weather charts (C3) and your knowledge of the rainfall pattern associated with the fronts (see p. 57) to explain the pattern of air pollution and wet deposition shown in C4.

Chapter 4
People and climate

Introduction

Despite rapid advances in technology, we are by no means free from the influences of climate. Two thirds of the estimated world costs from natural hazards are attributable to major climatic causes. For example, in 1976 people in Britain were using standpipes to collect their drinking water (Fig. 4.1). All the mains supplies had been turned off in some areas and many reservoirs stood dry, their muddy floors cracking in the heat of the sun. People were beginning to think that the climate had changed because there had been an almost unprecedented eighteen months with very little rain. Fortunately this drought was terminated by a month of very heavy rainfall and within a year the reservoir levels were back to 'normal'.

The possibility of climatic change

The disruption to water supplies in Britain was paralleled by severe problems in much of Europe. It showed that, although we can deal with small scale hazards, we are most unlikely to be able to deal with large shifts of climate without planning and preparation on a scale hitherto unthought of. It is already well known that large climatic shifts have occurred within the last 10 000 years, as we have emerged from a cold period dominated by ice sheets. There is no reason to assume that the climate will not shift back to such conditions or alternatively become much warmer in the near future.

A moment's thought will show that our whole lifestyle is geared to the present climatic 'norms': the clothes we wear, the amount we budget for heating, the legislation for housing insulation and design, the tourist industry, where we go for holidays, what crops farmers can grow and what yields they can expect, are all related to climate. Indeed the list of climatically influenced activities is almost endless. And as a result any major and permanent shift

Figure 4.1 *Standpipe in north Devon during the drought of 1976*

in climate could have the most severe repercussions on lifestyles. For example, people get very used to water coming from their taps. In Britain this is achieved by storing just 2 per cent of the annual river flow in a few well-located reservoirs. Only a dry period such as 1976 can challenge this supply. But if the climate were progressively to get drier then a larger proportion of the runoff would have to be stored. Not only would more land have to be used for reservoirs, but the cost would be enormous. So people have a right to be concerned about the possibility of climatic change.

The fact that the climate is changing is indisputable. There are many indicators of the change and all point towards similar trends:
(a) biological records such as the pattern of tree ring growth in long-lived species such as the

64

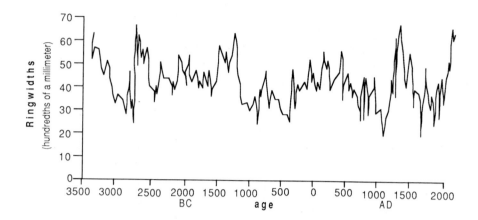

Figure 4.2 *The long record of the Bristlecone pine (this is unusual)*

Bristlecone pine of California (Fig. 4.2);
(b) geological records such as deep sea sediments or the pattern of radioactive oxygen trapped in Antarctic ice caps (Fig. 4.3);
(c) historical records of the advance and retreat of ice caps and cold, warm, dry or wet summers and winters (Fig. 4.4);
(d) meteorological records.

The change in Europe from a cold climate to a warm one over the last 10 000 years has not been a steady progression. Using the sources of data mentioned above it is possible to reconstruct the climatic fluctuations and place them in the context of historical events (Fig. 4.5). One widely reported event that occurred in the seventeenth century was the 'Little Ice Age'. This was the time when the River Thames at London froze over regularly in winter and when painters like Breugel were able to produce their famous scenes on the frozen Dutch polders (Fig. 4.6). The upland pattern of Bronze Age burial mounds seems to indicate that these people chose some of the least hospitable landscapes for their homes. In fact, a glance at Fig. 4.3 shows they lived at a time when Britain was very much warmer than it is today, and that the upper slopes of, for example, Dartmoor in Devon would not have been inhospitable even at 500 m above sea level.

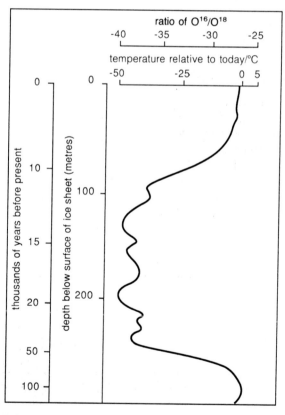

Figure 4.3 *Ice core from Camp Century, Greenland. The variations in the ratio of the two radioactive oxygen types reveal the trend in temperature over the last 100 000 years*

In the 1640s government officials were sent in several consecutive years to the once fertile and highly productive valleys around Chamonix in the French Alpine foothills to investigate the low payment of taxes. They reported:

The glacier 'Des Bois' advances a musket shot every day. Even in the month of August, towards the said land of Chamonix. We have also heard it said that there are evil spells at work among the said glaciers and that the people implored God's help to preserve them against the said peril. The people sow only oats and a little barley which throughout most of the seasons of the year is under snow, so that they do not get a full harvest in three years, and then the grain rots soon after. The people there are so badly fed they are dark and wretched and seem only half alive.

Clearly here they are reporting the consistent surge of the local glacier. Glacier response to climate is known to be quite slow and hence this is an indication of climatic conditions causing an increase in mass budget of the glacier over perhaps decades. The rate of advance (provided we are able to discover the distance of a musket at that time) indicates the size of the increase of mass budget and thus enables some insight into either the degree of increase of snowfall or reduction in average summer temperature. Increased rainfall is perhaps reflected in the way the grain is reported to rot, as is the fact that the people had chosen to try to grow moisture tolerant crops.

Figure 4.4

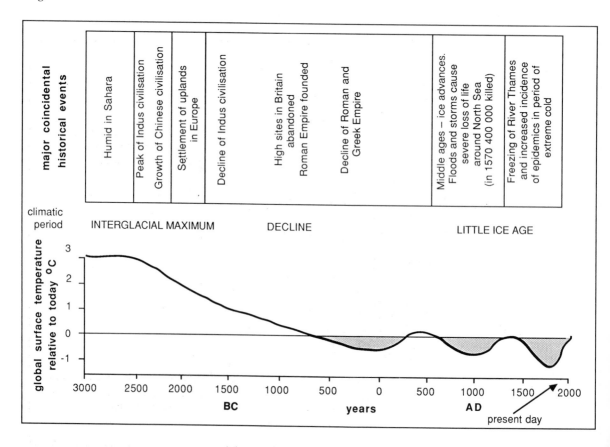

Figure 4.5 *The relationship between climate and historical events*

Figure 4.6 *A scene which today's climate makes it hard to imagine*

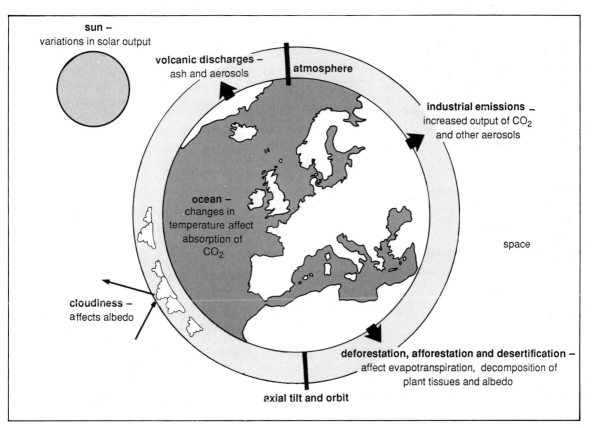

Figure 4.7 *Factors that may influence the Earth's climate*

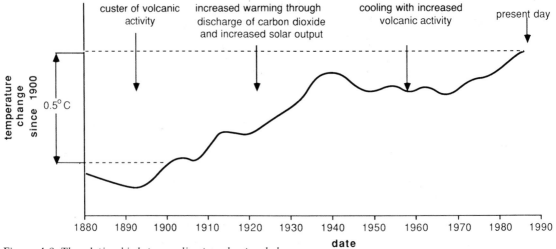

Figure 4.8 *The relationship between climate and natural phenomena*

Natural reasons for climatic change

The atmosphere responds to external influences (Fig. 4.7). Prime among these are changes in received energy from the sun which can either occur due to variations in solar output, or by changes in the earth's tilt or orbit. Changes in tilt and orbit occur only slowly and are very probably responsible for the shifts into and out of the major climatic changes such as those that produced the Ice Ages. Such long term cycles would indicate that, after the recent cold period ended about 12 000 BC, the climate warmed to a maximum about 4000 BC and has since been cooling. Thus, if this trend continues, a combined change in tilt and orbit will take the earth back into another Ice Age within the next 5000 years.

Changes of climate that occur over shorter periods of time, such as centuries or decades, are not so easy to identify or to explain. We have two 'natural' candidates to explain much of the climate change over the last century (Fig. 4.8):
(a) degree of volcanic activity; and
(b) changes in solar output.

(a) Volcanic activity

Volcanic eruptions may affect climate both locally and on a global scale depending on the nature of the eruption. With eruptions of the Mt St Helens type the effects are local because the ejected material is thrown only into the troposphere where particles are easily removed by rainfall. However, with eruptions like El Chichon in Mexico, much material is thrown into the stratosphere where it remains for many years, only slowly falling towards the earth's surface.

Of the materials thrown into the stratosphere, oxides of sulphur dominate. These spread out to form a veil encompassing the whole of a hemisphere in as little as two to three months. This then slowly extends over the whole globe. The effect of the veil is to absorb incoming radiation, thereby altering the energy budget of the lower troposphere and initiating a period of cooling.

Volcanic eruptions in recent times have caused a temperature decrease of up to 1.5°C from the long-term average for up to two years. If eruptions happen to be clustered in time, then the cumulative effects may be considerable. For example, in the early years of this century there was a cluster of eruptions, and this coincided with a period of cooling (Fig. 4.5). At Pamplemousse Gardens (Mauritius) this also coincided with a period of unusually wet weather (Fig. 4.9).

(b) Changes in solar output

The energy radiated into space by the sun largely depends on the rate at which convection occurs within the sun's outer layers. Changes in this output show a close relationship with global temperature fluctuations during this century.

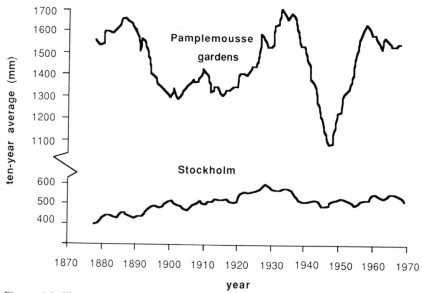

Figure 4.9 *The pattern of climate in Mauritius*

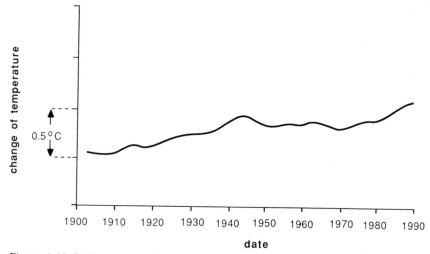

Figure 4.10 *Evidence of global temperature rise*

How could people cause climatic change?

Recently many meteorologists have become convinced that the climate is going to change dramatically within the next few decades, not due to the hand of nature, but to the influence of people on the global weather machine. The change is rather easy to identify because it has produced a steady rise of temperature throughout the present century, just at a time when natural cycles would indicate a decline to be due (Fig. 4.10).

As people notice their increasing effect on the environment (accelerated erosion, deforestation, pollution of oceans and atmosphere) it is natural also to question their impact in causing long term changes to the climate. There have already been conscious attempts to increase (or decrease) the amount of rainfall and thus produce higher crop yields, although so far these attempts (mainly through cloud seeding) have been on a local scale.

It is now quite clear that the reason for the climatic warming shown by recent records is the

69

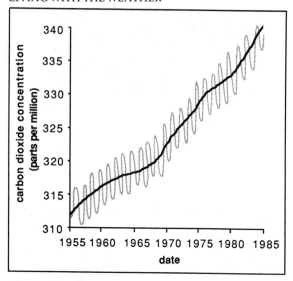

Figure 4.11 *Changes at Mauna Loa*

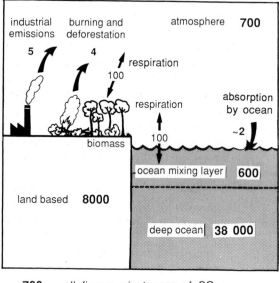

700 all figures gigatonnes of CO_2

← → average annual transfer rates

→ average annual increase this century

Figure 4.12 *Carbon dioxide in the Earth's system*

odourless, colourless gas called **carbon dioxide** that people create when they burn oil in motor cars, gas or wood in stoves and coal in power stations. The mean monthly concentrations of atmospheric carbon dioxide measured at the Pacific observatory of Mauna Loa, Hawaii, show a clear correspondence with global temperature changes (Fig. 4.11).

Although just half a degree in the last 50 years may not seem a great change, this has to be put in the context of its effect on the global climate: the 'Little Ice Age' of the seventeenth century saw global average annual temperatures dip just 1–2°C below those of today, while during the last major Ice Age global temperatures were only 5°C lower. Thus, if the meteorologists' predictions are correct, people in the next century will be faced with the conflict between retaining a lifestyle dependent on burning carbon-based fuels and the prospect of changing the global climate irreversibly. This is why it is important to understand the likely impact of increasing carbon dioxide levels.

The greenhouse effect

Carbon dioxide accounts for no more than 1.5 per cent of the tropospheric gases, yet it is extremely important because it is a large molecule which, although transparent to the incoming short wave solar radiation, absorbs strongly in the long wavelengths radiated back to space by the earth. This absorption makes our world much warmer than it otherwise would be. Indeed, without the absorption effects of the carbon dioxide (commonly known as the 'greenhouse effect'), the earth's troposphere might be over 25°C cooler and life on earth impossible. Because carbon dioxide has important effects at low concentrations, people can influence the global temperature relatively easily.

Figure 4.12 shows the quantities of carbon in different parts of the active earth system. Note the rates of transfer between these reserves. By burning fossil fuels and forests we cut short the long natural cycle. Although insignificant at first, the rate of burning has accelerated to such an extent that the amount of carbon dioxide gas is now increasing substantially. So far we have released 400 billion tonnes of carbon dioxide back to the atmosphere. Since the beginning of the century the carbon dioxide content of the atmosphere has increased from 290ppm to 315ppm in 1980 and predictions to AD 2050 suggest a doubling of pre-industrial levels that may top 600ppm. If this were true the global annual average temperature might rise by 2°C.

We are also cutting down more and more

forests. In 1950 a quarter of the world's land surface was under forest; now it is less than a fifth. Most of the forests are cut down and burned; the land is used for agriculture. But the amount of carbon stored in crops on farmland may be less than a fiftieth of the carbon contained in the trees they replaced. The loss is especially great in the tropics where the productivity of the trees is so high (Chapter 12). The replanting of trees in northern latitudes cannot hope to make up for these losses. The result is that deforestation may be putting as much carbon dioxide into the air as burning all fossil fuels.

The implications of climatic change

A global average temperature rise of 2°C seems likely by the middle of the next century, but the rise will not be uniformly spread. Thus some regions will see hardly any change, while others will show severe signs of modification. The poles, for example, may witness a 5–10°C rise in temperature. If this were to cause a melting of the ice caps then sea level would rise by 80 m, quite sufficient to inundate nearly all of the world's great population centres. But even if only part of the ice were to melt the repercussions could be horrendous. For example, the most likely ice regions to melt are those on the Antarctic shelves. At present these floating masses of ice are grounded on the rock of the shelves. This prevents ice on the higher inland areas from surging towards the ocean. But if the warming caused these grounded flows to break up then there would be nothing to prevent an ice surge. Estimates suggest that such an event would cause an 8 m rise in sea level, still quite enough to drown many of the world's cities. In such circumstances the Thames barrage, for example, would be completely drowned.

There are also other, perhaps even more important effects of a potential global warming. Warmer conditions might allow more crops to be grown in the developing world because the dry lands would receive more rainfall. But these would still not be capable of being the most productive regions in the world. In the American prairies computer models suggest a

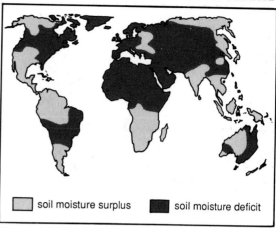

soil moisture surplus   soil moisture deficit

Figure 4.13 *Predictions of changes in the soil moisture in a* $2 \times CO_2$ *world can be achieved using powerful computer models and simulations of the atmospheric circulation. Note the dry mid-latitude summers*

1°C higher temperature combined with a decrease of 10 per cent in the rainfall and a lowering of the soil moisture at the start of the growing season (Fig. 4.13). If this were to occur then yields would fall by 20 per cent. And it just so happens that the present surplus produced by the prairies and corn belt is 80 per cent of the world's surplus – an amount that makes the difference between life and death to the 100 countries that have to import grain to feed their populations.

The difficulties of responding to rapid change are immense. Agricultural research stations need time to develop new strains of crops that may be able to cope with the changed conditions; farmers will have to retrain to new, more appropriate forms of farming. And it is likely that the real impact of the global warming will gain pace quickly: it will create a great period of uncertainty and instability. Any decisions we might need to make have to be taken now. But who would be prepared to restrain their use of energy on the basis of a computer model whose imagined effects will not be with us until the next century? A recent estimate of the cost of scrubbing carbon dioxide from the gases released in power stations shows that the process would use up 16 per cent of the output of the power station and increase the capital investment of building the station by up to 15 per cent. In turn this would cause up to a 70 per cent in-

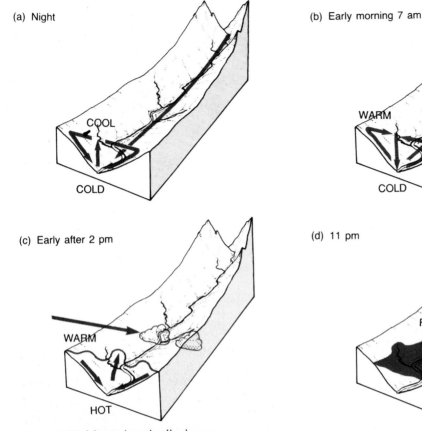

(a) Night

COOL

COLD

(b) Early morning 7 am

WARM

COLD

(c) Early after 2 pm

WARM

HOT

(d) 11 pm

Fog

Figure 4.14 *Mountain and valley breezes*

crease in electricity prices. Changes to power bills of this order would cause world-wide economic chaos and would be impossible to implement. Only a vastly improved efficiency of fuel use will solve this problem.

The climatic effects of local variations in relief and land use

The global pattern of air flows dominates the regional climate. But there is still considerable variation at the local level. The main factors that influence local climate are:

(a) exposure to radiation gain or loss;
(b) exposure to wind;
(c) amount of local heat generated (domestic fires, vehicle exhausts, etc.);
(d) presence of bodies that store heat (lakes, seas, etc.).

Valleys, for example, experience considerable diurnal fluctuations in wind direction, temperature and humidity (Fig. 4.14). At night the hills, exposed to the sky, radiate heat freely and the ground cools quickly. Air cooled by conduction with the ground becomes more dense and begins to flow as a **mountain breeze**, displacing warm, less dense air from the sheltered valley sides (Fig. 4.14(a)). Eventually a cold pocket of air accumulates in the valley bottom. Humidity is now high in the cold, still air and fog may become a real hazard.

By morning cold air fills the valleys (Fig. 4.14(b)). But as the hills are bathed in sunlight, they warm, and the warmed air in contact with them begins to rise, drawing cold air up from the valley as a **valley breeze**. This is a much less noticeable feature than the mountain breeze and is quickly terminated as the sheltered valley soaks in the heat of the rising sun. By mid-morning the valley is the warmest area and often becomes a heat source for cumulus clouds (Fig. 4.14(c)).

Student enquiry 4A:
Climatic considerations on the M25

The M25 is one of the largest civil engineering activities ever undertaken in the UK. Its purpose is to provide an orbital motorway 'box' which will allow traffic to bypass London and thus relieve central congestion (A1). The M25 is basically a 'green field' motorway, passing through London's Green Belt in order to cause the least possible disruption to existing urban areas. The route of the M25 and its relationship to geology and topography are given in A2. Here we will concentrate our attention on two small stretches of this major undertaking and the way the local climate plays a major role in the practical use of the road.

A New Civil Engineer supplement

A1

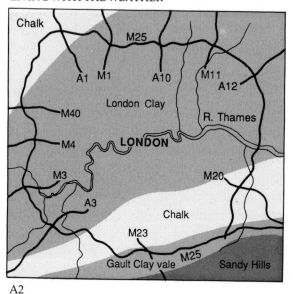

A2

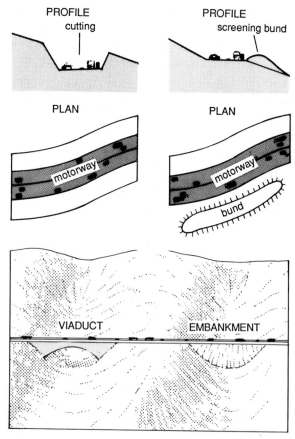

A3

South of the River Thames the geological setting of the route is largely dominated by the chalk of the North Downs. The route skirts the western edge of the Darent valley on the chalk outcrop. Just to the north of Riverhead to the junction with the M23, the route over the steep-sided chalk valley would be prohibitively costly and so the M25 is routed south across the narrow Gault Clay outcrop. Here it crosses the heads of many chalk dry valleys before being routed back on to the chalk at Reigate Hill. From here it descends into the Mole and Wey valleys where it crosses the London Clay. After this, and completing the swing round to join the M4, the M25 is taken on to extensive river terrace deposits.

The local councils have been instrumental in making sure that the environment was protected as well as possible. Thus the motorway has been taken into cuttings and the material so excavated has been formed into landscaped embankments where otherwise the motorway would have impinged visually on the landscape. These embankments (called **bunds**) are about 2 m high and parallel the motorway as it crosses the North Downs (A3).

The meteorological office provided the vital weather link for the construction teams by telling them when weather conditions would be suitable for pouring concrete and giving it time to harden. But they have also been involved in an unexpected way: to predict the incidence of fog.

In still, calm weather, the M25 has proved to be one of the most fog-prone motorways in the country. A4(a) shows the location of the 30 places where the problem is most troublesome. There have been frequent pile-ups with many people killed (A4(b)).

A4(a)

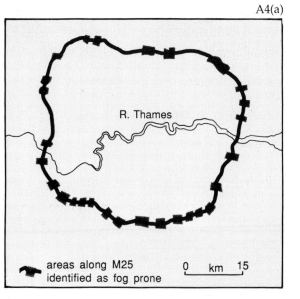

areas along M25 identified as fog prone

0 km 15

1. Explain why the section of M25 that runs at the foot of the North Downs might be so prone to the effects of local fog and note the weather conditions most likely to be the cause of problems.

2. Describe why local landscaping to hide the motorway may have made the motorway fog situation worse. Suggest modifications to the bunds that may help to relieve the fog build-up.

3. Make a judgement about the advantages and disadvantages of a viaduct and an earth embankment from the point of view of liability to fog (A3). Sketch out for each case the way you think fog will move.

4. From all these considerations, and bearing in mind the need to reduce visual impact of the motorway as well as reduce the fog hazard, trace out and justify an alternative route for the M25 in the Leatherhead to Weybridge (Gault Clay Vale) region.

A4(b)

A pile-up in fog on the M25

Sea and land breezes

Water bodies can absorb insolation, spreading it through considerable depths. By contrast, the land has a low thermal capacity. On a sunny day the upper few centimetres of land can therefore become much hotter than the sea. This causes a thermal gradient with air rising over the (low pressure) land and drawing an airflow from the sea and on to the coast as a cool **sea breeze** (Fig. 4.15(a)). Furthermore, the air above the heated land often becomes unstable and cumulus cloud develops by mid-morning. Thus it is common to see the coastal region bathed in sunshine, whereas inland regions become overcast. A regional wind (say as part of a depression) will either reinforce the sea breeze effect,

driving the cloudy area further inland, or it will counteract it, bringing the cloud back over the coast (Fig. 4.15(b)).

The most famous example of a sea breeze dominating the local weather occurs along the Californian coast near San Francisco (Fig. 4.15(c)) where a cool current upwells off the coast. As warm air flows are pulled on to the coast by inland heating, or driven inshore by the normal westerly airflow, rapid advection occurs and the air quickly cools to below its dew point temperature. Deep turbulent mixing caused by the air being dragged over the sea and land thickens the resulting fog. The zonal wind serves to drive the fog deeper inland before the sun can burn it off.

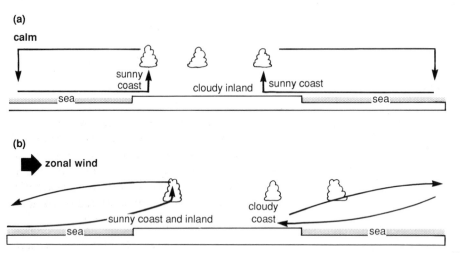

Figure 4.15 *Land and sea breezes*

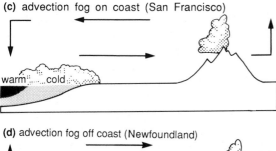

(c) advection fog on coast (San Francisco)

warm cold

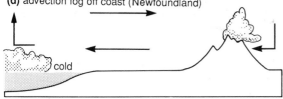

(d) advection fog off coast (Newfoundland)

cold

Figure 4.15 (cont.)

In Britain the coastal counties from north-east Scotland to the Wash of East Anglia regularly experience fog whose character is, in principle, not unlike that of San Francisco. However, in this case it is not an upwelling cold current just off-shore that cools air and causes condensation, but a long tongue of cold water that hugs the coast. Conditions are often particularly foggy and cold when high pressure atmospheric systems waft air from the North Sea over the land. At these times, while the rest of the country basks in sunshine, the east coast remains clammy and cold, shrouded by persistent fog.

The most persistent fog of all occurs off Newfoundland (Fig. 4.15(d)). In this unusual situation the advection effect brings warm air that has passed over the gulf stream over coastal currents that have come from the Arctic. This fog is very persistent and represents a seasonal problem and a hazard for shipping.

B1

Student enquiry 4B: Local winds and human activity

1. A farmer wants to plant a new orchard (B1) and also develop a camp site for tourist caravans and tents. He wants to give individual berths with a shelter of the kind shown. This can provide shade and wind protection, but only in one direction. He also knows that orchards are very sensitive to frosts in spring. He is less sure of the requirements of the camp site residents. He is thinking of putting a close boarded fence between the campsite and the orchard to keep trespassers at bay during the season when the trees bear fruit.

Describe the climatic consequences of these actions on:
(a) his success with fruit tress; and
(b) his success with campers.
Detail the requirements of both trees and campers and suggest how the scheme could be revised to benefit both trees and campers.
2. B2 and B3 show the coastal regions of Chicago and San Francisco. Assuming economic and social factors are not important, where would the most desirable residential area be in terms of any local climate effects (consider both summer and winter).

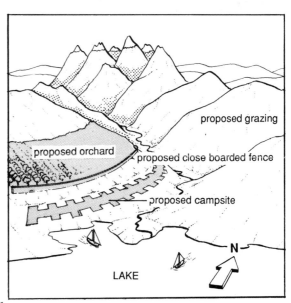

proposed grazing

proposed orchard

proposed close boarded fence

proposed campsite

N

LAKE

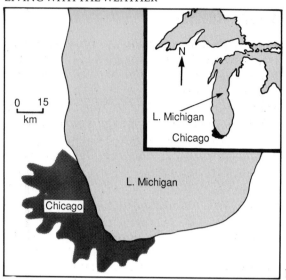

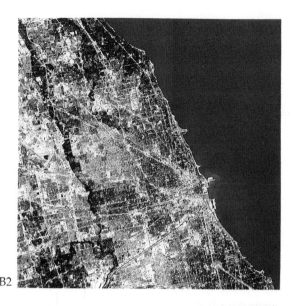

B2

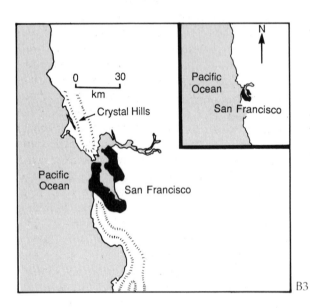

B3

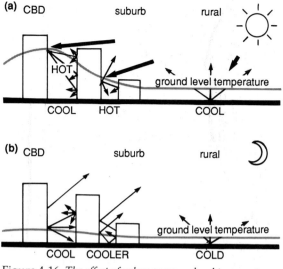

Figure 4.16 *The effect of urban areas on local temperatures*

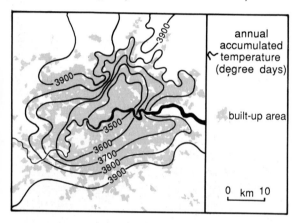

Figure 4.17 *London's heat island*

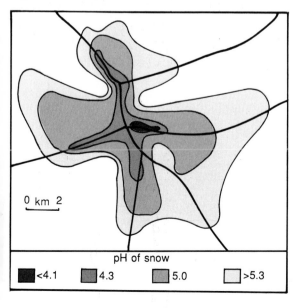

pH of snow

| <4.1 | 4.3 | 5.0 | >5.3 |

Urban climates

There are significant climatic contrasts between city, suburban and nearby rural areas. For example, high rise buildings tend to trap radiation so that heat generated by buildings stays largely within the building space (Fig. 4.16). This helps to elevate the urban temperature. The degree of urban influence depends on a number of factors, including zonal wind speed (a certain threshold speed will ventilate any city), and the character of the urban development (closely spaced office blocks will create a more distinctive local climate than detached houses in large gardens). The famous heat island created by London (Fig. 4.17) is a clear example of a local urban climate.

The urban atmosphere is particularly liable to pollution as a result of vehicle, domestic and industrial emissions either as dust and suspended particles or as gases (including the components of acid rain). In cities, dust particles can be as great as 4 million per cubic centimetre and directly contribute to the poor visibility experienced in many urban areas. About 70 per cent of urban gas pollution comes from vehicle exhausts. On a still day, and especially with anticyclonic weather, pollution will settle over a city as a **pollution dome**, the effects being particularly noticeable in the poorly ventilated areas of high-rise offices near the CBD (Fig. 4.18). A breeze will then spread the pollution as a plume. The Thames valley, for example, gets its worst pollution on days when easterly winds spread air from London; south-east England gets its worst pollution when easterly flowing polar continental air spreads pollution from the European mainland in winter. Urban pollution can therefore be a local effect that has a regional impact.

Figure 4.18 *Trapped pollution in an urban area with no heavy industry is measured by snow acidity values*

Student enquiry 4C: Urban pollution

Table 4C1

A	B	C	D	E	F	G
12	12	13	14	13	12	12
0	1	4	5	4	0	0
3	3	5	7	5	3	3
10	11	9	11	11	10	10
18	20	18	25	24	20	21

1. C1 shows a townscape in cutaway profile. Copy the profile on to the bottom of a graph sheet. Now plot the changes in temperature from Table 4C1 as graphs, plotting each one above the profile. Label each graph with one of the following:
(a) for *calm* conditions summer (i) early morning; (ii) late morning;
(b) for *calm* conditions winter (i) early morning; (ii) late morning; and
(c) for late morning conditions, autumn, strong (10 Kt) breeze.
Assess the climatic quality of areas within the valley floor for residential development.
2. Use the information on local variations of acid snow (Fig. 4.18) to draw an acid rain profile for the town. This will show the local sources of airborne pollution. Where are they? Which residents would suffer most?

3. C2 shows the profiles of solid pollutants away from a local motorway. Explain how these pollutants (which might include lead based aerosols) could affect local residents and land uses. Suggest areas of further tree planting that would be effective in containing the spread of road-generated pollution.
4. C3 shows a variety of conditions that might influence industrial pollution. Describe each condition. C4 shows a sketch of a hypothetical town in a hilly landscape. It is to be submitted as part of a planning application by an international company who want to establish a silicon chip production plant. The plant will use processes that emit a range of atmospheric pollu-

D

E

F

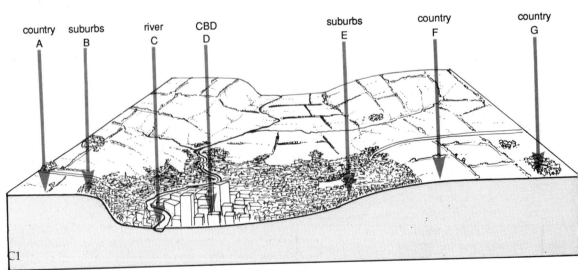

country A   suburbs B   river C   CBD D   suburbs E   country F   country G

C1

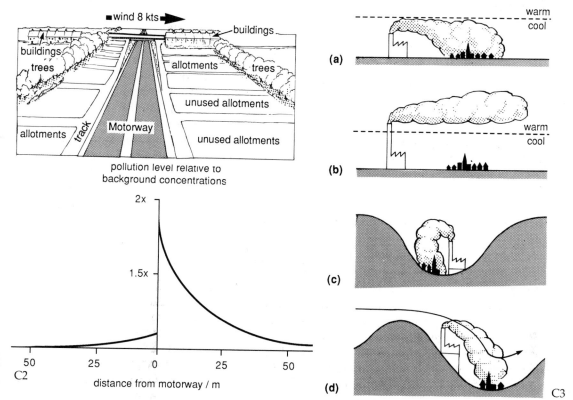

wind 8 kts →

buildings
trees
allotments
buildings
trees
allotments
track
Motorway
unused allotments
unused allotments

pollution level relative to
background concentrations

2x

1.5x

50   25   0   25   50

C2

distance from motorway / m

(a)   warm / cool

(b)   warm / cool

(c)

(d)   C3

tants. It seeks planning permission at site X. You have been asked by the planning officer to produce a report on the environmental impact of the plant on the local climate so she can decide where it should be sited.

The planning officer concludes that, due to the pressure for employment in the area, she will be obliged to grant planning permission.

However, the local council has two alternative sites of a suitable size available. Attempts could be made to steer the firm to either Y or Z if there were a strong case on environmental grounds. She needs some further advice on which site to offer the firm so that the local residents will be least affected climatically by the plant and so the environmental lobby will produce the fewest objections. Make up a dossier with scientific support for your final recommendation.

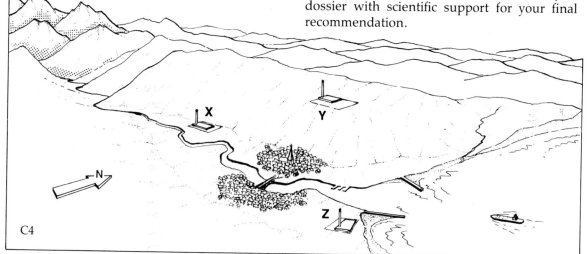

X
Y
Z
N
C4

Key terms

Acid rain: rain with a pH of less than 5.5 and caused by man-made pollutants, usually gases, that are acidic when mixed with water.

Adiabatic Lapse Rate: the decrease (or increase) in temperature of a body of air rising (or sinking) through the troposphere. For dry air DALR = 1°C/100m; for saturated air SALR = 0.6°C/100m.

Air mass: a region of the troposphere which has uniform characteristics gained by long residence in one position (example source regions: arctic and subtropical high pressure belts).

Anticyclone: a region of diverging and descending (warming) air.

Blocking high: a pool (region) of high pressure that becomes detached from the general easterly progression of highs and lows in the mid-latitude westerlies. Once detached it becomes more or less stationary and deflects air streams to the north and south. Regions under a blocking high experience prolonged drought.

Cirrus: high level layer cloud dominated by ice crystals. It has a characteristic whispy appearance.

Climate: the pattern of weather, usually regarded as the statistical average of the last 35 years of meteorological records.

Convection: overturning in the air resulting from excessive ground heating.

Cumulus: pillow-shaped cloud resulting from condensation of unstable convected air.

Depression: a region of converging and ascending (cooling) surface air in which two air masses of contrasting properties meet.

Dew point: the temperature at which condensation occurs.

Environmental curve: a graph (profile) of temperature against height for the troposphere. It is measured with a radiosonde ballon ascent.

Extra-tropical cyclone: a mid-latitude depression.

Front: a zone where two contrasting air masses meet and interact. The polar front is the most marked and is associated with the polar jet stream and the formation of mid-latitude depressions. At the surface the cold front follows a warm sector; the warm front precedes it.

Greenhouse effect: a term used to explain why the earth's average troposphere temperature is 25°C warmer than if there were no cloud, carbon dioxide, and water vapour or droplets in the air. These elements absorb terrestrial heat before it escapes to space and re-radiate part of this back to the ground.

Heat island: a region of enhanced temperature over an urban area. It is most common in winter and at night.

Horse latitudes: zones of calm beneath the sub-tropical high pressure regions.

Hurricane, typhoon: an intense tropical cyclone with high speed winds.

Hygroscopic nuclei: aerosols – small particles of salt, clay, hydrocarbons from exhaust systems, etc. – suspended in the air and which form nuclei on which water can condense to form droplets.

Inter-tropical convergence zone (ITCZ) is the region where tropical air flows meet. It is an irregular zone that follows the seasonal progress of the overhead sun. It is signified by convectional rain.

Insolation: short wave radiation from the sun.

Jet stream: a very rapidly moving air flow with a wave-like motion, embedded in the upper troposphere. It is usually associated with major temperature changes within the air. Jet streams are thought to 'steer' the mid-latitude depressions and anticyclones.

Lapse rate: the decrease in temperature of air with height (or pressure).

Monsoon: Arabic word for 'season', relating to a tropical or sub-tropical climate in which the wet season begins very abruptly.

Nimbo: rain producing.

Occlusion: a region where the warm sector of a depression is completely lifted off the ground.

Pollutant: aerosols produced by people.

Relative humidity: the proportion of water vapour in the air compared to the maximum it could hold (measured in per cent; maximum 100 per cent).

Sea breeze: a sea-land air flow caused by local coastal convection currents that develop because of land-sea temperature contrasts.

Stratosphere: the shell of atmosphere beyond the tropopause and containing insolation absorbing ozone.

Stratus: low to medium level layer cloud produced by the bulk uplift of stable air at a front or over mountains, or bulk cooling of an air layer (anticyclone in winter).

Sub-tropical high pressure: a region about 30° latitude N and S, underlain by the world's great deserts, where air subsides as part of the general atmospheric circulation (poleward edge of the Hadley cell).

Terrestrial radiation: long wave radiation from the earth.

Trade winds: constant winds that blow between the sub-tropical high pressure regions and the ITCZ.

Tropopause: the sharp zone separating troposphere from stratosphere

Troposphere: the shell of atmosphere closest to the earth's surface.

Westerlies: the mid-latitude variable winds that blow predominantly from west to east and which carry depressions and anticyclones around the mid-latitudes.

Theme: Managing landforms

Chapter 5
Slopes

Introduction

Only a very small proportion of the earth's surface is absolutely flat. Most of it is made up of slopes (Fig. 5.1). Notice the wide variety in steepness, size and shape of slopes in the photographs – all slopes are essentially unique.

The slope of the land is of considerable importance to:

(a) farmers, who may be restricted in choice of land use or forced to adopt specific conservation or land use systems – or even terrace land; and

(b) engineers and those who have to build homes and roads, or install pipelines and cables, or excavate cuttings and construct embankments and spoil tips while ensuring that the slopes they use or create remain stable and safe.

Slopes are both natural and man-made and all are dynamic – they are subject to both gradual and rapid change. Slopes collapse, or fail quite frequently. In many cases the result is only a small scale inconvenience such as a partly blocked road or railway line (Fig. 5.2), but the results can be large and horrific, involving avalanches and mudflows of immense proportions that cost many lives (Fig. 5.3). Clearly it is vital that the mechanisms that cause slope instability are understood before building on or near them.

Figure 5.1(a) *Landscapes of slopes.*

Notice the slopes can be classified as straight, convex or concave. Do particular slope types occur in specific parts of the landscape?

Figure 5.2 *A small debris fall hampers traffic in Utah, USA*

Figure 5.3 *Huascaran disaster, Peru, 1970*

Factors involved in slope formation

To understand the processes and changes associated with slopes, it is helpful to think of a slope as a **system** with inputs (water, frost, soil etc.) and outputs (material, water, etc.) (Fig. 5.4). The inputs and outputs are linked together by paths of movement, e.g. soil creep, landslides.

The slope system can best be described as a **cascading** system since it involves the progressive movement of matter and energy. You can see how this operates in Fig. 5.5. Consider, for example, material on a steep slope by the sea. Waves break against the lowest section, directly abrading or plucking material away and steepening the slope. Gradually the slope becomes sufficiently oversteepened for loose debris just out of reach of wave action to begin to slide and tumble to the foot of the cliff. If sufficient material accumulates quickly a scree slope may temporarily be formed before wave

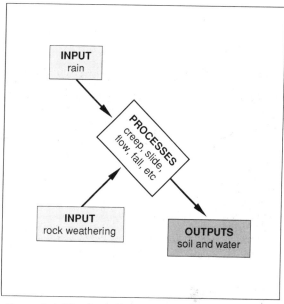

Figure 5.4 *The slope system*

Figure 5.5 *Cliffs at Whitby, Yorkshire – an example of an active debris cascade system*

action removes it. However, once out of equilibrium, the cliff above has to adjust over all its area. Thus sliding material near the lower cliff removes the support it was providing to material higher up, so that this, too, slides away. In this way adjustments are made over all the slope in the form of a **debris cascade** (Fig. 5.6(a)). And as long as the waves keep removing material from the base of the slope, so adjustments will occur above.

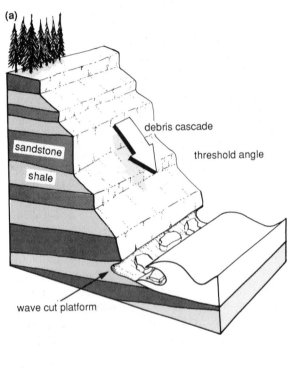

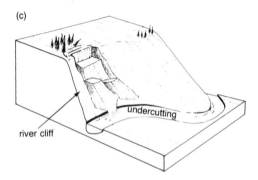

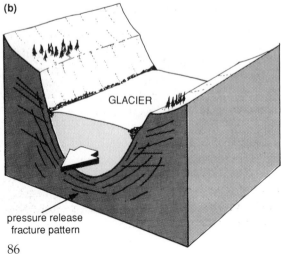

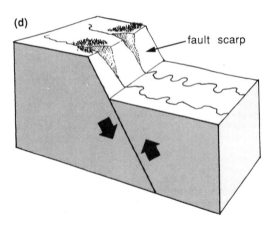

Figure 5.6 (a) *The principle of debris cascade.* (b) *Steep slope created by glacial erosion.* (c) *River cliff created by migrating meanders.* (d) *Fault scarp created by rifting*

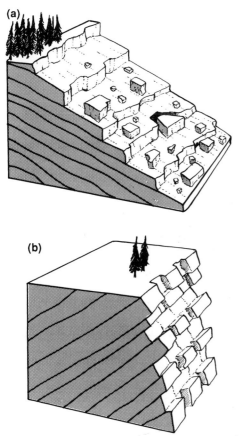

Figure 5.7 (a) *Slope with dip away from land. Weathered blocks easily fall clear; slope is similar to dip of beds.* (b) *Slope with dip into land. Weathered blocks are retained on the slope and there is a tendency for a cliff to form*

From this example you can see that the most important factors are:

(a) the undercutting of a slope;

(b) the weathering of material so that it can move; and

(c) the changing external conditions such as saturation by percolating water, throughflow or a rise in the ground-water table.

Slopes are normally created by erosional agencies such as rivers, waves or glaciers or by tectonic processes such as faulting or the building of volcanoes (Fig. 5.6(b), (c), and (d)). The material of which the slope is made has a major influence on slope development because it controls such factors as (a) the rock structure and dip, and thus the tendency for the rock to remain stable at a steep angle; (b) the size of physically weathered debris. The complex cliff shape in Fig. 5.5, for example, results from the interbedding of two rocks with contrasting properties; the sandstone is structurally much stronger than the shale and stands at a steep

angle.

Some rocks dip towards the slope. Weathering of such rocks tends to encourage material to fall away when it has been weathered, whereas material weathered from strata that dip back from the slope tend to stay in place (Fig. 5.7).

The influence of weathering

All forms of weathering produce material of lower bulk density than the material from which it is derived. Weathered products are small and do not fit together well. Because of this, weathered material, be it scree or soil, also has less structural strength and is more prone to move.

Slopes can be categorised as:

(a) transport-limited slopes, where the rate of transport is less than the rate of weathering of new material. These slopes are soil and vegetation covered. Many slopes in humid temperate and tropical environments are soil-covered.

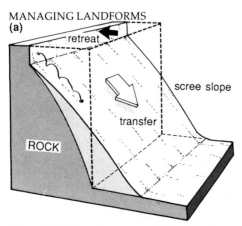

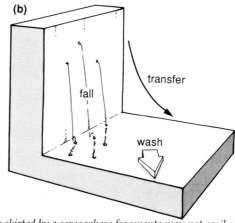

Figure 5.8 (a) *A slope susceptible to frost shatter is frequently skirted by a scree where fragments may not easily be removed.* (b) *A slope created in massive sandstone. Debris created is of individual particle size and easily washes away*

Soil results largely from chemical weathering (decay) of exposed solid rock or some other material. Weathered products consist mostly of small platelet-shaped particles called clay minerals. Soil is thus a mixture of fragments of unweathered rock (stones, sand, etc.) in a matrix of clays. Soil clay minerals have the special property of being cohesive (sticky) when damp. Topsoil is usually bound together further by an intricate web of plant roots and stuck together by humus. However, soil processes often cause clays to be washed from the topsoil into the subsoil, leading to a concentration of clay platelets in this zone. These translocated platelets often block soil pores and make the subsoil more prone to saturation.

(b) weathering-limited slopes, where the rate of transport across the slope is greater than the rate of weathering of new material. Such slopes always show exposed rock and a thin, discontinuous mantle of coarse debris (Fig. 5.5). Slopes that are not soil covered are less common. In a few cases bare rocks occur because they are virtually chemically inert and rarely support soils except in flat landscapes. Quartzite is a striking example of this, but some acidic igneous rocks (high in silica) also weather slowly. However, bare rocks mostly occur either in cold or very dry environments where chemical weathering cannot be very effective. In these environments mechanical breakdown dominates.

The most common mechanical weathering process is frost shatter, whereby water becomes frozen in rock fractures, expands and forces surface fragments from the bulk rock. In this way dislodged fragments may be prised from a stable to an unstable position. Frost shatter produces a wide size range of angular rock fragments, largely depending on the fracture pattern of the rock. These tend to rest against the lower slope and form a scree (Fig. 5.8). Some massive rocks (such as many sandstones) are not susceptible to frost shatter because there are no fracture lines. Weathering thus has to remove particles one at a time.

Slope movement

There is a delicate balance of forces acting on slope material, and there are certain **threshold conditions** which, if passed, tip the balance in favour of movement. There are many types of movement, many related to particular shapes of slopes as shown in Figure 5.9.

The main processes of direct gravity influenced movement are:
(a) fall;
(b) slide; and
(c) flow.
All these are rapid movements. There is also the virtually imperceptible movement process called:
(d) creep and frost heave.
The first process (a) applies to loose, noncohesive rock debris only; the other three processes (b–d) involve the interaction of soil and water or frost. In addition much material is moved by:
(e) water running over or through slopes.

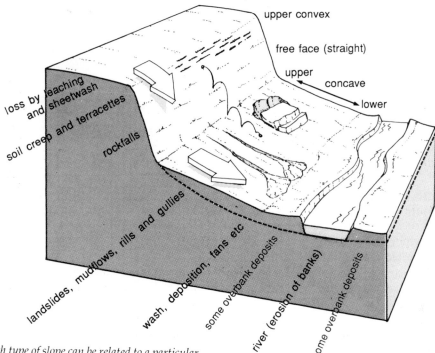

Figure 5.9 *Each type of slope can be related to a particular type of process*

(a) rock fall

A particle of weathered material remains at rest on a slope if the frictional resistance to movement is greater than the downslope stress produced by the particle weight (Fig. 5.10). At a certain threshold angle 'Ø' the stress equals the maximum frictional resistance. This angle is called the **threshold angle for stability**. If the angle of slope is steeper than this value the particle with move. Most steep bare slopes on which rockfall is a dominant process are commonly called cliffs; another, more technical term is **free face**.

On a cliff material will fall as it becomes released by weathering and will often accumulate as a scree at the cliff foot. The angle of the scree is the angle of rest of the weathered material and this, of course, is just below the threshold angle for movement.

Rockfalls from cliffs mostly do little damage to property because they occur either at coasts or in sparsely populated uplands. However, one dramatic example of rockfall hazard occurred in Wales. The photograph, Figure 5.11

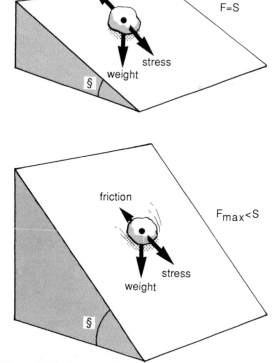

Figure 5.10 *Rock stability on a slope*

89

illustrates the danger of rockfalls to some of the people of Blaenau Ffestiniog who had built their homes in the shadow of some vertical cliffs. But the threat of cliff collapse had not impressed the people who had built their homes below the potentially unstable rock faces. They seem to have believed that the cliff was indeed 'as solid as a rock'.

In the nineteenth century the potential for disaster had already begun to worry engineers. The probable consequences of frost weathering forced them to sling massive chains around the more precariously poised boulders, bolting the chains to sound rock above. However, this did not solve the problem, and year by year the cliff weathered further. The severe winter of 1981/2 brought this problem to a head, and by 1983 the cliff had begun to look more like a construction site as engineers undertook more complete remedial measures.

(b) and (c) rapid mass movements

On a more gentle transport-limited slope, there will be a soil cover and particles will not move singly. In this case we need to consider a block of soil on a slope (Fig. 5.12). However, the situation is just the same as for a rock particle, movement occurring if the threshold angle 'Ø' is exceeded. Soils, however, can hold back water because of the slowness of percolation and throughflow. Alternatively saturation could occur through a rise in ground water levels. In this case a further effect becomes important – the buoyancy (or upthrust) effect of saturation (see upthrust in Fig. 5.12).

Think of the effects of saturation on soil particles in the same way as standing in a barrel which is slowly being filled with water. As the water rises it becomes progressively more difficult to stand firmly on the bottom because much of your weight is taken by the water. And so it is with saturating soils. As the pressure of the soil on the slope decreases, so the magnitude of the friction also decreases and the soil can move much more readily or at a less steep angle than when it is dry or just damp.

Water is by far the most important external influence on slope stability, which is why many slopes fail during or immediately after periods of heavy or long duration rainfall. Its effect is to

Figure 5.11 *Construction in progress in 1983. What choices are now being pursued?*

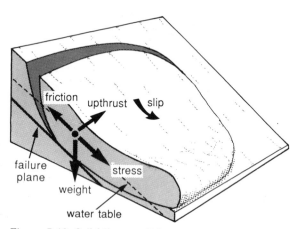

Figure 5.12 *Soil failure conditions*

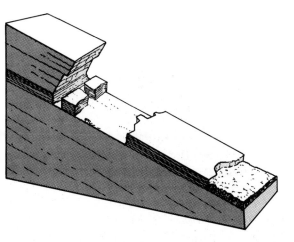

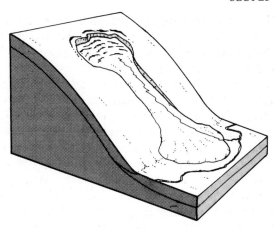

Translational slide–Movement is predominantly along planar or gently undulatory surfaces. Movement frequently is structurally controlled by surfaces of weakness, such as faults, joints, bedding planes, and variations in shear strength between layers of bedded deposits, or by the contact between firm bedrock and underlying detritus.

Flow–Movement of mass such that the form taken by moving material or the apparent distribution of velocities and displacements resembles that of viscous fluids; velocity ranges from slow to extremely rapid.

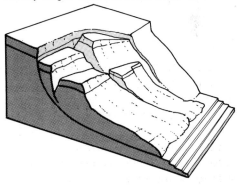

Fall–Mass travels most of the distance in free fall, by leaps and bounds, and rolling of bedrock or soil fragments.

Complex–Landslide incorporating two or more types of movement.

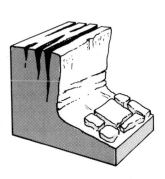

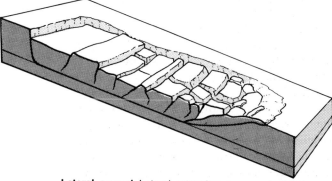

Topple–An overturning movement that, if unchecked, will result in a fall or slide.

Figure 5.13 *Types of slope failure*

Lateral spread–Lateral extension movement of a fractured mass; some spreads are without a well-defined basal shear surface; others include extension of rock or soil resulting from liquefaction or plastic flow of subjacent material.

91

Figure 5.14 *Landsliding induced by meander undercutting*

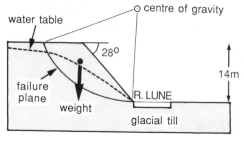

Figure 5.15 *The mechanism of a rotational slide*

reduce the threshold angle for movement 'Ø'. If this falls below the slope angle movement will occur. However, slope length also plays an important role because a slope of constant angle becomes less stable as it gets longer. On moderate and steep slopes, where the threshold angle for soil stability can be exceeded under saturated conditions, episodic collapse (landslides/flows) is usually the dominant landforming process (Fig. 5.13).

The main categories of movement are **slides** – whereby the soil moves as a unit and slips over a failure plain – and **flows** – in which the soil liquidifies and moves as a fluid. However, there are many graduations between the two main categories because, during sliding, friction often causes the soil to be shaken up so much that liquefaction occurs and the material completes its movement as a flow. Flows can travel over much shallower angles than slides.

Typical areas for landsliding are at river cliffs where meandering rivers undercut and therefore steepen the adjacent slope (Fig. 5.14) and

at sea cliffs. Whether shallow or deep-seated slips form then depends on the nature of the slope material (Fig. 5.15). If soil overlies solid rock shallow slips are the norm; if there is deep unconsolidated material such as glacial till in a sea cliff or alluvium in a river cliff, then deep-seated rotational slips will tend to dominate. Thick clays crack in dry periods and provide channels for water entry and the build-up of saturated zone when rains return.

In the Jackfield area of Shropshire, England the rapidly downcutting River Severn has cut a gorge into horizontally bedded sandstones and shales, initiating shallow landslides. Furthermore, water draining through these material percolates through the sandstones but is held up above the shales, so that in many cases water rises up into the soil. This situation is particularly common after a prolonged period of winter storms.

A large shallow slide began to form from such causes in Jackfield in 1951 (Fig. 5.16). The area had previously been regarded as stable and a railway line, a road and several houses had been constructed. Since then the slide has continued in most winters, causing the destruction of the houses and interrupting the road and railway. As Figure 5.16 shows, the road, many times repaired, today resembles nothing more than a fairground roller coaster. It is impractical either to drain the slide or to stabilise the road at an economic cost, although the local authorities have valiantly tried to keep open communications within the village.

Flows, strictly called **debris flows**, are more common in areas with ill-sorted materials. In these cases there is limited clay to hold the soil together and movement readily causes the particles to shake loose. Loose, coarse-grained materials include weathered material mantling semi-arid slopes, volcanic ash, gelifluction material and some glacial tills.

Debris flows contain no more than 20 per cent water. The large proportion of solids in the slurry that is formed give great strength and the material resembles fast-moving wet concrete. The strength factor allows the flow to carry huge boulders as well as trees, cars, pieces of bridge, etc.

Areas prone to debris flows can be identified

Figure 5.16(a) *Shallow slides near Jackfield*

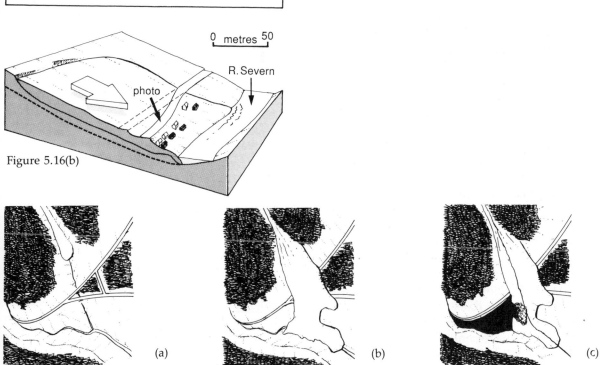

Figure 5.16(b)

Figure 5.17 *Sequential diagrams showing how the Polallie Creek debris flow caused a flood on the East Fork flood river*

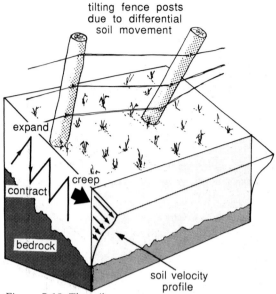

Figure 5.18 *The soil creep process*

by (a) slopes mantled by unsorted debris (usually gravelly or muddy sand); (b) deeply incised channels near steep headwaters; and (c) streams with bank deposits (levees) containing part-buried trees and other coarse debris.

At approximately 9 pm on Christmas Day 1980, a disastrous debris flow burst out of Polallie Creek Canyon on the slopes of Mt Hood, Oregon, USA, owing to sustained wet conditions followed by an intense rainstorm. The flow was triggered by a small landslide that occurred in the headwaters of the Polallie Creek. As the unconsolidated debris slipped it vibrated into a debris slide. The flow gathered more material as it moved on, tearing down trees in its path. It then rushed across the main Oregon State Highway 35, damming the East Fork River. The river was flowing at near flood levels, so it took only 9 minutes for a lake 4 ha in area and up to 12 m deep to form. At this point lateral pressure from the lake waters, and erosion due to dam overspill caused a catastrophic collapse of the saturated debris-slide dam. Eight kilometres of highway were washed away or badly damaged, 1 person was killed and $13 million of damage was done. This was a spectacular example, but debris flows and landslides are by no means uncommon and cost more in repair bills than any other hazard in the USA.

(d) creep and frost heave

Soil creep and frost heave are the imperceptible downslope movements of surface soil due to wetting and drying or freezing and thawing respectively. When soil becomes wet the clay minerals absorb water and the soil swells. This movement occurs mostly at right angles to the slope (Fig. 5.18). As water is taken from the soil by plant transpiration the soil shrinks again, this time primarily under the influence of gravity in a downslope direction. As a result a ratchet-like motion occurs. Freezing and thawing produces the same effect, but orders of magnitude faster. Soil creep is largely a summer phenomenon, frost heave dominates in winter; both are minor processes and rarely cause concern to people.

(e) water

Water flows over the surface under two conditions:

(a) when rainfall intensity exceeds infiltration capacity; and

(b) when water tables rise to the surface.

The conditions under which these situations arise are described more fully in Chapter 10. In humid temperate regions it is rare to find surface flow sufficiently fast to entrain particles and cause erosion because rainfall intensities are low and any water flowing over the surface is trapped and slowed down amidst a dense network of plant stems and roots. Important areas of surface erosion thus primarily occur on ground disturbed by the activities of people. However, in other regions the rainfall intensities are much higher and the ground level vegetative cover is less complete. Semi-arid regions, deserts and the humid tropics all experience erosion by surface runoff.

Slope erosion from flowing water often begins as **rainsplash**, whereby raindrops falling directly on an exposed soil surface impact and scatter water and clay particles (Fig. 5.19). Mud spatter is a clay suspension which, as it gradually infiltrates the soil surface, separates out, so that the clay tends to fill the small pores of the soil and reduce infiltration capacity. Eventually a surface **crust** is produced which is almost impermeable. In consequence a progressively

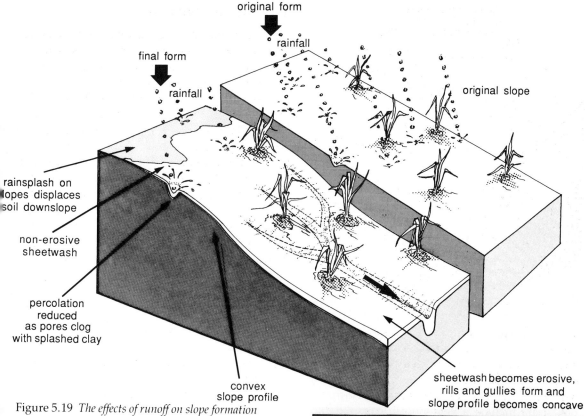

original form

rainfall

final form

rainfall

original slope

rainsplash on
slopes displaces
soil downslope

non-erosive
sheetwash

percolation
reduced
as pores clog
with splashed clay

convex
slope profile

sheetwash becomes erosive,
rills and gullies form and
slope profile becomes concave

Figure 5.19 *The effects of runoff on slope formation*

Figure 5.20 *A volcanic ash slope, Washington State,
USA. The fill and gully network has created concave
regions that link together and form the source of a stream*

greater part of each rainstorm flows over the
ground surface.

In areas where there is limited infiltration
and incomplete vegetation cover, the water
flows over a slope as a sheet (**sheetflow**). With
added contributions from rainfall sheetflow becomes faster and the volume of water greater
downslope. Eventually a threshold speed is
reached which allows the sheetflow to pick up
(erode) soil particles. With time sheetflow gradually becomes focused into a coherent network of shallow channels called **rills**. Some
rills will trap more water than others and will
develop progressively into **gullies**. Gullies are
an established part of a drainage network and
are not easily removed. Indeed, by channelling
water and focusing it into more efficiently
shaped channels, gullies are self-reinforcing.
At the heads of the gullies there is a break of

slope down which sheetwash cascades. This is a high energy location and one where erosion is rapid, leading to headward growth of the gully.

Because sheetwash, rills and gullies transfer water more efficiently downslope, they are able to transfer and erode over progressively shallower gradients and, indeed, slopes dominated by running water erosion develop the classic concave profile of river channels (Fig. 5.20).

Water can also erode either by carrying materials in **solution** or by carrying materials through a network of sub-surface **pipes** in the soil. These processes do not have direct visual impact on the landscape, but removal in solution can be as important as all other processes combined on gentle slopes. When pipes become large their roofs often collapse and open channels (gullies) are thus created.

Student enquiry 5A: Prediction and remedial solutions for unstable slopes

---

Most rapid mass movements have a long history and show tell-tale scars on hillslopes. They are often most clearly identified on aerial photographs. If old sites can be identified some forward planning can be attempted.

1. Spanish Fork lies near a gap in the Wasatch hills of Utah, USA. Here the steeply dipping rock strata include a very poorly consolidated shale rock. Landslides have been initiated in this formation all over the area. Rivers have increased the likelihood of slides where they run along the strike of the rock, steepening the slope for considerable distances. The Wasatch mountains are difficult terrain for people, and communications congregate in valley bottoms, frequently following the river banks. Debris flows that move down valley sides towards the river thus stand a great chance of seriously disrupting the local communications. Furthermore the area is prone to flooding if late melting snowpack runoff is compounded by an early summer thunderstorm.

The Spanish Fork area had received 50 per cent above average rainfall for the previous two years before the dramatic movement on 14 April 1983. This had resulted in a high soil moisture and water tables in all soils. These antecedent conditions, coupled with decades of unnoticed internal weathering, finally triggered the slide at Thistle (A1, A2, A3).

Using A1 to A3 describe what appears to have happened and the way the slide has affected the communications and local residents.

2. The final remedial solution chosen was to drain the lake that formed behind the landslide dam by constructing a rock tunnel and permanently diverting the small stream. Why were the roads and railways still diverted and the lake drained instead of bulldozing the flow away?

3. A4, A5 and A6 give information for the region surrounding the spectacular Mam Tor landslide in Derbyshire, England. What are the similarities between the Mam Tor and Spanish Fork slides both in terms of natural processes and human impact?

4. Now obtain an Ordnance Survey map of the Mam Tor region. Rebuilding the road would be one solution. What would be the arguments for and against this solution? It has also been suggested that rerouting of the A625 should take place either by widening the Winnats Gorge road (through areas owned by the National Trust) or by taking a route near to Trek Cavern (a tourist attraction). Draw a morphological sketch map of the area, indicating the areas where slope processes would make road construction difficult or hazardous. Use this map as a basis for commenting on the possible rebuilding or rerouting. Explain what other factors besides cost and slope stability would need to be taken into account.

A1 (a) *Area before the slide;* (b) *see page 98*

A2 *The landslide toe area*

A1(b) *The lake created by the slide*

A3 *Half-flooded house after the lake had been drained*

A4 *The Mam Tor slide*

A5

A6

Slopes in the humid tropics

The humid tropics are characterised by high temperatures and rainfall. Even though most areas of the humid tropics experience rainfall for only part of the year, sufficient water remains deep within the soil for intense chemical weathering to reduce all materials to clays. In areas where there are basic rocks such as basalts, the type of clay formed (montmorillonite) shrinks and swells dramatically with changes in water content. Most tropical soils have been forming for millions of years and depths of tens of metres deep are not uncommon, and over a hundred metres has been recorded (Fig. 5.21).

The situation with regard to slopes can be summarised as 'the rate of weathering is greater than the rate of hillslope transport which in turn is greater than the rate of incision by rivers'. As a result many valleys have gentle slopes. Indeed, rivers characteristically appear to wander aimlessly across almost flat plains. Usually weathering and the centre of the valley are unrelated, while rapids and waterfalls only occur with particularly resistant rock bands such as quartzite (Fig. 5.22). Landscapes are thus often characterised by abrupt breaks of slope (scarps) separating almost level surfaces. Only in highland zones does a significant shift in climate produce valleys of the kind found in temperate lands.

The reason for the lack of river incision, despite the large volumes of water discharged during the rainy season, is that the water has few tools with which to abrade. Because most of the material has been reduced to clay, there is little coarse load to abrade the rock and lower the bed. Residual quartz pebbles do occur, while the nature of soil formation often yields residual iron nodules (laterite), but because these are large, they tend not to be moved by surface wash and are not usually available to the stream.

With very gentle slopes, the main transport processes must be surface wash and other processes involving running water. Tropical storms have a very high intensity, and although they may at first appear to be protected by the forest canopy, rainforest trees are so tall that it is possible for the raindrops falling from the canopy to regain their terminal velocity before they splash on the ground. Also, because the canopy cuts out the light to the ground, there is naturally a fairly exposed soil surface. As a result, the main agency restraining soil loss is the surface network of tree roots.

Today it is commonplace to find the rivers of tropical humid regions having the consistency of soup in the rainy season. However, the suspended sediment load they carry today is not natural, but a result of erosion of cultivated ground. Scenes of high sediment loads in rivers demonstrate that surface wash and rainsplash is quick to act on exposed ground, leading to the rapid formation of rills and gullies. This is important information for both engineers and those concerned with soil conservation.

Landslides and other mass movements are uncommon in most of the undisturbed areas of the humid tropics, partly because many areas have gentle slopes, and also because the intricate network of tree roots binds the soil together to resist movement. However, landslides do occur on steep slopes during the wet season because, although the clays are strong when unsaturated, they become plastic and lose most of their strength when wet.

Figure 5.21 *A deeply weathered soil, typical of the humid tropics. No solid rock can be seen in this road cutting*

Figure 5.22 *Characteristics of humid tropical landscapes*

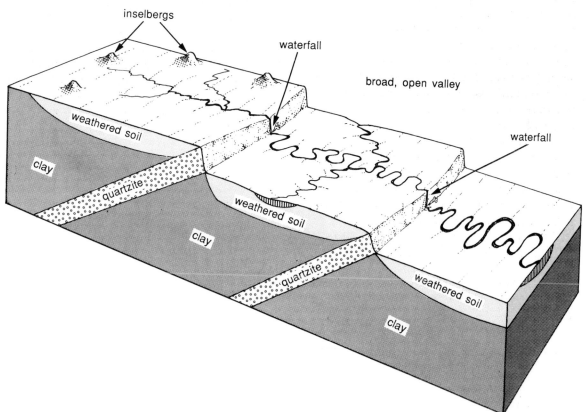

Key terms

Buoyancy: the ability of water in saturated soil to take up some of the pressure between grains, making their movement easier. Total buoyancy in soils causes liquefaction and material then flows.

Concave slope: one whose angle decreases downslope.

Convex slope: one that becomes steeper downslope.

Debris cascade: the sequential movement of weathered debris down a slope following removal of material from the slope base.

Factor of safety: the relation between the applied stress on a soil, and the stress needed to cause movement.

Fall: movement through the air of intact rock masses.

Flow: movement of non-cohesive saturated material down a slope.

Gelifluction: downslope flow of material above a frozen subsoil (often taken to mean the same as solifluction).

Gully: a deep water-cut channel in soil large enough to disrupt mechanised farming.

Heave: the sawtooth downslope movement of clay-based surface materials by swelling and shrinking with changes in moisture content.

Landslide: general term to mean rapid mass movement across a failure plane.

Leaching: transport of dissolved material through a soil by water.

Mass movement: the bulk movement of material where flowing water is not the main transport process. It includes rockfalls, avalanches, landslides, debris flows, soil creep and gelifluction.

Overburden pressure: the part of the weight of the soil that acts into the slope. It is opposed by the buoyancy force in saturated soils.

Particle movement: the transport of debris in flowing water such as leaching, rainsplash and sheetwash.

Rainsplash: soil material splashed from the surface by the impact of a falling raindrop.

Rill: a small channel in topsoil cut by flowing water.

Rock avalanche: cascading of loose rock debris down a slope, most of which is propelled into motion by the impact of other falling or rolling debris.

Rotational slip: the rotational movement of thick, cohesive material about a theoretical centre.

Scree: a fringe consisting of loose accumulations of physically weathered coarse rock debris at the foot of a slope.

Sheetwash: transport of material by unconcentrated overland flow.

Slide: movement of intact cohesive material across a failure plane.

Slump: rapid mass movement where a slide collapses into a debris flow.

Soil: for slope movement purposes, soil is taken to be any unconsolidated material.

Soil creep: imperceptible surface soil movement due to heave.

Strike: a direction taken on the surface of a rock stratum at right angles to the dip.

Terracette: small elongated steps of topsoil found on steep slopes.

Threshold slope: the maximum angle of stability of weathered material. Material accumulates to the threshold angle approximate to the value of static friction, but collapses to the angle controlled by the value of dynamic friction. Threshold angles for unsaturated materials are often about twice the angle for the same material when saturated.

Transport-limited slope: a soil-covered slope where the weathered material is produced more rapidly than it can be removed by transport processes. Common in humid temperate and tropical environments.

Weathering: the slow *in situ* change of surface materials when subject to the effects of temperature and/or water. **Mechanical weathering** involves disintegration, **chemical weathering** involves the creation of new materials, mostly clays.

Weathering-limited slope: a bare slope where transport can always remove any newly weathered debris. Common in arid, semi-arid and cold environments.

Chapter 6
Coasts

Introduction

For more than a thousand years people have lived and farmed along the Holderness shore of Lincolnshire, England. But those who choose to live or farm near the sea find their future very insecure for, each winter, the cliffs retreat and eat into the precious land. Today the cold North Sea washes across the area where once there was thriving farmland and villages (Fig. 6.1). The presence of the villages is now only remembered through the maps and documents made centuries ago although, as the photographs show, the problem is no less real today.

Holderness is made up of glacial till dumped as the last of the ice retreated 12 000 years ago. This material, largely unconsolidated clay, pebbles and boulders, produces low cliffs which are not much of a barrier to the fierce north-easterly storms that send the waves crashing against them. The Holderness coast is not very heavily populated today, but severe erosion can currently be found on many densely populated shores. Today, even in places where the numbers of people requiring protection are small relative to the cost of any engineering work, there are still vociferous demands for action to be taken. One of the most famous examples of this is at Barton on Sea in Hampshire (Fig. 6.2).

The coastline is not just a pleasant environment to live near, it is also an important resource. There are huge quantities of sand and gravel, vital for the construction industry. Ecologically, the coastal environment represents a unique habitat both for flora and fauna.

It is a major location for recreation with hundreds of kilometres of resorts hugging the coast. Some industrial activities also require coastal locations, e.g. steel and chemical works. Ports and harbours need to be dredged in order to keep them clear and safe for shipping.

In all, the coastal environment is under great pressure and it must be handled carefully. Ill-considered schemes can affect natural processes and radically alter the coastline to the detriment of other users. The coastline thus needs careful management. This chapter will first consider the natural processes operating to shape coastlines. It will then examine the interaction of natural processes with human activities.

Wave processes

Most people think that rapid erosion occurs when soft rock outcrops at the coast. On the surface this appears to be the case at Barton; clearly the local residents think the weak sandstone cliffs are primarily to blame for their difficult situation (Fig. 6.3). But in fact their troubles do not begin at the coast, but tens of kilometres out to sea, as ocean waves are driven in over a progressively shoaling (shallowing) seabed (Fig. 6.4).

Waves are set in motion by the stress of the wind blowing against the ocean surface. Thus water acquires energy from wind depending on (a) the **duration** for which the wind blows; (b) the distance over which it blows (the **fetch**); (c) the **velocity** of the wind; and (d) the **decay**

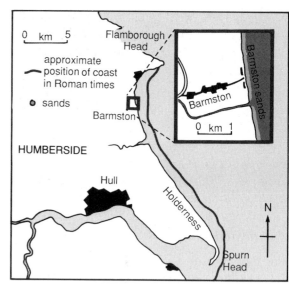

Figure 6.1 *Coastal erosion on the Holderness coast*

Figure 6.2 *Collapsing cliffs threaten this hotel at Barton on Sea*

Figure 6.3 *Christchurch Bay: solid geology*

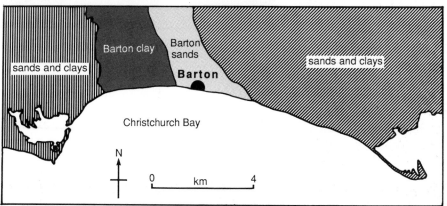

(a)

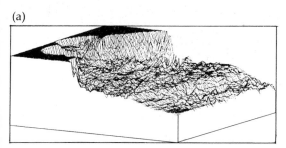

Figure 6.4 *The sea bed and its influence on waves approaching Barton on Sea*

(b)

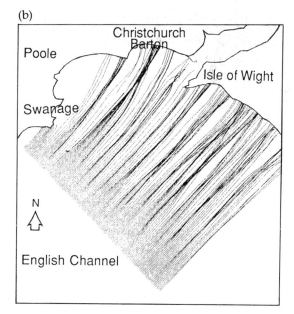

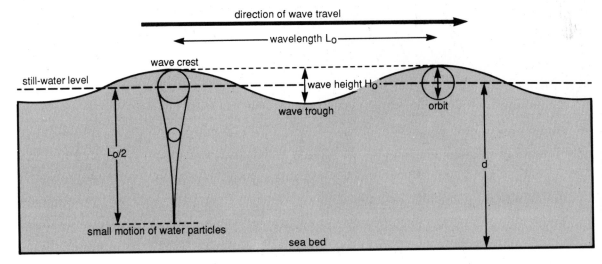

Figure 6.5 *The nature of ocean wave motion*

distance beyond the region of generation. Ocean waves transfer energy as a wave *shape* only. Thus a wave crest moves forward because the surface waters are making small linked orbiting motions (Fig. 6.5), not because the water moves forward in bulk.

Clearly, strong winds blowing for a long time over great distances will be able to pump the maximum energy into the waves. Waves eventually rise (**set up**) to such a steep angle (120°) that they become unstable and collapse; the maximum height of waves possible in any given set of environmental conditions thus largely depends on the wavelength. Waves that have reached their collapsing height produce a **fully arisen sea**. Fully arisen seas are not common because of the long time (days) wind must blow over the same growing waves.

In practice, storm winds set up waves which have a relatively short wavelength for their height (wavelength 10–20 times height); these are steep-sided waves. **Storm waves** are unstable and quickly collapse when the wind dies down; when they move outside the storm generating areas they therefore tend to decay quickly, leaving only the more stable, broad based types of wave to travel outward. These broad-based waves are called **swell waves**, and have a relatively long wavelength compared with their height (30–500 times). They lose energy only slowly and can travel for thousands of kilometres before decaying completely.

Although wave forms can travel for large distances in deep water, in shoaling conditions the orbiting water starts to brush against the sea floor. The orbiting effects of water extends down to about half a wavelength. Some oceans swell waves have wavelengths of over 200m and even water 100m deep will therefore influence their progress. Frictional contact with the seabed both distorts the shape of the orbits into an oval, and slows the water. If part of a wave reaches shoaling water ahead of the rest, it will slow down. As a result a straight crest will begin to distort into a curve, a process called **wave refraction** (Fig. 6.6).

Waves approaching, an irregular shoreline with a smoothly shoaling bed begin to 'wrap themselves' around the coast, concertining at headlands and expanding in bays. In Fig. 6.6 the approaching wave crest of uniform height and speed has been divided into segments of equal length. Each segment of the wave therefore has the same energy. The figure also shows the changing length of wave segments as they reach the coast. The lines drawn to connect consecutive places on the advancing wave are called **orthogonals** and they trace out the path of each wave segment. The wave near the headland begins to shorten, while the wave in the bay lengthens. Because the wave energy is fixed, any change in crest length must be compensated by a change in wave height. So waves that shorten become higher and waves

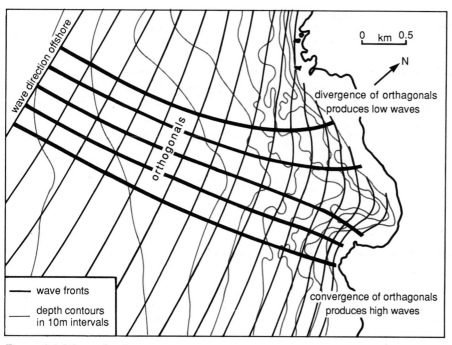

Figure 6.6 *Wave refraction patterns*

that lengthen become lower. Thus it is common to find high waves breaking on a headland while those in the bay are small. Thus wave action is more powerful at headlands.

The simple pattern described above is only true for an evenly sloping seabed. When the seabed shoals irregularly the waves are refracted in a complex way, and regions of concentrated energy can only be predicted using computer-generated refraction diagrams. In Fig. 6.4, for example, the seabed shoal pattern causes waves to converge, and energy to be concentrated in some parts of the bay as well as on some parts of the headlands. This is a major factor in understanding the erosion of the Barton cliffs.

What is the effect of breaking waves?

As waves move inshore they reach a zone where the amount of water shoreward of the wave is insufficient to keep the water orbiting. At this point the wave begins to break (Fig. 6.7). The character of the breaking wave depends on the steepness of the beach and the shape of the wave. In general, waves that **spill or surge** forward direct most of their energy up

the beach, sending up a powerful **swash** and transporting sediment. These waves, which are common both to gentle and steep beaches respectively, tend to pile up sediment at the head of the beach (Fig. 6.8). This is the characteristic pattern associated with swell type waves. By contrast, those that break and **plunge** directly down on to the beach, comb much sediment seaward. In this case there is a weak swash which does not tend to travel far up the beach and a strong **backwash**. Plunging waves are associated with short wavelength storm waves.

The result of these different breaker actions is to keep a **dynamic balance** in the coastal zone, the beach profile continually building landward and being combed seaward by successive swell and storm waves (Fig. 6.8). Building is marked by broad ridges called **berms**, downcombing by erosional **terraces** and the formation of a submerged bar at the low tide limit. The effect of **tides** is to make the breaking waves reach to a different distance up the beach each day, so during a period of falling tidal (spring to neap) the pattern of berms and terraces tells much of the recent storm/fine weather pattern. Beyond the limit of normal waves there may be **sand dunes**, formed by wind blowing sand from the

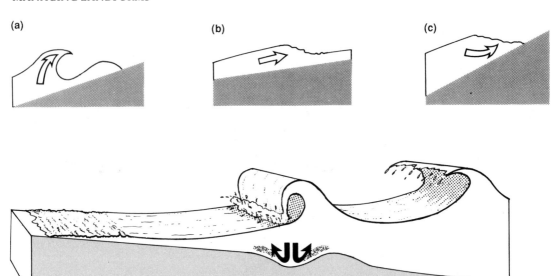

Figure 6.7 *Patterns of breaking waves.* (a) *Plunging on moderate beach slope.* (b) *Spilling/collapsing on gentle beach slope.* (c) *Surging on very steep beach slope.* (d) *A wave breaking as it approaches the shore*

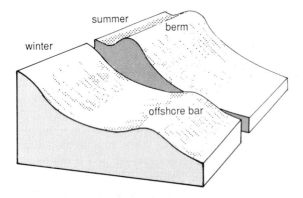

Figure 6.8 *Contrast in beach profile between summer (swell dominated) and winter (storm dominated) waves*

Figure 6.9 *Sand dunes on the coast at Harlech*

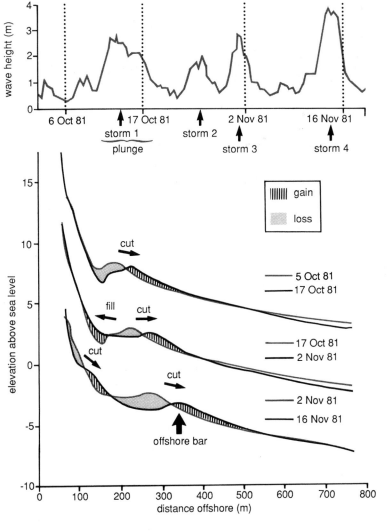

Figure 6.10 *Effects of four storms on the beach and nearshore at a profile line south of Duck, North Carolina, USA*

beach when it is dry and exposed during low tide (Fig. 6.9). Dunes are an important reservoir of sand during storms but they also prevent the onshore movement of storm breakers.

Beach profiles may change on a *daily* basis as swell waves give way to storm waves, and on a *weekly* basis due to tidal effects. But they also change on a *seasonal* basis because storm waves tend to be a 'winter' phenomenon with swell waves more common in 'summer' (Figs. 6.8, 6.10). However, because storm waves carry more energy than swell waves, a single storm with plunging breakers can comb down suffic-ient material to require several months of rebuilding by spilling waves. If several con-secutive storms occur the amount of material

combed away may take years to rebuild. The nature of this dynamic balance has extremely important consequences for coastal engineer-ing.

Beaches contain a wide variety of sediment sizes, from fine sands to shingle. The size and character of the beach material and the slope of the beach are related to the forces to which the beach is exposed and the type of material available on the coast. Material comes from the following sources:

(a) Rivers generally bring fine sand and mud.

(b) Direct erosion of cliffs supplies a wide range of sediment sizes. Glacial till cliffs on the east coast of England, for instance, provide large boulders as well as fine clays and some sand;

109

whereas eroded chalk cliffs (e.g. southern England) produce large quantities of flint shingle. **(c)** Currents and waves carry sediments (mostly sand and gravel) from deeper water on to the beach.

Finally, it is important to know that not all material found on the beach is part of active processes. For example, some beaches or shingle barriers and bars such as Chesil Beach were produced during the period of rising sea level that followed the retreat of the last ice sheets. Similarly the **barrier islands** of the USA Atlantic

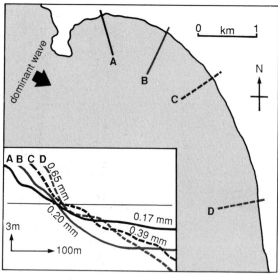

Figure 6.11 *Relationship between sediment size, beach gradient and exposure to wave attack, Half Moon Bay, California. Notice the log spiral shape of the bay*

and Gulf coasts, 90 Mile Beach in east Australia, and many others owe their existence to beach building during the post-glacial rise of sea level. Thus it can be extremely foolhardy to rely on the erosion of cliffs to replace shingle excavated from the beach whose existence is entirely due to onshore processes in an earlier period of earth history!

In general, the larger the size of sediment on the beach, the steeper its angle. However, the most exposed parts of a coast will have waves with such large amounts of energy that only coarse sediment such as shingle will be able to remain. Thus there is also a characteristic relationship between beach sediment, gradient and exposure to wave energy around a bay (Fig. 6.11).

Sediment transport

As water is driven onshore by the advancing wave fronts it tends to pile up on the beach. In extreme circumstances this gives rise to a **storm surge** of water that may raise sea level by several metres. However, there also has to be a return flow of water. Often this occurs as an **undertow** which, if highly concentrated, is called a **rip current** (Fig. 6.12).

Most waves approach beaches at an angle. Thus the water is partly driven along the shore, and this gives rise to a **longshore current**. All these currents are able to move sand-sized sediment along and off the shore. Breaking waves, on the other hand, move sediment in a

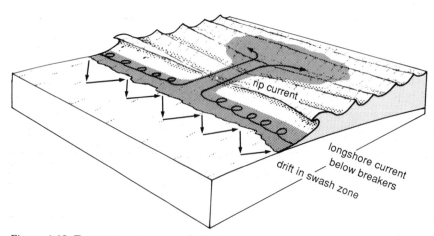

Figure 6.12 *Transport systems near the beach*

rachet like motion because the angle of run up of the swash is different from the downslope return of the backwash. This motion (**beach drift**) can move cobbles as well as sand within the breaker zone. Beach drift is the most easily observed transport process, but the effects of currents are equally important. Together they cause a complex pattern of sediment transport called **longshore drift**.

The pattern of currents at La Jolla canyon, California (Fig. 6.13) shows the complex set of currents typically produced and the source regions of cliff erosion associated with places of concentrated energy. There is a dominant direction of wave approach and currents, and sediment eventually moves to the south, but locally there are regions of flow reversal. Such patterns can readily be identified by placing a set of floats just seaward of the breakers and charting their progress.

It has been found that most coasts have a pattern of currents that effectively divide beaches into semi-closed cells. These are called **sediment cells** (Fig. 6.14) and each can have one or more of:

(a) source region (offshore, cliff, river, etc.);
(b) transfer zone (the region over which long-shore drift operates); and
(c) sink region (spit, offshore sandbank, etc.). Knowledge of sediment cells is very valuable to all those trying to plan for coastal management. For example, it is more sensible to permit sediment removal from a sink region than from a transfer zone or source region because these latter areas would cause greater erosion.

Influences of the land on coastlines

The shape of a coast is not just the result of wave action: it is also related to the nature of the materials that make up the land. For example, coastlines are either composed of rock strata which lie parallel to the coast (described

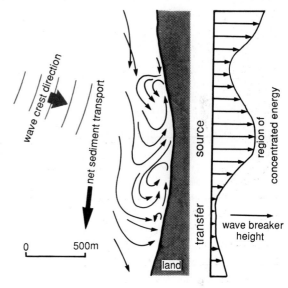

Figure 6.13 *The complex current and sediment movements at La Jolla Canyon, California*

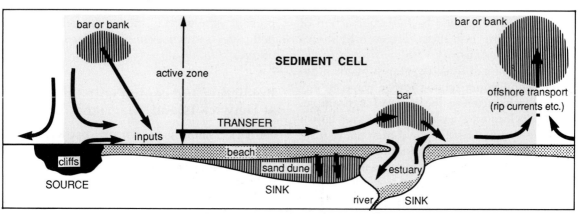

Figure 6.14 *The sediment cell and sediment budget concept*

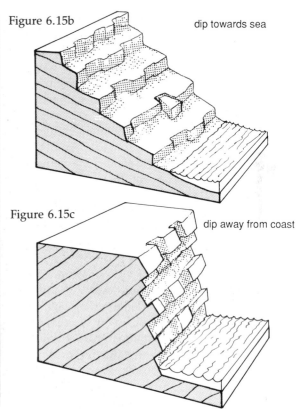

Figure 6.15b — dip towards sea

Figure 6.15c — dip away from coast

Figure 6.15a *Lulworth Cove, Dorset*

as **concordant** coasts) or, much more commonly, intersect the coast at some angle (described as **discordant** coasts). When a variety of rocks are exposed to attack, waves will tend to excavate those strata that offer the least resistance, either because they are physically soft and are susceptible to direct abrasive forces of sediment-laden waves, or because they have a complex and intricate fracture or fault pattern which can be exploited by hydraulic action of waves crashing into them. Figure 6.15 shows some examples.

All stretches of coast develop towards a dynamic equilibrium related to the wave energy and the character of the rocks. For example, soft rocks located at a place where waves have a high energy will readily yield material to form an extensive beach. The formation of the beach will absorb wave energy and it will therefore become liable to various forms of littoral drift. Clearly rocks in sediment sink regions will be less liable to attack than those in source regions and cliffs may not form. Thus it is certainly pos-

sible to find the same strata yielding several distinct landforms depending on its position with respect to a sediment cell.

The classic coastline shape of bay and headland usually occurs when there are stretches of coast with markedly differing resistance to erosion. Nevertheless, dynamic equilibrium is also reached, such that sediment transfers to the bay and shelter by the headlands both prevent excavation of the bay beyond a certain point; yet another example of dynamic equilibrium.

Predicting and coping with flood risk at Fenwick Island, Maryland, USA

Fenwick Island is a narrow barrier island, formed during the post-glacial rise of sea level (Fig. 6.16). Its surface now rises just a few metres above sea level, and its exposed position along the mid-Atlantic seaboard makes it extremely vulnerable both to hurricanes and to winter depressions. The island has poorly

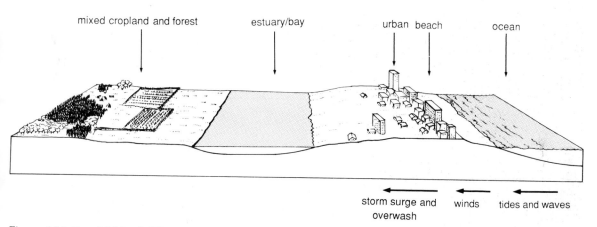

Figure 6.16 *Fenwick Island, USA*

fertile sandy soils and was not attractive to early settlers. However, the prospect of a wide sandy beach as a source of recreation made the island attractive in later years and Ocean City was established in 1870. Since then development has been rapid (Fig. 6.17) and, although the permanent population is still only 4000, in summer holiday-makers swell the population to over 200 000. Large numbers of hotels and self-catering flats (condominiums) have been built for the tourists, and of course a prime requirement is a view and proximity to the beach. Further there are vast areas devoted to permanent caravan sites and to mobile caravans. Paradoxically, as development has increased, the most stable and least hazard prone (back) regions have remained undeveloped, while the exposed ocean front has seen more or less continuous urbanisation. Together, housing developments total over $100 million. In 1962 a large storm swept over part of the island and caused considerable damage and loss of life; most of the new urbanisation lies within the zone inundated by this magnitude of storm surge (Fig. 6.18).

The average rate for beach recession on barrier islands in this region is 60 cm/yr, yet despite this, new developments continue to crowd as close as possible to the beach. They do not seem aware that, in a few years time, they will not have to go to the beach, for the beach is coming to visit them.

Coastal protection

In this section we will evaluate some of the protection measures available to people whose job it is to manage the coastlines. Many factors need to be considered. Coastal management involves:

(a) an understanding of the nature of littoral processes (i.e. researching an adequate data base for decision making);

(b) increasing public awareness of the real

Figure 6.17 (a) *Recent development along the shore front of Ocean City*

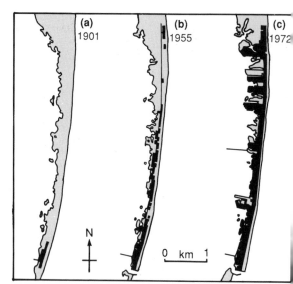

Figure 6.17 (b) *Extent of urban or built-up development on Fenwick Island, 1901–72*

nature of littoral processes, both to stop any unnecessary panic and also to encourage remedial action at a suitable stage;

(c) political decisions concerning the priorities of spending money on coastal protection as opposed to pressing housing need, social services, etc. and the way the coastal land is zoned for planning purposes to reduce future hazard to dwellings.

The role of education

Due to the lack of public education in coastal management, even people living by the coasts are usually surprised when high energy waves damage property, erode land or cause loss of life. The normal reaction in most developed countries is to call upon the local authority to prevent the alternation of their coastline. However, because there is usually no nationally co-ordinated coastal management programme and the responsibility for action is often left in the hands of local authorities with small finances and responsibility for only short lengths of coastline, many sea defences and coastal protection strategies are somewhat short sighted in nature. *It is therefore commonplace for chosen strategies only to attack the symptoms and not the causes of erosion.* This occurs mainly through lack of understanding. Public awareness is that

Figure 6.18 *The dashed line on this 1978 photograph approximates the storm surge penetration distance during the storm of March 1962*

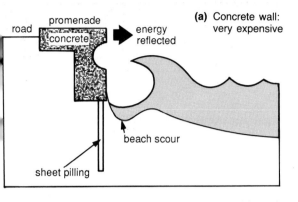

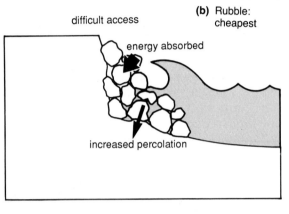

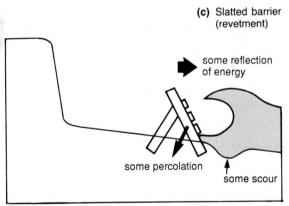

Figure 6.19 *Defence systems*

erosion requires a substantial engineering structure to combat the problem; there is a credibility gap in advocating any other approach. Of course in some instances the rather unsightly civil engineering constructions described above prove effective. However, too frequently such methods do more damage than good in the long run and such schemes 'whether concerned with sea defences or coastal

protection cannot succeed unless the works are developed in such a way as to retain a good beach' (Professor Clayton, 1982).

People need to be made aware that the primary purpose of retaining a beach is to protect the land from the assault of the sea by absorbing most of the energy of wave attack. In fact the only long term way to be sure of retaining a sandy beach for holiday makers and of protecting coastal homes is to maintain natural longshore drift rather than obstruct it. Often, however, this can conflict with desired uses of the coast and a compromise must be sought.

The coastal defence works available

Figure 6.19 illustrates some engineering solutions to coastal erosion. It is usual to build concrete (sea) **walls** to prevent beach erosion and to complement these with wooden **groynes** emplaced to trap sediment on beaches. If the specific coastal environment is understood well, and if carefully used, these structures can be most effective, often in combination with one another and with **beach nourishment**. Whatever the case, the cost of any coastal defence structure is high and the benefits claimed must be seriously assessed.

The most expensive structure is the **sea wall** (Fig. 6.19(a)). The purpose of the wall is to prevent erosion by presenting a physical barrier. It is also designed with such a shape that approaching waves are reflected back to sea. However, there are some problems with such a simple, rigid structure. First of all, it makes access to the beach very difficult. Water is also restricted to the lower beach because the upper beach is covered with the wall, and this makes the water table rise in the lower beach. With less chance of percolation, not only do waves run up the beach with greater power, but they get reflected back by the wall and thus add greatly to the power of the backwash. In many cases this can give the same results as plunging waves, that is, the beach sediment is gradually combed down and the beach gradient flattened. In some cases sea walls have caused the redistribution (commonly called 'loss') of so much beach that the base of the sea wall has become exposed and the wall then undermined.

An alternative approach has been to use

115

Figure 6.20 *Half Moon Bay*

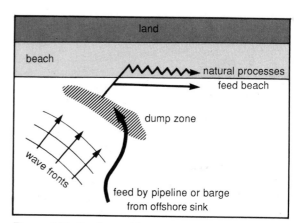

Figure 6.21 *Beach nourishment system*

material dumped on the foreshore (Fig. 6.19(b)). Here the idea is to provide rocks of such weight that they cannot be moved. This may be material as small as shingle, but in high energy environments alternatives include dumping irregularly shaped masses of concrete and even old motor cars on the beach (Fig. 6.20). This is a cheap solution but particularly unsightly. It greatly restricts access to the beach and, by again preventing waves from reaching the top of the beach, it keeps water on the lower beach, and increases the chance of scouring.

Some people favour the use of slatted walls or **revetments** (Fig. 6.19(c)). These unsightly structures are build with the intention of allowing water to break on the slats then cascade down between them, thus reducing the impact of the backwash and scouring. However, most revetments have slats too close to achieve the cascading effect and they behave much like a sea wall.

Groynes are commonly used to slow down longshore drift and retain a beach. However, these may cause added problems unless carefully constructed and are, in any case, unsightly.

A quite different technique is to pump sand back onshore from suitable offshore source regions. This is called **beach nourishment** (Fig. 6.21). No structure is created and no obvious signs of activity are seen by the general public except, perhaps, for the movements of a dredger. Beach nourishment is an ongoing process, unlike the construction of structures where activity occurs in short bursts. Beach nourish-

ment would obviate the need for groynes. This is the only method which acts *with* natural littoral processes to maintain a good beach and thus absorb the energy of wave attack. However, care must be taken to dredge material only from sediment sinks or so far offshore that it does not take away from regions of natural transfer.

Further defence can be attempted by reducing the landslide hazard. Thus a cliff saturated with water is more liable to fail than one that is freely draining. It is clearly advantageous to lower the water table in this type of cliff and it is common to introduce drainage pipes into cliffs of weak materials where geological conditions make them liable to saturation (see also Chapter 5).

Problems of beach nourishment

Whereas beach nourishment has been commonly practised in the USA over the last 30 years it has still not become an integral part of coastal protection in the UK. The largest project to date was completed as long ago as 1974 on the beaches of Bournemouth on the south coast of England. £1 million was spent at that time.

Marine extraction around the British shores is not without its problems. There are obvious potential hazards to the workforce and equipment from the highly variable weather experienced around the British shores, and days when working is impossible will be more frequent than in places, such as the USA, where seabed extraction is more common.

The potential market for beach nourishment using dredged material includes the main coastal resorts in the south and east of England. This is because they are in areas with soft rocks or unconsolidated cliff materials and where cells are open and littoral transport considerable. By contrast the west coast is primarily a hard rock area with pocket beaches, many closed sediment cells and small littoral sediment transfers.

At the town of Cromer 6000 m^3 of beach sediment have been lost from the bay over the last ten to twelve years, lowering the beach and allowing waves to damage the sea wall and pier. Professor Clayton has suggested that a feed averaging 10 000 m^3 a year (e.g. initial feed of 50 000 m^3, followed by a triannual topping of 30 000 m^3) would totally reverse the trend. The estimated cost is £15 000 in sand each year, a sound economical alternative to the repair or replacement of the sea wall that would cost well in excess of £1 million (prices at 1982). Cromer is dependent on its beach as a tourist resource and this theoretically should make such a scheme even more attractive.

The best example on the East Anglian coast for potential sand feeding is a 20 km stretch of beach near Clacton on Sea. The beaches along this region have eroded to their lowest levels for 5000 years. This may mostly be due to continued readjustment by the coast even though sea levels are now somewhat stable. However, some contribution to the high erosion rate is also made by dredging in the Felixstowe harbour mouth. By removing sand and gravels at a rate of 250 000 m^3 a year for sale inland as aggregate, the natural feed has been reduced. Beach feeding would again seem a particularly sensible alternative to, or could be used in combination with, coastal protection works so far used. The existing protection works are, despite their skilful emplacement, after 23 years of operation beginning to show serious signs of undermining suggesting their imminent collapse. Sand feeding in this case could again be achieved through a bypass from across the Felixstowe channel. From the point of view of tourism, the area has a catchment of much of London and south-east Essex.

There have been some unfortunate experiences in the past, most notably the disaster at Hall Sands, when gravel dredged offshore for Plymouth Dockyard caused a virtually complete loss of beach material and the destruction of a fishing village. Great care will need to be exercised to ensure this does not happen again.

Environmental problems of dredging

Potential environmental problems from dredging activities at sea are of three general types:
(a) alteration in the balance of erosion, transport and deposition of sediments in the littoral zone;
(b) interference with other users of the area; and
(c) disturbance of marine ecosystems.
The disturbances from marine sand and gravel operations are, however, dependent both on the mining method and the environmental conditions of the area, emphasising the specific need for research information on the region of extraction.

Because wave patterns might be altered by dredging patterns and this may, in the long term, carry political penalties, the question also arises as to the seaward extent of the active littoral zone. The tests by the Hydraulics Research Station made at Worthing by tracing pebbles tagged with radioactive silver led to the conclusion that 'shingle movements offshore of the 18 m contour will be negligible at all times. However, at the moment the rule of thumb estimate in legislation for the limit to which dredging operations affect inshore-offshore sediment transfer is taken as 5 km'.

Some investigations have established large nearshore areas of sand banks whose exploitation would not seem to affect the seabed contours greatly and are in sites where they could be useful to beach nourishment. A good example is in the East Anglian region. Here a series of banks, comprising Newcome, Holm, Corton and Scroby sands near Lowestoft, contains over 10^9 m^3 of sand. Even large beach feeding operations involving the removal of 10^6 m^3 of sand from the banks would not cause any change in wave attack on the shore.

Student enquiry 6A (decision making topic): The coastal protection of Frinton and Walton, Essex

Frinton and Walton form two small coastal resorts built on top of low cliffs. The cliffs and foreshore are formed principally of a tenacious but poorly consolidated clay (known as 'London Clay' by geologists), and capped by a permeable deposit of sand (known as the 'Red Crag').

The Crag often serves as a reservoir for rainwater. Runoff therefore partly takes the form of springs at the clay/sand junction near the cliff top.

Many people have settled at Walton and Frinton, particularly on retirement. Convalescent and retirement homes are common (e.g. the Samuel Lewis home). People come to the area to be within view of the sea and thus both settlements are stretched out along the cliff edge. People have been aware of the naturally large rate of cliff recession for at least 100 years; by the time of the first Ordnance Survey mapping in 1874 there was already a substantial groyne field built into the beach. Nevertheless, continued pressure to have a sea view has increased rather than slackened the urge to build near the sea front, despite the obvious handicap of an unstable cliff. For over a hundred years people have, therefore, engaged in battle with the 'encroaching' sea. Their varying degrees of success are traced out by successive Ordnance Survey mappings (A1).

Enquiry 6A also contains (a) A2, a photograph of the area covered by A1; (b) A3, a geological cross-section showing the cliff instability; (c) A4, sea defence works; (d) A5, a photograph taken to the south of Frinton showing the typical coastal development and ensuing problems; and (e) a map, A6, showing Frinton and Walton with respect to the direction of dominant wave approach and the coastal sediment budget.

1. Using the evidence available, make a detailed assessment of the coastal problem facing

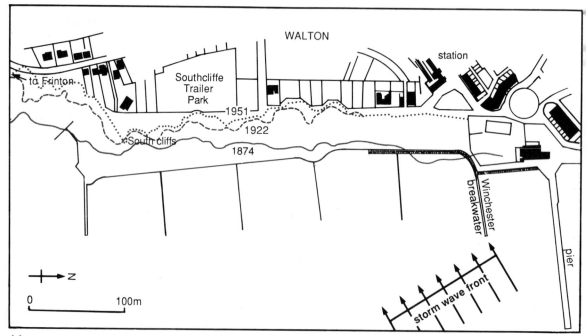

A1

A2

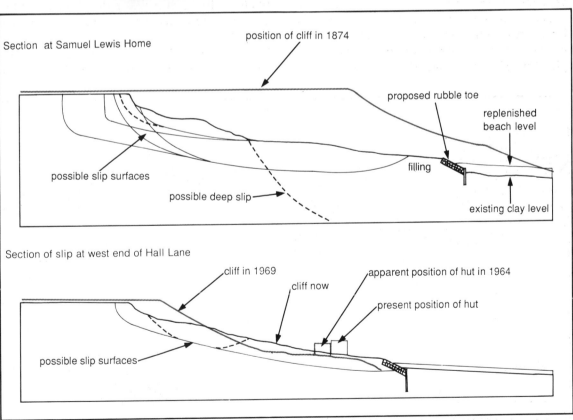

Section at Samuel Lewis Home

position of cliff in 1874

proposed rubble toe

replenished
beach level

possible slip surfaces

possible deep slip

filling

existing clay level

Section of slip at west end of Hall Lane

cliff in 1969

cliff now

apparent position of hut in 1964

present position of hut

possible slip surfaces

A3

Frinton and Walton Urban District Council.

2. Make a tracing of the Walton area map A1. Research has indicated that between 1874 and 1922 the cliffs retreated at an average of 1.04 m/yr. This rate slowed slightly to 0.86 m/yr between 1922 and 1951. Assuming retreat to be currently 1.00 m/yr, carefully mark on your map the predicted cliff top for 1981 and 2001. Comment on the planning implications of your results.

3. Describe the sea defence works shown in A4. What was each installation intended to do in preventing further erosion?

4. The works were carried out between 1967 and 1969. Study the map Al. Consider the following points, then comment on the degree of success the sea defences have had in protecting Walton. Has erosion continued? Has it continued uniformly? Have any changes been made to the roads as regards access to the cliff top? Are there any other protective measures evident?

5. Draw up a summary report suitable for presentation at a District Council meeting, which would be comprehensible to the other (non-expert) members of the Council. The report should explain (a) the nature of coastal processes and problems caused; (b) how a natural process can become a hazard; and (c) areas of greatest concern. You should conclude with a suggested scenario for action or inaction.

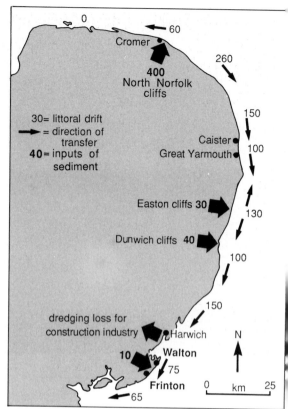

A6 *The East Anglian sand budget established using both computed values and those calculated using observer observations. All figures in thousands of cubic metres per year*

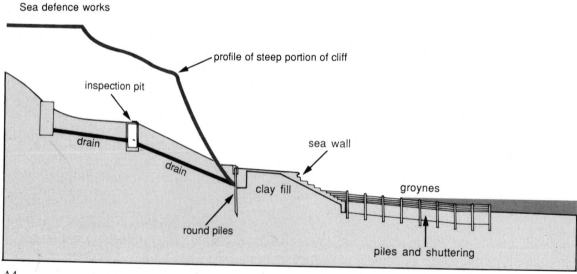

A4

A5

Figure 6.22 *Barges in central London carrying London's waste to the North Sea for dumping*

Pollution in the coastal zone and oceans: problems and solutions

In the earlier sections of this chapter we examined the action of waves on the land and people. In this final section we take a brief look at the effect of people on the water, for it seems very common for people to regard the dumping of waste out at sea in terms of 'out of sight, out of mind' (Fig. 6.22). Here we ask how valid such an argument is.

There are many types of wastes that are released into the coastal zones or in the deeper ocean zones. They are;

(a) domestic sewage;

(b) industrial wastes;

(c) dredged material from rivers and harbours;

(d) radioactive wastes;

(e) oil; and

(f) heat (e.g. from power stations).

Waste is disposed of either directly by pipeline or by dumping, or indirectly by tipping it into rivers or discharging it into the air. For example, five European countries dump sewage sludge, the concentrated leftovers from sewage treatment works, into the North Sea, with most coming from Britain (Fig. 6.23). Britain also dumps much industrial waste at sea, about 2.5 million tonnes per year. Three quarters of this is fly ash from power stations and colliery waste after coal treatment. Fly ash dumped off the Northumberland coast has been blamed for reduced lobster catches, and colliery waste is claimed to have polluted fisheries as well as creating an eyesore. Other dumped wastes include acids, which are neutralised in the sea, and small quantities of toxic wastes, mainly from the process called scrubbing which removes potential airborne pollutants from incinerators. These wastes come mainly from the pharmaceutical, chemical and textile industries. They are mostly too wet or too smelly to be suitable for dumping in tips on land.

The problems caused by sewage disposal are widespread. In Caister, Norfolk, for example, the outfall pipe for the town stops just seaward of the bathing beach and causes gross pollution. Local current and atmospheric patterns combine to create serious problems:

(a) because it is often misty the level of sunlight that could destroy sewage bacteria is too low to perform an effective job;

(b) the area is surrounded by sand banks and so the coastal circulation is contained near the beach;

(c) an onshore wind often blows in summer. This causes surface currents to bring sewage back on to the beach;

(d) currents also bring wastes into this area from Yarmouth, 7 km away.

The EEC has recognised that there can be pollution problems and has established regulations to protect bathing beaches. Unfortunately the bureaucratic definition of 'bathing beach' is 1000 visitors per kilometre and, because surveys have shown that Caister beach does not have this degree of usage, the local authorities are not being forced to improve the situation, even though the remedy of a longer pipe is not that difficult (Fig. 6.24).

The North Sea has a very complex pattern of currents that resemble intermeshing cogwheels. If you choose the right spot, these flows can be used to carry British wastes well away from the shore only to accumulate in the Wadden Sea off the west coast of Germany. Here there is considerable evidence of a build-up of toxic chemicals in sea mammals, but, as

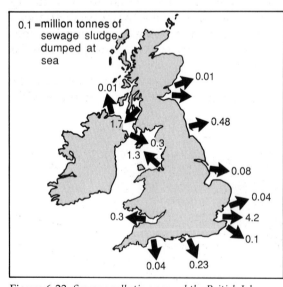

Figure 6.23 *Sewage pollution around the British Isles*

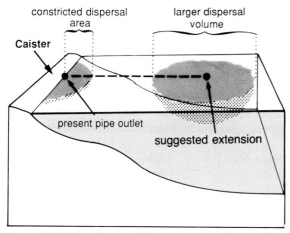

Figure 6.24 *Possible ways to increase sewage dispersal*

with acid rain, absolute proof of the connection between offending source and recipient sink is difficult to obtain.

Polluted oceans

The North Sea may be a convenient dumping ground for British wastes, and powerful currents may cause it to disperse, but such fortuitous circumstances are not always available. The Mediterranean region provides the best example of a stinking sea, because it is a closed body of water with slack currents and bordered by seventeen independent states. Here, many of the countries are just beginning a phase of industrialisation with all its attendant pollution problems.

Figure 6.25 shows a model of the flows and pollutants in the Mediterranean Sea. Figure 6.2 shows the actual pattern of flows and the location of the major sources of industrial pollutants. It is hardly surprising that there is widespread pollution of bathing beaches throughout the area. Figure 6.26, for example, shows only those beaches affected by oil pollution, many others are affected by sewage, radioactivity and heavy metals. The problem is very large. For example, flushing of refinery waste and ballast tanks in ships sends up to 1 million tonnes of oil into the Mediterranean Sea a year. Even though the discharge zones are restricted to two areas (Fig. 6.27) the problem is not solved because the places chosen are regions of low oxygenation and so added oil does not oxidise readily and the chances of destroying the natural ecosystem are that much greater.

Fouling the Caribbean

In the Mediterranean the interests of developed world countries are directly at stake. Yet despite increasing concern it is proving almost impossible to get all countries to ratify treaties to reduce the input of sewage and oil. The Caribbean Sea/Gulf of Mexico is a nearly closed water body lying almost entirely within the developing world. It is not as polluted as the Mediterranean ... yet. But what of the future as it becomes progressively exposed to many pressures for development?

A glimpse of some of the problems can be gained from the case of Ixtoc 1: the world's

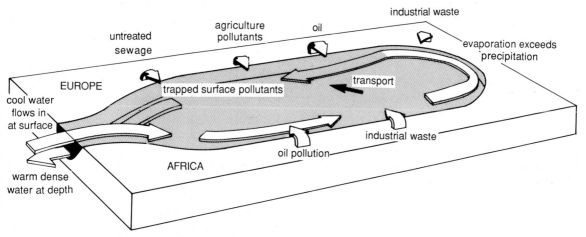

Figure 6.25 *A model of flows and pollution in the Mediterranean Sea*

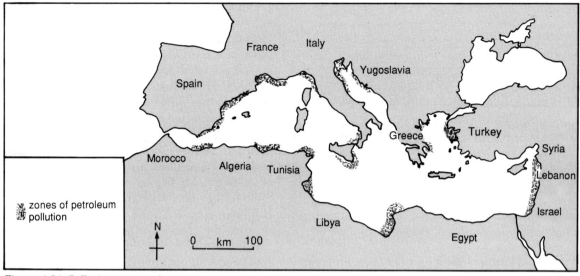

Figure 6.26 *Pollution zones in the Mediterranean Sea*

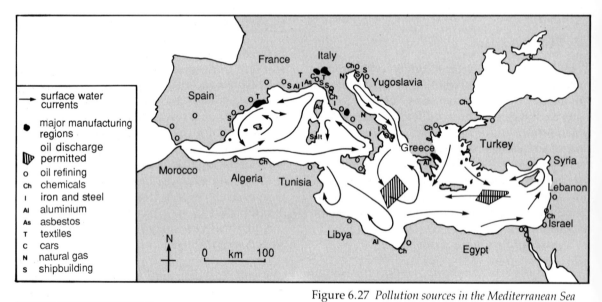

Figure 6.27 *Pollution sources in the Mediterranean Sea*

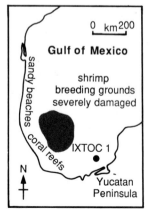

Figure 6.28(a) *Location of the IXTOC 1 blow-out in the Gulf of Mexico*

largest oil spill (Fig. 6.28(a)). On 10 December 1978 Petroleos Mexicanos (PEMEX) started to drill the Ixtoc 1 exploration well about 80 km off the coast. By the end of May 1979 the well had reached 3600 m. Then came trouble with the circulation of the drilling mud. On 3 June during attempts to seal the well it blew out and caught fire. The explosion and fire destroyed the drilling platform which then sank to the seabed, damaging the casing of the well. This allowed oil and gas to mix with the water close to the sea floor, beginning the largest marine oil

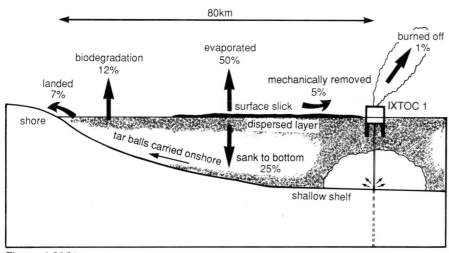

Figure 6.28(b)

spill in the history of oil exploration.

Initially the spill was estimated at 4500 tonnes per day; when the well was finally capped on 23 March 1980 – 290 days after the blow out – a total of about 475 000 tonnes of oil had been lost. The oil that was lost during the blow-out polluted a considerable part of the offshore region of the Gulf of Mexico as well as much of the coastal zone, which consists of sandy beaches and coral islands enclosing lagoons. The oil was saturated with gas and consequently hit the surface as water droplets and gas bubbles in oil. Much of the gas was burned as it emerged but only a very small proportion of the oil was burned.

The oil was of a light type and thus comparatively water-soluble. It began to form a slick, the texture of chocolate mousse, 1–4 cm thick, up to 5 km wide and 60 km long. Gradually the lighter parts of the oil were lost by evaporation, leaving the rest. As the remaining droplets became heavier they began to sink through the water to the bottom. When oil reached the beaches it was deposited as tar balls with little stickiness (Fig. 6.28(b)).

Mechanical recovery of the oil by the clean-up squads accounted for less than 5 per cent; evaporation removed over 50 per cent. Bio-

chemical degradation of the oil would have destroyed another 15 per cent; about 30 000 tonnes (6 per cent) landed on the Mexican beaches; the rest of the oil, or about 25 per cent, sank to the bottom of the Gulf. Attempts to clean the beaches were ineffective and mostly consisted of bulldozing the oil into trenches on The beach; booms pulled across the inlets to some lagoons to stop oil entry were also ineffective.

The continental shelf in the area of Ixtoc 1 is a highly favourable area for a diverse and productive ecosystem with a commercial potential greater than 8 kg/ha; the shrimp populations are of great commercial value and these were disrupted for many years. In general the oil killed marine life near the well by its toxicity and through its stickiness. It is probable that 2.5 per cent (15 000 km^2) of the Gulf of Mexico was poisoned. The oil that sank to the bottom, however, was not sufficient to cause harm to the benthic (bottom-dwelling) communities. By contrast the oil had drastic effects on the coastal communities such as crabs, although the molluscs (e.g. clams) were not very affected. These are, however, merely indications of the range of the potential damage: the actual extent of the damage caused by the world's largest oil spill will never be determined.

Student enquiry 6B:
Planning to reduce pollution

Enquiry 6B gives information on a number of past pollution incidents and present pressures.
1. Make a report on the history of pollution in the area, explaining all the implications of past incidents and present pressures. Include maps to show the areas most vulnerable to the different forms of pollution.
2. Make a realistic assessment of the chances of reducing further pollution, explaining the basis for your assessment. You should include a detailed description of the various possible strategies.

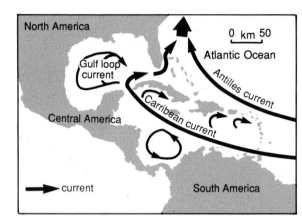

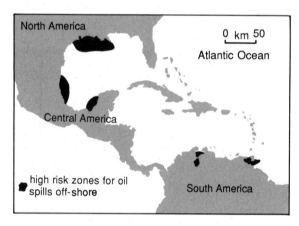

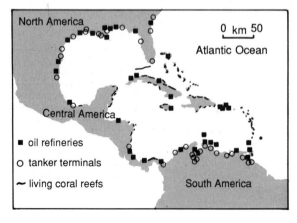

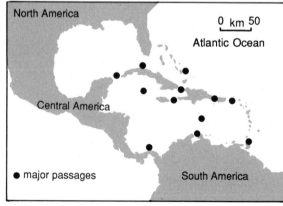

Who will save the Caribbean?

Stephanie Yanchinski

Six months ago the nations which rim the Caribbean Ocean, and the United Nations Environment Programme, put the finishing touches to an ambitious intergovernmental plan to control the pollution that threatens their environment. The plan is not asking for much – $8.2 million over the next three years; but it is having some growth pains. The Americans mouth words about supporting the plan in general but refuse to contribute any money, while Britain awaits direction from its dependencies about what to do. Meanwhile, year by year, month by month more coral reefs are bombed, and more tankers spill their oil.

The Caribbean countries take their pollution problems seriously: over the past decade they have created more than 100 national parks. So why have they turned to an international organisation, the United Nations Environment Programme, for help?

Certain geographical features of the Caribbean basin aggravate the problems caused by pollution. Unlike other semi-enclosed seas such as the Mediterranean, there is a continuous flow of fresh water through the region. No fewer than seven major river systems empty directly into the Caribbean, including the Mississippi, the Rio Grande and the Orinoco.

One of the most worrisome pollution problems is oil. The Caribbean is potentially one of the most important oil-producing regions in the world. Each day the region yields about 8 million barrels of crude oil (more than 3 million from offshore rigs) and the capacity of refineries in the area amounts to more than 12 million barrels per day. From 1973 more than one-sixth of the world's oil was produced in the region or shipped through it. At any given moment, approximately 25 loaded supertankers and 75 smaller vessels are travelling on Caribbean waters. Oil spills in coastal waters through accidents and washing and operational discharges amounted to more than 76 million barrels in 1978.

Inadequate sewage treatment is another serious pollution problem. In 1974 it was estimated that less than 10 per cent of the Caribbean sewage systems had treatment facilities and that sewage generated by 30 million people is dumped untreated into the Caribbean. Many resort hotels are equipped only with "package" sewage treatment plants that are often overloaded or inadequately maintained. So often sewage is discharged near to beaches.

Caicos may play host to American sewage

British administrators, who last week took direct control of the Turks and Caicos Islands in the West Indies, are being made an offer they may feel unable to refuse – £18 million a year, in return for allowing the island of West Caicos to become a dumping ground for sewage sludge from the US.

Conservationists, including the government's own advisers at the Overseas Development Agency (ODA), warn that sludge could wreak havoc with the crystal clear waters around the island. This could jeopardise the islands' two main industries, fishing and tourism. Ironically, one victim could be a £5 million "Club Med" scheme to set up a luxury holiday resort on the neighbouring island of Providenciones. The scheme has attracted controversy because of a subsidy from the ODA.

The sewage, contaminated with a range of heavy metals, comes from a dump in Philadelphia which is to be cleared for housing. Growing environmental concern in the US about toxic wastes has made its export a commericaly attractive solution.

The income from the scheme could provide relief for Britain from grants which are currently paid to support the islands. During 1986 these will amount to £5 million.

The plan has aroused controversy within both the islands' former government and Whitehall. The waters around the island are some of the cleanest in the Caribbean. The area supports a thriving fishing industry and West Caicos itself is home to much wildlife, including flamingos, herons and humming birds.

The coastal waters of the Caribbean Sea are its most productive but, at the same time, most vulnerable zone. The balance of marine plants and animals, precisely adapted to their environment, is easily upset by pollution. The West Caicos island comprises highly porous oolitic limestone, which is peppered with holes. The ODA's report says: "There would be little to prevent any large quantity of sewage from penetrating the holes and reaching the sea." Lake Catherine – a saline lake on the island – could quickly become polluted.

In March 1983, 27 nations – including 12 Commonwealth countries – signed the Cartagena Convention, intended to protect and develop the marine environment of the Caribbean. The convention contains a commitment to establish national parks and protect threatened species. So far, the Turks and Caicos Islands have no national parks, planning controls or other formal mechanisms for preventing environmental damage.

New Scientist, 31 July 1986

Key terms

Backwash: the seaward return of water following the uprush of waves on a beach.

Bar: a submerged or emerged embankment of sand or gravel built on the sea floor in shallow water by waves and currents.

Barrier beach: a bar essentially parallel to the shore, the crest of which is above normal high water.

Berm: a nearly horizontal part of the beach built up by the deposit of material by wave action.

Breaker: a wave breaking on a shore, over a reef, etc. Types:

(a) spilling: water spills down the front face of the wave with breaking occurring over a substantial distance. Spilling wave motion tends to push material landward, building up the beach steepness;

(b) plunging: crest curls over air pocket and breaking occurs with a crash. Plunging waves tend to transport material seaward, combing down a beach and making it less steep;

(c) collapsing waves: break over the lower part of the wave; intermediate between (a) and (b) but tend to drive material onshore; and

(d) surging waves: where the base of the wave rushes forward from under the wave and the wave slides up the beach face, pushing material landward and increasing beach steepness.

Bypassing: the artificial transfer of beach material from the updrift (accreting) side of an inlet or harbour to the downdrift (eroding) side.

Clapotis: is the standing wave form produced by the reflection of a non-breaking wave train from a surface that is near vertical; clapotis imposes push/pull stresses on the surface.

Ebb current: is the tidal current that occurs with a falling tide and drags material away from the shore.

Fetch: the horizontal distance over which a wind generates a wave train.

Groyne: a shore protection structure built (usually perpendicular to the shoreline) to trap littoral drift or retard erosion.

Hydraulic action: the stress put on a cliff or man-made structure by breaking waves, often causing the air trapped by the wave to be forced into cracks within the rock and forcing blocks free.

Littoral zone: the zone seaward of the shoreline to just beyond the breaker zone.

Longshore current: is the littoral current in the breaker zone that moves parallel to the shore; it is usually generated by waves breaking at an angle to the shoreline.

Longshore drift: is the littoral drift of material due to longshore current and swash effects.

Mole: a massive land-connected, solid fill structure which may serve as a breakwater or pier.

Nourishment: the process of replenishing a beach.

Orthogonal: on a wave refraction diagram, a line drawn perpendicular to the wave crests. Tracing orthogonals is a way of plotting the path of the advancing wave.

Pier: a structure, usually of open construction, extending from the shore. Piers do not impair littoral drift.

Refraction: is the process by which the direction of a wave moving in shallow water at an angle to the contours is changed; the part of the wave advancing in shallow water moves more slowly than the part still advancing in deeper water, causing the wave crests and orthogonals to bend towards alignment with the underwater contours.

Rip: a strong current flowing seaward, being the return of water piled up on the shore by incoming waves and wind. It normally flows below the advancing wave and is commonly called an undertow.

Runnel: a trough formed in the foreshore by breaking waves.

Shingle: any beach material coarser than gravel.

Shoal: a shallow part of the seabed.

Spit: a small point of land projecting into a body of water from the shore.

Storm surge: a rise above normal water level on the open coast due to the action of wind stress on the water surface and possibly due to reduction in atmospheric pressure.

Storm wave: a wave of relatively short period and substantial height set up and still influenced by winds.

Swash: The uprush of water on to the beach face following the breaking of a wave.

Swash drift: the longshore movement of sediment on a beach due to the ratchet-like movement of swash and backwash.

Swell: wind generated waves that have travelled out of their generating area; such waves have a regular and long period.

Terrace: a near flat bench *cut into* the beach (contrast with berm).

Tombolo: a bar or spit that connects an island to the mainland.

Undertow: a misnomer for rip current.

Wave height: the vertical distance between a crest and the preceding trough.

Wavelength: the distance between two corresponding places on adjacent waves (i.e. between crests, troughs).

Wave period: the time for a wave crest to move through a distance of one wavelength.

Wave train: a series of waves from the same direction.

Chapter 7
Cold environments

Figure 7.1 (a) *A house is damaged due to throwing of permafrost soils.* (b) *Avalanche devastation*

Introduction

Cold environments present people with two challenges:
(a) how to survive the intense winter cold; and
(b) how to use the land without disturbing the delicate land-forming processes associated with seasonal freezing and thawing.

Figures 7.1(a) and (b) indicate some of the problems that can beset the unwary: in one case a building has subsided as the central heating melted the upper part of the frozen ground; in the other case an avalanche has devastated a small ski resort in the High Alps, causing some loss of life and a great deal of damage.

This chapter is concerned with cold environments, often known as **periglacial environments**, their natural processes and the challenges they offer all who wish to develop such hostile parts of the world.

What is a periglacial environment?

Most of the area with which we shall be concerned is known as periglacial. However, it is difficult to define the word periglacial by one simple set of environmental figures (Fig. 7.2). Apart from being very cold for part of, or all of the year, a common characteristic is that **frost action** is a dominant process and most areas are underlain by perennially frozen ground, known as **permafrost** (Fig. 7.3). Much of the area is

cloaked by a low form of shrubby vegetation called **tundra**. The land is mostly too cold and hostile to farm.

Periglacial environments can be of three main types:

(a) Cold dry climates with severe winters ('Siberian' type). These have very low winter temperatures, short summers and perennially frozen ground extending to great depths.

(b) Cold humid climates with severe winters ('Arctic' type) which have long cold winters but more precipitation than the Siberian type, and summers in which some rain may fall. Here freezing is less intense or prolonged although perennially frozen ground is widespread. Mountainous areas with an Arctic climate have deep snows and are often free from perennially frozen ground. In this case spring melting gives intense freeze-thaw cycles in valleys.

(c) Cold climates with a small annual temperature range due to proximity to the oceans or high altitudes ('cold island' type). In both cases there is a frost cycle almost every day but no perennially frozen ground.

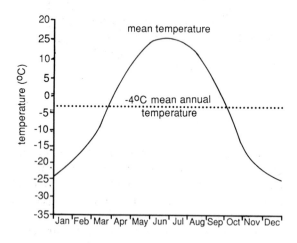

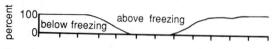

Figure 7.2 *Characteristic climate data for a region of continental climate within the discontinuous permafrost zone*

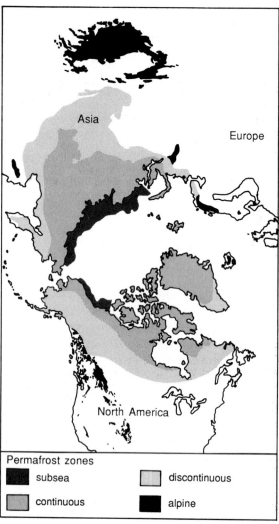

Figure 7.3 *Distribution of permafrost in the northern hemisphere*

The direct effect of permafrost on natural processes

To understand the problems faced in managing this environment it is helpful to look at the nature of frozen ground and the phenomena it produces. Frozen ground occurs in two forms:

(a) as seasonally frozen ground (**active layer**) which remains frozen only through the winter season and melts each spring; and

(b) the perennially frozen ground (**permafrost**) which remains continuously frozen for a period of at least two consecutive years.

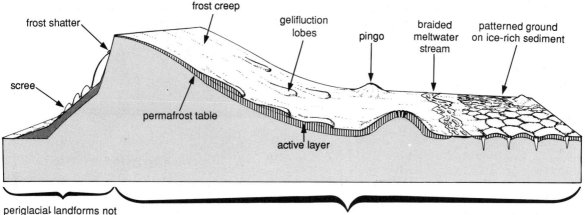

Figure 7.4 *The range of permafrost landforms*

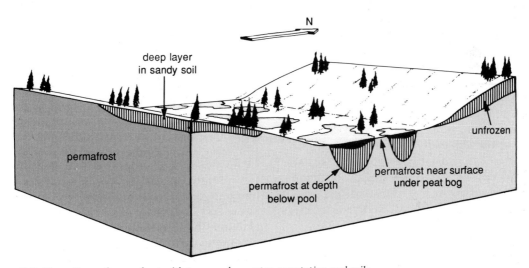

Figure 7.5 *The pattern of permafrost with topography, water, vegetation and soils*

Permafrost is largely confined to polar and sub-polar regions, but it still covers 20 per cent of the world's land surface. For example, half of the USSR and Canada and over 80 per cent of Alaska, all of Antarctica and even 20 per cent of China are underlain by permafrost. There are two main regions of permafrost:

(a) the area of **continuous permafrost** where all land is underlain by permafrost except under lakes and rivers that do not freeze to the bottom.

(b) the area of **discontinuous permafrost** where the type of sediment and surface vegetation exercises a great control on permafrost distribution. Here permafrost is most common under peat bogs, which dry out and give an insulating surface blanket in summer, but which wet up and transmit the cold readily in autumn. In many bog areas the permafrost often comes very near the surface whereas in gravels it is frequently absent.

There is no clear boundary between each type of surface condition, and so in some areas discontinuous permafrost occurs, giving patches of frozen ground interspersed with those that melt each spring. This phenomenon points to the strategic role of the ground materials and slope in determining the nature and importance of permafrost (Fig. 7.4).

The importance of ground materials is found in their water holding capacity (Fig. 7.5). Thus

131

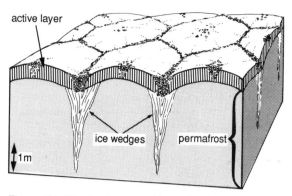

Figure 7.6 *The development of ice wedges beneath the active layer occurs on gently sloping or flat land in the ice-rich sediments*

some sediments, such as sand, have large pores that drain rapidly and do not hold large volumes of water into the winter freezing period. When freezing causes ice formation in such materials the expansion that occurs as water is frozen into ice causes little increase in sediment volume. By contrast, clays and silts can retain much water in their capillary pores and these sediments will expand considerably as the contained water freezes. Most expansion occurs in the direction of least resistance and thus results in **frost heaving** of the surface. Frost-susceptible soil often attracts additional water from below as it freezes and this causes the development of ice veins, wedges and lenses (Fig. 7.6).

In spring, the ice melts from the surface downward. Because the underlying region is still frozen it is impermeable, and the additional water drawn into the upper soil during freezing now causes saturation. These wet, active layers often resemble a sludge and will deform even when people walk on them. Ice-rich sediments will not only settle as the ice returns to water and the volume reduces by 9 per cent, but more importantly there will be a loss of bearing strength or ability to support structures because the material is saturated. The active layer varies in thickness according to its moisture content: it is often as little as 30 cm in wet, organic sediments, but up to 3 m in well drained gravels.

Saturated soil without bearing strength on slopes is liable to a slow flow process called **gelifluction**. Areas subject to this kind of activity can be identified from the air by their distinctive lobate or terraced pattern of disturbance and they can be distinguished in observation trenches by flow structures and buried soil layers (Fig. 7.7).

The active layer reaches its maximum depth in late summer. At this time over a metre of soil may be unfrozen and water can be transferred down slopes by throughflow. As the autumn progresses, however, refreezing sets in and the freezing front begins to penetrate further and further down into the active layer. Throughflow trapped between these two frozen zones behaves as though in a closed pipe. The downslope end of such a 'pipe' may be under considerable hydrostatic pressure, much like any other enclosed column of water. If the freezing zone is thin at any point, the water pressure may thus be able to arch up the surface frozen soil. As winter progresses this water body is frozen into an ice lens. Such features may build year after year into considerable hills and are called **pingos** (Fig. 7.8; see also Figs. 7.13 and 7.14).

Problems of the permafrost zone

Four fundamental types of permafrost-related land use problems are:

(a) thawing of ice-rich permafrost with subsequent subsidence;

(b) frost action, generally made worse by poor drainage caused by permafrost;

(c) freezing of buried sewer, water and oil lines; and

(d) freezing of trapped throughflow.

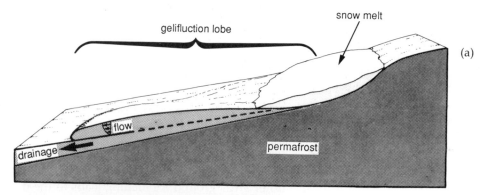

(b) Figure 7.7(a) *Gelifluction on slopes. Note the snow patch feeding water into the gelifluction lobe.* (b) *Patterns of lobes on a Swiss maintainside.*

Figure 7.8 *The pingo has caused arching of overlying sediment in the Mackenzie Delta, Canada. The core is a lens of almost pure ice*

(a) Thawing of permafrost

This occurs not only under heated structures such as houses but also under unheated structures such as roads, airfields, agricultural fields and parks. When settlement and subsidence occur due to ground thawing the landform is described as **thermokarst**. This landscape, which contains sink holes, tunnels and caverns, has some similarity with limestone karst. Thermokarst mounds develop where land has been cleared, such as the front gardens of houses. They are often 15 m in diameter and stand up to 3 m high. It must be curious watching your gar-

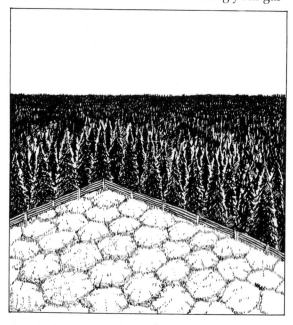

Figure 7.9 *Low-angle, oblique aerial view of thermokarst mounds in an abandoned agricultural field in Alaska*

den grow – literally. Thermokarst mounds begin forming 2 or 3 years after an area is cleared and the ice begins to melt. Trenches form where the melting ground ice that once comprised ice wedges causes differential settlement. Local depressions first appear and surface water collects in these. This water helps speed thawing until well defined trenches appear, leaving the central silt sediment as an upstanding mound. Some polygonal patterns develop in areas that once had a network of ice wedges (Fig. 7.9); in other areas ground ice melting leads to the development of deep pits rather than regular patterns.

All thermokarst features present hazards for farmers because they make the use of machinery virtually impossible. Similarly airstrips are impracticable to maintain on ground that is continually developing trenches and pits. Repairing roads and railway tracks is especially expensive. For example, settlement of one section of track near Fairbanks, Alaska, requires annual maintenance costing over $1 million. Settlement continues even though the railroad is over 50 years old.

A new housing project built on the floodplain in Fairbanks was severely affected by subsidence after a year. Paved streets, and even garages had begun to subside dramatically, although the houses were untouched. This was because the ice-rich silt at the house locations had been dug out for 9 m depth and replaced with a gravel pad whereas the roads were only dug out to 2 m. Summer warming of paved areas and watering of nearby lawns were the main contributors to rapid melting (Fig. 7.10).

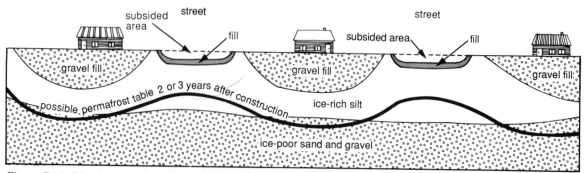

Figure 7.10 *Disruption of ground in Fairbanks suburbs*

There are some occasions when melting the permafrost has beneficial effects. For example, on ground with *low* ice content and a thin permafrost the removal of the vegetation will cause the permafrost to thaw out. This will actually turn a poorly drained area into one with better drainage and greater agricultural potential because drainage will not be confined to a thin active layer.

(b) Frost action, generally made worse by poor drainage caused by permafrost

As a general rule people try to disturb the permafrost as little as possible. On ice-rich sediments they often remove part of the active layer and replace it with a gravel pad. Alternatively houses are built on piles so they do not rest directly on the ground but have an air gap. Both designs add considerably to the cost of construction

The best way to avoid the problems caused by frost action is not to build on poorly drained materials. If it is absolutely necessary to build on these materials then special precautions will have to be taken. Either the subsurface drainage will have to be improved or the surface will have to be insulated from melting by covering it with gravel or moss. If the structure has to support a considerable weight then it cannot be 'floated' on an insulating blanket and piles must also be driven into the ground. Piles will be frost heaved out of the ground unless they are driven right through into the permafrost region. Most piles are dry augered and then backfilled with a silt-water slurry. As the slurry freezes it 'cements' the piles in place. As a rule of thumb the pile has to be driven into the permafrost to twice the depth of the active layer.

Frost heaving occurs very quickly. One season is all that is required to destroy roads or buildings that are not constructed properly. Houses, for example, must be completed in the summer season and their floors and basements heated to prevent the build-up of seasonal frost beneath their foundations. There are many instances where building sites left unfinished at the start of winter have become unusable by spring because all the previous construction has been cracked and heaved during winter.

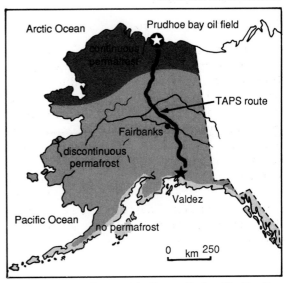

Figure 7.11 (a) *Route of the Trans-Alaskan Pipeline System (TAPS) through three permafrost zones*

The factor that has most impeded progress in cold areas has been the difficulty of maintaining communication systems rather than dwellings. Dwellings can be sited on materials of low susceptibility to heave much more readily than airports, railways, roads and pipelines. These have to cross the landscape in reasonably straight paths and this frequently means they have to be built over less than desirable materials.

Achieving effective communications requires very expensive engineering solutions, so routing structures away from the most susceptible regions is a great money saver. For example, a large part of the $8 billion project to carry oil from Prudhoe Bay to Valdez (Fig. 7.11) was spent in overcoming frost heave problems. Part of the problem is that oil coming directly from wells is hot and any pipe buried in ice-rich sediment would have melted the ground. The resultant settlement would almost certainly have led to pipe rupture. Thus for 615 of the 1284 km the pipeline was carried on trestles above ground. To support it 123 000 piles were driven into the ground in pairs (Fig. 7.11(b)). Cross beams were slung between each pair of piles, with the pipe resting on the cross beams. To prevent the piles being jacked out of the ground and pipe rupture, the piles were not only driven deep into the permafrost, but they

Figure 7.11 (b) *Elevated section of the pipeline*

water supply; most reservoirs have to be deep enough so they will not freeze right through during the winter, and the intense cold makes the transfer of fluids particularly troublesome. When the Trans-Alaskan pipeline was being built, for example, the heavy construction machinery had to be left permanently switched on because if the oil and fuel froze the machines could not be thawed and restarted. Similarly obtaining water from a reservoir is only the first hurdle of supply, because no amount of lagging will insulate the water pipes from such penetrating cold. A similar problem confronts the distribution of sewage from homes; there is a real danger of sewage becoming frozen in underground pipes and blocking the system.

The only real answer that has so far been found to this problem is to provide heating along the entire length of a pipe. Usually this is achieved by heating all pipes together in **utilidors** as they pass through tunnels or over the ground on piles (Fig. 7.12).

were also fitted with self-operating refrigeration plants (see as fins on Fig. 7.11(b)). Inside the hollow piles is ammonia gas. Whenever the ground is warmer than the air the gas rises to the top of the pile, is cooled through the fins and then liquifies, where it sinks to the bottom. In this way heat is carried away from the base of the piles and they are never subject to thawing.

(c) Freezing of buried sewer, water and oil lines

Permafrost imposes some heavy penalties on people who live in cold environments through the winter. There is difficulty finding a winter

(d) Freezing of trapped throughflow

Alexander Tihonorovov was showering in a heated bath house one winter day in a northern valley in Siberia. As he washed he noticed cold water welling up between the floor boards and covering the floor. Alarmed he rushed outside and could only stare as water began to pour from the windows, freezing into great cascades (Fig. 7.13). Within hours the building was filled with ice up to window sill level and the building was ripped apart by the force of expanding ice.

Ground water can be a problem in permafrost regions. It can flow downslope and become

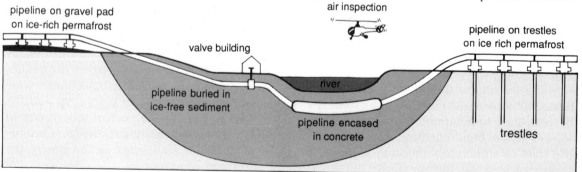

Figure 7.11 (c) *Overcoming permafrost hazards on the Alaskan pipeline*

trapped at the slope base above the permafrost table but below the thickening frozen zone of the active layer. As water accumulates the hydraulic head can become so great that it is able to break through a place where the frozen zone is very thin. This was the case with Alexander's house, because heat from the dwelling had kept the winter's frozen layer very thin.

Where springs emerge at the foot of a hill or are artificially produced by road and rail cuttings, then the seeping water will freeze and produce 'icings'. Icings may also be produced from elevated highways and railbeds. Autumn frost penetration is more rapid beneath these artificial materials than in natural materials with a vegetation cover and so the active layer freezes to the permafrost more quickly than elsewhere. If this occurs on a slope it will block natural throughflow and water will accumulate, trapped upslope between the freezing active layer and the permafrost (Fig. 7.14).

As the frozen soil ruptures it may produce a sound like a cannon shot. Breached water will flow over the surface and freeze. Icings like this can cover roads and railbeds and add considerably to maintenance costs.

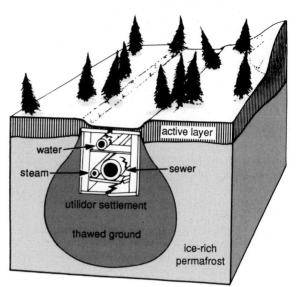

Figure 7.12 *Heat from the utilidor has thawed the ground and allowed the irregular subsidence of the utilidor that resulted in broken pipes*

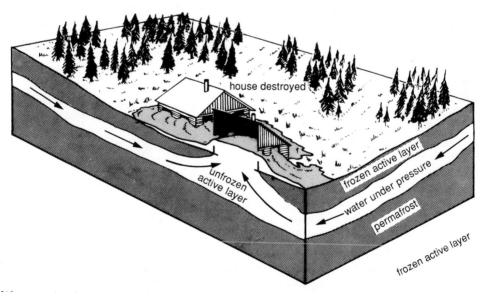

Figure 7.13 *Water moving downslope under hydrostatic pressure is trapped between the thickening seasonal frost layer and the underlying permafrost table. The unfrozen ground beneath the heated building provides an exit for the water, and it bursts through the floor, filling the building and pouring out of the windows into the sub-zero weather. As the water freezes, the building is filled with ice*

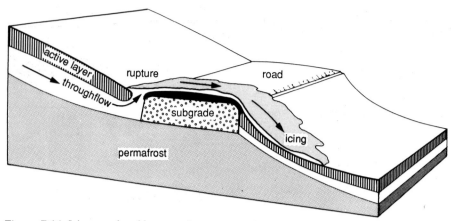

Figure 7.14 *Icings produced by ground water rupturing during the autumn freeze*

Student enquiry 7A:
Surviving in the Fairbanks area

To discover some of the problems associated with periglaciation, we shall look in some detail at the environment of Fairbanks, Alaska (A1).

Fairbanks experiences a continental climate. Temperatures dive as low as −20°C in winter and precipitation totals a mere 300 mm per year. However, the low evapotranspiration from the sparse and woody vegetation means that the effective precipitation (i.e. that which remains in the ground) is quite high. This, coupled with only gently sloping or floodplain land, produces considerable areas of swamp.

The discontinuous permafrost zone is not totally inhospitable (although it may be expensive, due to high heating and insulation requirements). There are warm summer days with long hours of continuous sunshine. These not only help compensate people for the long cold winter, but are an important element for the development of the natural environment. With care, the land can even be used agriculture. Despite the short summers grass will grow and cleared land can be prepared for pasture.

1. Study A2 which shows the general extent and thickness of permafrost in the Fairbanks area. Describe and account for its thickness and extent.

2. Explain why fields A and B would have very different agricultural potentials even though

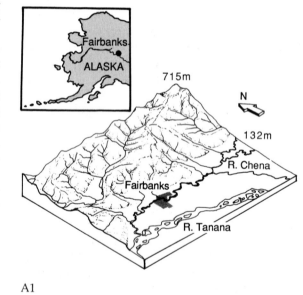

A1

they are adjacent.

3. Examine the geological map of the Fairbanks area (A3) which shows locations of different types of surface sediments and the street plan of the town. Using the information about boreholes draw on tracing paper contours of the permafrost table. Describe the contour pattern and suggest how this might be helpful in planning the locations of town expansion.

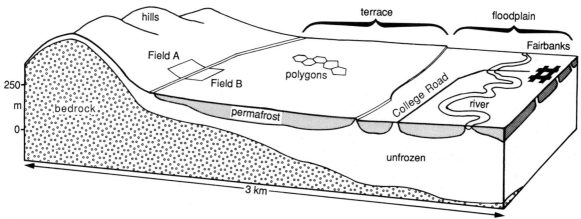

A2

4. Using the rule of thumb for pile depths draw out a tracing overlay showing areas for construction that would be cheapest to piledrive and therefore have priority in development.

5. The sanctuary of the Presbyterian Church in College Road was build on the floodplain sand and gravel (A4). Later a church school building was erected nearby, but unfortunately this building soon collapsed. The loss of one building and the provision of its replacement cost the church over $300 000 between 1955 and 1962.

(a) Study A4 and explain why the school building collapsed.

(b) Do you think the location of the 'new' school building is any better? Why?

6. One spring day Jack Smith closed the front door of his new $250 000 house in Fairbanks, Alaska and wondered why the door had been sticking lately. His wife also complained that when the kitchen floor was mopped all the water ran to a corner of the room. But this was only the start of their troubles. By the following autumn cracks had appeared in the foundations and walls and, after being dragged downwards some 12 cm, the water pipe to the house had finally ruptured. It was time to abandon the house for this challenge to the natural environment had been lost.

From information about each of the source materials in A3 suggest, with reasons, where Jack may have built this house.

Kitty Johnson in Fairbanks experienced an icing in her house of much the same character as Alexander's in Siberia. Suggest regions for the location of Kitty's ill-fated house.

7. Draw up, on a tracing overlay, a pattern of all hazards related to active layers. Shade in this map, graduating from blue as lowest grade hazard to red as highest hazard.

8. Explain why, in this particular floodplain region, a map showing the height of the permafrost is not as good a planning tool as a geological map showing character of materials.

9. Suggest some of the regions on which farming might be most and least successful in the Fairbanks area shown in A1. After considering slope, aspect and soil material, construct a tracing of agricultural land potential.

10. Give reasons why house building continues in ice-rich permafrost areas of Fairbanks despite maps which show the distribution of the hazard.

11. Fairbanks contains a number of hazardous zones in central locations. Explain how the city planners could use these zones to the advantage of the citizens.

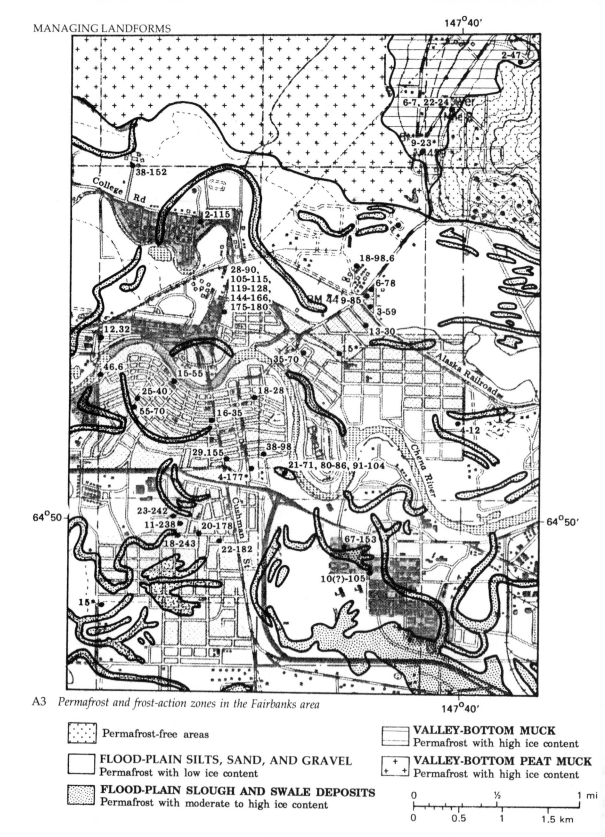

A3 *Permafrost and frost-action zones in the Fairbanks area*

Permafrost-free areas

VALLEY-BOTTOM MUCK
Permafrost with high ice content

FLOOD-PLAIN SILTS, SAND, AND GRAVEL
Permafrost with low ice content

VALLEY-BOTTOM PEAT MUCK
Permafrost with high ice content

FLOOD-PLAIN SLOUGH AND SWALE DEPOSITS
Permafrost with moderate to high ice content

21-64 Borehole location. First number indicates depth to top of permafrost; second
number indicates depth to bottom of permafrost or to bottom of hole, if bottomed
in permafrost. '*' indicates hole bottomed in permafrost.

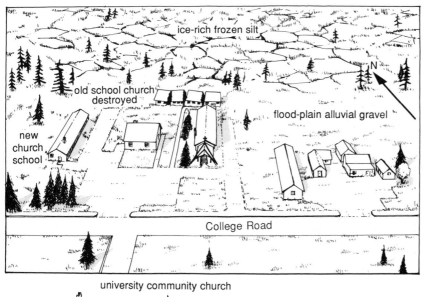

(a)

ice-rich frozen silt

old school church destroyed

new church school

flood-plain alluvial gravel

N

College Road

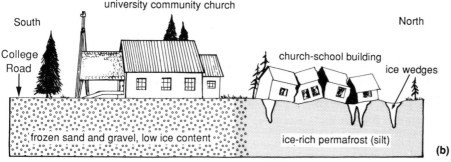

South

College Road

university community church

North

church-school building

ice wedges

frozen sand and gravel, low ice content

ice-rich permafrost (silt)

(b)

A4

Student enquiry 7B:
Exploration and development of Siberia

The development of Prudhoe Bay and the construction of the Trans-Alaskan pipeline are two of the most impressive engineering achievements of the century, although they have largely gone unnoticed. Now the USSR is out to exploit the potential locked up in its vast Siberian wastelands (B1, B2). Here Soviet geologists have discovered, in addition to the oil and gas already being piped out, some of the largest deposits of coal, iron ore, copper and tin in the world. The key to their exploitation is a project called BAM (The Baikal-Amur Mainline area). This is the area bordering the second Trans-Siberian railway, but this new line will be built far to the north of the present one, in land farther from the strategically sensitive Chinese border.

1. Suggest some reasons for the route of the first Trans-Siberian railway, explaining (with the help of Fig. 7.3) why it made a great southern loop instead of cutting across the north of Lake Baikal.

The BAM, whose designated area is seven time the size of Britain, will be subject to centralised development. The Soviet Academy of Sciences is involved in helping the planning of the BAM and overcoming the engineering problems associated with the permafrost zone.

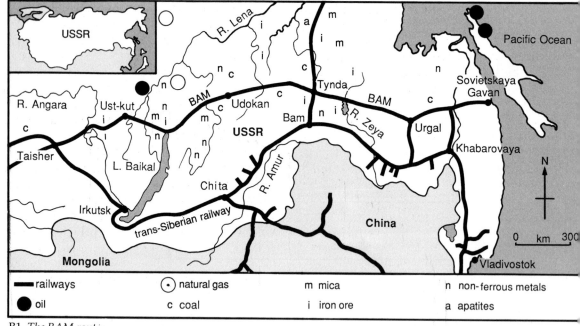

B1 *The BAM route*

Tapping a world resource

THE MINERAL reserves in the BAM zone are immense. There are 88 billion tonnes of coal and 7·7 million tonnes of iron ore, which is approaching 10 per cent of the known world resources. North of the railway lie huge gas fields and, further north still, gold and diamonds.

The key area in the early stages of BAM's development is around Nagorny where a giant open-cast mine is already extracting 13 million tonnes of coal a year. Nearby are massive iron ore deposits and an ore-dressing plant has been built to handle nine million tonnes per year. A coal-fired power station will establish the power for a giant metallurgical zone—provided the construction costs in this, one of the coldest spots in Siberia, do not prove too much.

Around Udokan are the USSR's largest deposits of copper, along with titanium, iron ore, rare metals and, conveniently placed to fuel metal preparation, coal.

Elsewhere are some of the world's most important deposits of tin, in the Khol-domi Valley, along with zinc, copper, lead, tungsten, bismuth and molybdenum. Refinement of many of these metals will use hydroelectric power from rivers draining into the northern shores of Lake Baikal. A series of power stations have already been built along the Angara River and at Ust-Ilimsky. At the eastern end of the railway, where again coal is in rich supply, the chemical industry will be important. Much of this will depend on the processing of wood.

BAM's planners believe that many more minerals await discovery as the development of the BAM zone progresses. In the Priokhoyte area there are thought to be commercial reserves of iron ore, phosphorites, non-ferrous metals and semi-precious metals. But above all there is timber. The USSR has more standing timber than any other country in the world: one fifth of it lies along the route of BAM, an estimated 4 billion cubic metres of timber in all. Their only concern is that, in such a cold climate, trees take longer to grow than elsewhere so the need to protect resources, as well as the environment, is correspondingly greater. □

B2 *New Scientist*, 1 November 1984

They also have responsibility for protecting the environment. One of their tasks is to set up new livestock farms and hothouses to feed the migrants who will have to live in this area.

2. Describe the problems of setting up such farms and how these problems could be overcome.

3. The USSR has more standing timber than any other country in the world: one fifth of it lies along the route of the BAM. BAM's planners hope to cut down much of the 100 million hectares of timber in the zone. What might the results of this be? If a replanting scheme is chosen suggest some ways in which tree survival and growth could be ensured.

4. The BAM railway crosses seven mountain ranges, has nine long tunnels through permafrost and 126 large bridges across broad rivers that freeze in winter and flood in spring. On BAM's route the permafrost is extremely deep; down to 1500 m. The Trans-Alaskan pipeline was often taken over piles on such difficult land, but the railway cannot be taken on piles for 2000 km. As a result a 4 m high soil embankment faced with rock fragments has been suggested for the track base. Sketch out a cross-section of the line and indicate some of the reasons why this might be a good idea.

5. Suppose you were the engineer in charge of building the railway. As chief director of operations you have to draft a set of operating and construction rules for the construction engineers and support crews so that they have a minimal long term impact on the fragile environment. You must include in this a short statement (including illustrative diagrams) for issue to the workforce who do not have a technical understanding of the environment so that they are aware of what damage they can do if care is not taken. Give reasons for the special precautions they have to adopt. You should make use of the following information:

The mountains have only a minimal soil cover. The intermontane landscape consists of low hills. Materials here are mostly fine-grained clays, silt and sand. Gravel is uncommon and confined to river beds. In this area the active layer thaws to about 1.5 m. In the past heavy tractors with caterpillar belt treads were used in summer to cope with the boggy ground, sometimes also using the bulldozing blade to remove the soft surface and make a road. Some of the scars from this process are still clear 40 years after they were made. Spring meltwater running over them is still causing erosion. Your contractors suggest several schemes: (a) the use of wide balloon tyres on vehicles to reduce the 'footprint' of the vehicles; (b) only working after the ground has become frozen and covered with snow; (c) the use of frozen lakes and rivers as roadways for as many of the winter routes as practicable; (d) the creation of ice roads and airstrips by pumping water on to the tundra at the start of the freezing season so that it forms a thin and even sheet of ice.

The challenge of mountainous terrain

Cold environments mostly occur in the polar regions where, because communications are poor, the settlement is scanty. However, small areas of seasonally cold climate do attract large numbers of people – these are the mountain ski resorts. Here the natural landforming processes show a different balance to the polar tundra. Rapid changes in temperature, for example, are both seasonal and diurnal. Most mountain areas also experience much higher precipitation than their lowland counterparts. Furthermore slopes are often steep, sometimes precipitous. Thus the dominant slope processes are not related to ice-rich sediment changes. Many of the slopes are weathering-limited, that is transport processes act faster than weathering so that any new loosened material is quickly removed and the slope left mostly bare. In these cases natural processes are dominated by rock falls and the effects of rapidly moving masses of snow – avalanches.

Weathering in steep slope environments proceeds largely through the process of **frost shatter**, whereby rain or snow melted by daytime warmth percolates into rock pores or fractures and freezes overnight. The resultant expansion on freezing may break surface rock

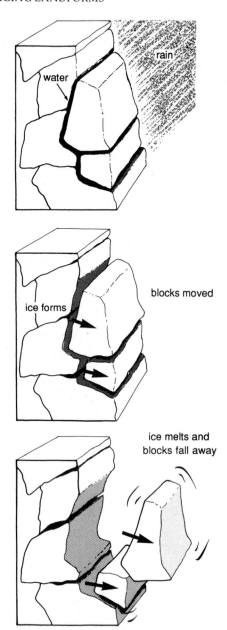

Figure 7.15 *The process of frost shatter and rock displacement on steep slopes*

fragments clear of the main rock body (Fig 7.15). The following morning, when air temperatures again rise and the ice melts, the fracture line that contained the ice is now the control slope for the shattered rock fragment. If this local control slope is below the threshold angle of stability it will not move. However in many cases the threshold value will be exceeded and the rock fragment will fall, perhaps hitting and dislodging further, otherwise stable fragments until they all finally come to rest. The results of this action are widespread and readily visible as the familiar scree slopes that skirt mountain cliffs.

The usual threshold angle for stability of coarse angular rock is about 40°, and material frost-shattered on more gentle slopes will not naturally fall away. Indeed, further weathering may allow the coarse debris to develop into a stony soil which will support trees. Many alpine regions have forests mantling slopes between 40° and about 20°. Below this angle forests may still dominate, although many will have been cleared for pasture.

The 20°–40° degree slopes are among the most critical in the landscape because they are also places on which snow can accumulate in an unstable fashion. It is unusual to find deep snow accumulating on very steep slopes, partly because such slopes are usually very exposed and the snow is quickly blown away, and partly because it quickly tends to collapse and fall away under its own weight. However, on the intermediate slopes snow falls can and do develop into deep drifts, particularly on slopes sheltered from the dominant winds.

Drifts form intermittently through the winter. Thus a snow storm may be succeeded by perfectly clear skies and some of the surface snow may even melt down to give a hard surface crust to the drift. In any case a certain degree of compaction will take place as pressure of the snow pack on the delicate snowflake spikes forces them to melt back into shape more reminiscent of ball bearings. Each subsequent snowfall is separated from that on which it accumulates by a difference in compaction and a discontinuity of crusted ice. During the winter many such discontinuities may form in an ever-deepening drift.

Multi-layered snow is in its thickest and therefore most unstable state at the end of the season of winter snows. In spring local melting takes place and small patches of snow are continually shifting their position. But this is the time when even a small fall of snow from, say, the overhang of a cornice, can disturb a large drift, exceeding the threshold angle of stability and setting an avalanche in progress (Fig. 7:16).

The avalanche hazard

Avalanches begin slowly, often inconspicuously as an unstable mass of snow slumps, causing one snow layer to slip over the crusted layer below. But within a few seconds the moving mass is gathering both speed and momentum (Fig. 7.17). Riding ahead of the main mass is a shock wave as air is pushed aside by the snow: above the surface the still powdery new snow is floated into the air as a powder avalanche, while the main, consolidated mass races across the rock below picking up loose debris along its track and supported on an almost frictionless cushion of air. Avalanches commonly reach speeds of over 300 km/hr.

Figure 7.16 *A powder avalanche*

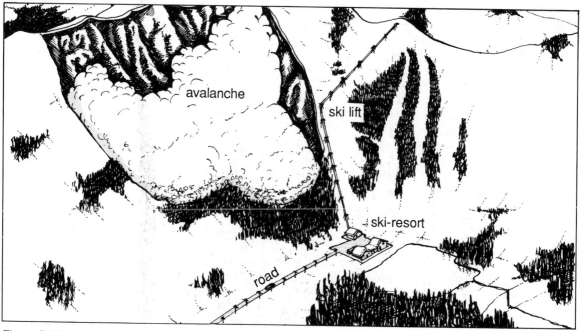

Figure 7.17 *Avalanche impact on inhabited areas*

Figure 7.19(a)

Despite these efforts to inform the public of impending avalanche danger, there continue to be many avalanche accidents throughout the United States. In 1985, there were 20 fatalities associated with avalanches; the ten-year average is 14 per year. Historically, avalanches have affected mostly mining towns, killing 15–100 people with each slide. Since the end of the mining boom, it is more common that victims are people involved in recreation activities. As mountain development continues, fatalities increase (enclosed are statistics for the US that show this trend taking place

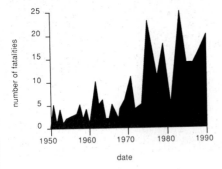

between the winter of 1950–51 and September of 1985).

The potential for catastrophic avalanche disasters within mountain towns, transportation corridors, and residential areas is great, as can be seen in these two examples:

1) Juneau, Alaska, has huge avalanche paths directly over its main city center. More than once the buildings have been hit: roofs of houses have been torn off, the high school has been damaged, and a boat harbor has been destroyed. Only by chance has there not been a catastrophe. All avalanche professionals recognise, however, that it is only a matter of time.

2) On any given Sunday, the Little Cottonwood Canyon area of Utah holds over 10 000 skiers, tourists, and residents. During each minute of the day, two thirds of these people are exposed to avalanche dangers. The diligence of the avalanche forecasters employed by each ski area, of the Utah Department of Transportation, and of the US Forest Service have prevented a major disaster so far, but there have been many close calls – especially when weather forecasts have been inaccurate.

I hope that the National Weather Service will recognise its current role in mitigating snow avalanche problems and continue to support the efforts of other agencies to avert disaster. Death by snow avalanche is not something that should be ignored, even over the summer.

Sincerely,
Sue A. Ferguson
Program Manager
USDA FS Utah Avalanche
Forecast Center

Natural Hazards Observer

An avalanche hits objects in its path with devastating force. The shock wave can literally blow a building to pieces, while the snow mass exerts direct pressures on obstacles in its path of over 100 tonnes/m^2.

Avalanches have an important role to play in the development of the natural landscape because their inertia enables them to carry rock fragments released by frost shattering from steep slopes to the gentle slopes of the valley bottom. Some 100 000 avalanches are thought to occur in the mountainous west of the USA alone each winter. Most occur harmlessly in unpopulated areas. But of course, they can also have a devastating effect on people caught in their paths (Figure 7.19(a)). Each year avalanches claim dozens of lives, destroy houses and block communication routes. And the hazard is increasing as more and more people don their ski outfits and head for the mountains

(see Figure 7.19(a)).

Avalanche control teams work in most populated mountain areas during the late winter and early spring. They try to break up any particularly threatening drift by using explosives or firing cannon into the cornices and high ridges.

There are many ways to protect areas against avalanches and an equal number of ways to make an area more avalanche prone. For example, natural forests act like anchors within the snow drift and make movement less likely. A forest below an avalanche-prone slope can absorb most of the impact and protect houses downslope. Many Alpine villages do not have forests near them just to improve the scenery! Andermatt in Switzerland, for example, has its forest protected by law (Fig. 7.18). Juneau, in Alaska, is renowned for its avalanche hazards:

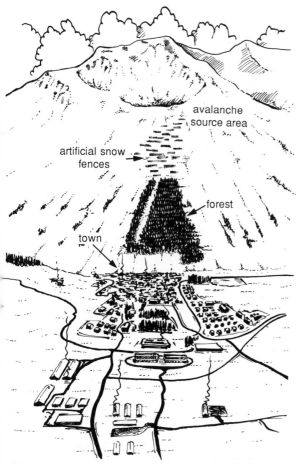

Figure 7.18 *A combination of natural and artificial barriers to protect Andermatt, Switzerland*

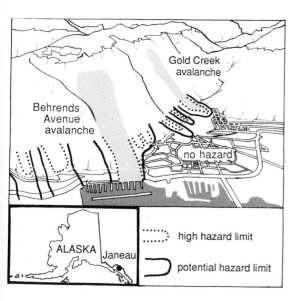

Figure 7.19(b) *Hazard zones at Juneau, Alaska*

Figure 7.20 *Fences designed to prevent avalanches*

they can readily be picked out as areas devoid of trees (Fig. 7.19(b)).

In areas where the controlled release of a potential avalanche is not possible, a number of protective measures can be taken, all designed either to stop the movement of drifts or to deflect them from important areas or homes. High on the slopes steel and concrete fences are built to slow and slop the avalanche before it gathers momentum (Fig. 7.20). Lower down, large earth and rock splitter wedges are placed to deflect the avalanche away from homes. And, of course, homes can be built in areas not normally affected by avalanches!

In many popular resort areas the tourists are their own worst enemy because they don't understand how the simple act of skiing in an unstable area can start an avalanche. One of the most dangerous times is immediately following a deep fall of fresh snow – just the time many cross-country skiers like best. At these times the golden rules are to avoid heavily laden 'chutes' and areas near the top of or below a cliff, and to learn what unstable snow sounds like when it is skied on.

Student enquiry 7C: Avalanche hazard analysis

1. Study the sketch of the valley shown in C1 and the photograph of a ski resort in the Colorado Rockies. On a tracing overlay divide the valley into hazard zones and shade these in, using blue for the lowest hazard through to red for the greatest. Suggest some safe ski routes that could be signposted and a small handout that would help people unused to the dangers of mountainous snow-covered terrain.
2. Read the article 'Acid rain may trigger Alpine avalanches' (C2). Now examine the following quotation: *'There's some danger in living in certain parts of the community, but I incline to the view that its greatly overstated. The government has bitten off more than it can chew in protecting everyone from everything. We would be wiser to caution people, but let them run their own affairs.'* Comment on the information and statement in the context of people in the cold zones.

C1(a)

Guide to defining hazard zones

no risk ☐   low risk ☐   intermediate risk ▥   high risk ▦

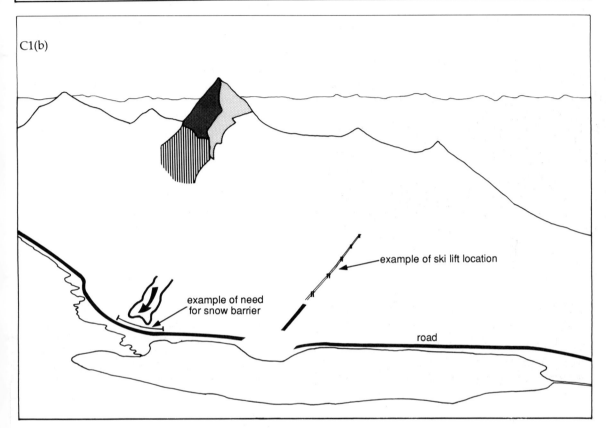

C1(b)

example of ski lift location

example of need for snow barrier

road

C2   **Acid rain may trigger Alpine avalanches**

The picturesque Alpine villages of Switzerland are filling up with skiers. But the winter holidaymakers may have more than high prices and crowded lifts to worry about this year. The forests that protect the slopes from avalanches are dying. Mountain villages may have to be evacuated as a result.

The mysterious decline of European forests, thought to be caused by air pollution, has reached the Alps. The Swiss Federal Office of Forestry reports that 36 per cent of the forests that cover much of Switzerland are diseased.

Villages perched high up in the Swiss Alps have traditionally been built in spots where forests provide some protection from avalanches. As the forests die, the protection disappears.

The problem is made worse by the fact that trees at high altitudes seem to be most at risk. The Swiss forestry office says 43 per cent of trees in the central

Alpine region of the country are sick. The Swiss environment minister, Alphons Egli, who was elected President of the country in a parliamentary vote last month, says: 'The situation in the mountain forests isn't just bad, it's dramatic.'

In the highlands of the mountain canton of Uri, for example, 90 per cent of white fir, and 50 per cent of red fir and pine are diseased. Some villagers in Uri are worried that little stands between them and disaster.

One such village is Bristen. The beeches, firs and pines on the slopes above the village are becoming infested with bark beetle. The spread of the beetles is often connected with air pollution, which may pre-dispose the trees to attack. Foresters in Uri have been cutting down infected trees in an attempt to halt the spread of the beetle. The villagers of Bristen have watched the disappearance of the trees with alarm. They are familiar with the ways of the Bristen-

Sick trees are all that hold back the snows

stock mountain that towers over their valley. In 1974, a number of trees were cut down on its slopes, and avalanches in the area increased dramatically.

Trees provide protection from landslides and rock-falls. In the forests above Bristen there are bare patches of ground, which increase the chances of a slide. The real worry, however, is snow, which can fall at speeds up to 250 kilometres per hour, and hit the ground with an impact of 50 tonnes per square metre, triggering avalanches.

Swiss scientists say that forests cannot actually stop an avalanche that starts higher up the mountain side. But they can "absorb" up to 10 centimetres of snow accumulation by carrying it on their branches. Also, snow under the trees is mixed with needles and debris, and is less likely to slide.

Bristeners are used to evacuating parts of the town when there is a danger of avalanches. Now they say that the houses that were considered safe refuges are in danger. The mayor of Bristen, Hans Murer, appealed last year to the canton's government for money to build concrete barriers, of the kind used to protect highways and other new constructions. He estimates that he needs three million francs to build an effective barrier.

Last summer, Bristeners built huge soil terraces above the town, and next year's plan is to plant young trees there. The Swiss forestry office warns that young trees at high altitude are most at risk of disease and it is not sure whether the strategy will work.

The forestry office estimates that 10 per cent of Alpine 'barrier forests' will lose their protective capacity in the next few years. This would put 150 000 people at risk, and threaten the safety of hundreds of roads and ski trails, which earn the region most of its income. The forstry office's scientists blame the damage on air pollution, including acid rain and fog, and ozone, which is created by the action of ultraviolet light on pollutants.

Car exhausts are the most important cause of ozone formulation in Switzerland. But, in a vote last month, the canton of Uri rejected a proposal to put a 20-franc 'forest tax' on cars.   *New Scientist*, 2 January 1986

Key terms

Ablation: the melting of a glacier or ice sheet.

Active layer: the surface layer of a region of ground ice which melts during the summer, allowing land forming processes to operate.

Avalanche: the rapid movement down a steep slope of snow and contained debris.

Ice-rich permafrost: ground containing more water in the form of ice than it could possibly hold if the water were liquid.

Frost creep: the slow downslope ratchet-like movement of the active layer by means of expansion and contraction during the freeze-thaw process.

Gelifluction: the process of slow flow of the active layer during the summer thaw season.

Gelifluction lobes: an elongate lobe of sediment produced by localised movement of the active layer. They most often form downslope of a snow patch.

Glacial till: material transported in the basal layers of a glacier or ice sheet and left unsorted as a mantle to a landscape after ablation.

Ice wedges: seep veins or wedges of ice, sometimes metres deep that grow down into permafrosted sediments. They are fed by melting surface snow in the spring.

Patterned ground: polygonally or circular cracked ground produced by intense freezing in the winter season. The margins of patterned ground are sometimes reinforced by ice wedges.

Periglacial: a region with a cold climate whose soil and rocks contain ground ice and whose landforms depend on processes operating during ice melting.

Permafrost: material with a temperature colder than 0°C for a period of at least 2 consecutive years. The material may or may not contain water in the forms of ice veins and lenses.

Permafrost table: the upper surface of the permafrost zone.

Thermokarst: a landscape containing depressions, tunnels and caves caused by the sub-surface melting of ice-rich permafrost.

Pingo: the Inuit word for hill; this is an ice-cored dome of sediment perhaps tens of metres high and hundreds of metres in diameter which is analogous to a surface blister. It grows only in water-rich sediment such as river floodplains that have been placed under hydrostatic pressure.

Utilidors: heated tunnels connecting dwellings in cold regions and designed to carry service pipes such as water and sewage.

Chapter 8
The dry lands

Introduction

Dry lands, those parts of the world which can be climatically classified as arid or semi-arid, include an immense variety of landscapes. Every inhabited continent has its dry lands, and in many cases they have been chosen as the locations of major cities (Fig. 8.1; Table 8.1).

All dry lands have water supply problems and these will be dealt with in the succeeding chapters; here we focus on landform management.

The drylands present several significant geomorphological hazards to people:
(a) the presence of aggressive salt;
(b) flash floods and unstable channels; and
(c) the instability of sand.

In order to meet the challenge of the dry lands environment we must first understand how these major factors influence landscape evolution.

Salt weathering

The dry lands environment owes much of its character to the special dominance of salt weathering. Dry lands experience high daytime air and surface temperatures for at least part of the year, low and erratic rainfall and a very high

Table 8.1

City	Population (millions)
Accra, Ghana	1
Ahmedabad, India	3
Alexandria, Egypt	4
Ankara, Turkey	2
Baghdad, Iraq	3
Baku, USSR	1.5
Beijing, China	10
Cairo, Egypt	10
Caracas, Venezuela	3
Damascus, Syria	1.5
Delhi, India	6
Guadelahara, Mexico	3
Hyderabad, India	3
Karachi, Pakistan	6
Kuibyshev, USSR	1.5
Lahore, Pakistan	2
Lima, Peru	4
Los Angeles, USA	5
Monterey, Mexico	3
Phoenix, USA	1
San Diego, USA	2
Tashkent, USSR	2
Teheran, Iran	6
Tiensing, China	6
Tunis, Tunisia	1

Figure 8.1 *Dubai City. Half a million people live here, but at what cost?*

potential evaporation. This means that, in regions where groundwater is near the surface, water, together with contained salts, is often drawn up to the ground surface by capillary action. Capillary action is most important in fine grained sediments such as clays, but it is also important in limestones and sandstones. As water evaporates at the surface the salts are left behind either as surface salt coatings – called **efflorescences** – or contained within the surface layers of the sediment.

Certain environments favour the development of salts in sediments or rocks:

(a) sabkhas, which are coastal regions underlain with saline groundwater; and

(b) playas, lakes in the centre of closed depressions which receive the drainage of internal basins (Fig. 8.2).

The accumulation of salt in certain preferred regions is only the first stage of what might be called the **'salt cycle'**. Efflorescences are liable to be blown by the wind and their salts redistri-

buted on bare rocks that would naturally have low salt contents (Fig. 8.3). Thus this redistribution of salt allows salt weathering to proceed over wide areas and cause rock splitting,

Figure 8.2 *The playa in Death Valley, California. The light colour is salt*

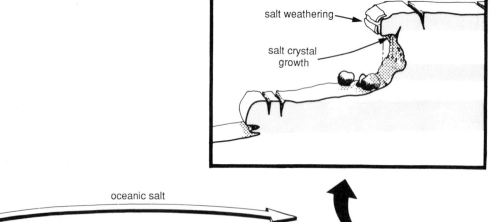

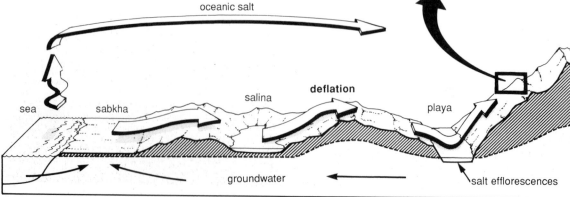

Figure 8.3 *Salt movements in arid environments*

granular disintegration and the creation of basal overhangs.

Salt weathering mainly occurs on exposed rocks as salt particles deposited in the wind are washed into rock pores during occasional storms. When the rainwater evaporates the salt crystallises in the pores. Salts can set up stresses in three ways:

(a) thermal expansion of salt crystals within pores;

(b) hydration of salts at times of high humidity; and

(c) growth of salt crystals in the pores over many wetting cycles.

Today salt attack is recognised as a major form of weathering, supplanting previously held ideas concerning rock weathering by 'heating and cooling', 'onion weathering' or wind abrasion as the cause of many dry land features (Fig. 8.4).

The salt hazard

The presence of salt attack on rocks is of considerable importance to people who live in the dry lands. For instance, structures whose foundations penetrate to zones near groundwater are very vulnerable. Concrete, in particular, is liable to disintegration and expensive steps have to be taken to isolate the concrete from the 'corrosive' environment (Fig. 8.5).

Figure 8.4 *A natural arch in sandstone. Once regarded as a feature of wind erosion it is now recognised as a result of salt weathering*

Care also has to be taken that concrete is not made from local materials containing high salt concentrations or this will lead to even faster disintegration (Fig. 8.6).

The greatest problems occur when construction takes place on soil with a shallow saline groundwater. This is common in dry lands because most settlements seek reliable water supplies (e.g. Cairo, Egypt beside the River Nile) or coastal sites for trade (e.g. Suez City, Egypt) and therefore are liable to be developed on sabkha environments. Development away from shallow groundwater zones will help to

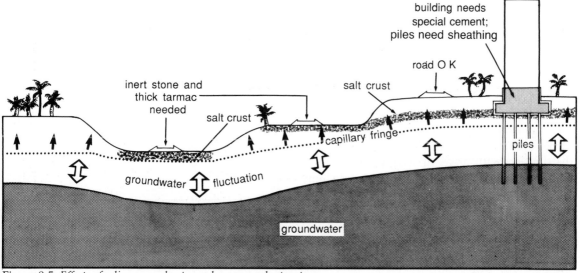

Figure 8.5 *Effects of saline groundwater on human-made structures*

reduce the impact of this problem but there is often a conflict between the site requirements of commercial trading objectives and the preferred locations of the construction industry.

Roads are as vulnerable as buildings where groundwater lies near the surface. Whereas salty soils can be used with impunity for unsurfaced roads, they can spell disaster when used under bitumen surfaces. Bitumen, because of its black colour, normally produces the hottest surfaces in a dry land. Thin bitumen surfaces can allow evaporation of water under these conditions, and this encourages further capillary rise of water from below. The salt, however, is deposited at the soil-bitumen junction where is accumulates, attracting more and more salt until it causes salt blisters to grow, heaving the road surface into small domes or causing cracks to develop. This problem requires the use of special, impermeable bitumen and a thicker cover, both features which cost more than normal. Clearly it is best to locate or even relocate roads away from groundwater areas before surfacing them for the first time.

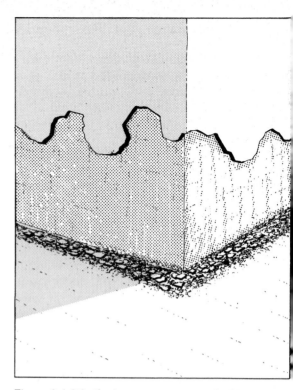

Figure 8.6 *Weathering on a new concrete building*

Student enquiry 8A: The importance of salt weathering

Enquiry 8A contains a map produced to show the aggressive salt conditions prevailing in Bahrain. Place a tracing overlay on top of the weathering map and mark out those places where foundation problems are likely to be most severe. Separately mark on the regions into which urban areas can expand with the least problem from aggressive salt. Now find a map of Bahrain and compare the urban population distribution with areas of weathering, discussing what proportion of the urban area may suffer problems.

A1

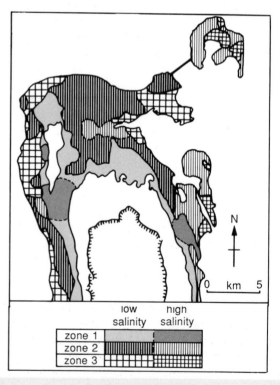

Figure 8.7 *A dry 'gulch' in the USA. This is a typical ephemeral channel. The channel features indicate the nature of flood flow*

Water in dry lands

Dry lands are not completely without rainfall and all areas receive rain and/or snow from time to time. Usually this is in the form of heavy convectional storms over very limited areas. Except for **exotic** rivers that cross dry lands and are fed by distant, more humid regions (e.g. Nile, Colorado), rivers are characteristically **ephemeral** in character, forming raging torrents soon after rainfall, but drying out completely between storms (Fig. 8.7). There is rarely sufficient flow to carry sediment great distances and many landforms result from this local sediment transport. Essentially, therefore, most dry lands show a pattern of just two major systems:

(a) mountain basins with steep slopes and thin sediment veneer; and

(b) the mountain front (piedmont) plain with its covering of sediments.

Depending on the nature of the environment, dry lands can respond to local rainfall events in two ways:

(a) on uplands with steep slopes, the rubble-like surface materials retain little water and there is an almost instantaneous response of runoff to rainfall. Indeed, in mountainous terrain it is very common for the runoff to occur in the form of a **flash flood** in the deeply incised valleys (locally called canyons, arroyos, wadis,

etc.). In some cases such flows are nearly sediment free and they behave as ordinary rivers; in other cases, where there is considerable fine-grained sediment to be entrained by the rushing water, these two constituents combine to produce a substance that has the consistency of liquid cement and is called a **debris flow**;

(b) on lowlands with gentle slopes and considerable sediment cover (such as sand dunes) runoff rarely occurs even at the height of storms.

The combined effects of these types of response mean that weathered material is transferred from uplands to lowlands, but rarely moved away from lowlands. This tends to lead to large depths of sediment accumulation in lowlands proximal to mountains. Even these transfers occur at a slow rate because of the low rate weathering and infrequent runoff events. Thus dry land environments frequently show many features that are relics of erosion during wetter climatic periods. Meanders in wadis and many mountain valleys are some typical 'fossil features'.

Some of the most active features formed are **alluvial fans**, cone-shaped landforms created where mountain torrents debouch on to low-gradient plains. Water previously confined to a definite channel is able to move freely over the landscape, the channel efficiency is lost, the gradient slackens and water infiltrates into the

155

playa

pediment

mountain
front

butte

Figure 8.8 *Features of arid mountain fronts*

existing sediment. As a result the water flowing over the surface has insufficient energy to carry the coarsest particles and these are deposited to increase the size of the fan. As more and more water is lost into the fan so further deposition occurs. As storm follows storm the water gradually builds up a steep alluvial fan on which dividing (braided) channels form and reform. A mature fan has an entrenched and almost stable channel near the mountain front, with a less stable channel pattern where the fan is building actively outward near its base.

Water that flows away from an alluvial fan may sink into the sediment of the plain and be lost. In other cases it may flow to the centre of a lowland basin and accumulate to form a temporary lake called a playa lake. There are several forms of playa, their characteristics depending on whether the lake is the result of surface run-off or a rise in groundwater level. If a playa lake results from a rise of groundwater the soils near a playa are normally heavily saline and the salt left behind after the lake has evaporated leaves a characteristic salt encrustation.

156

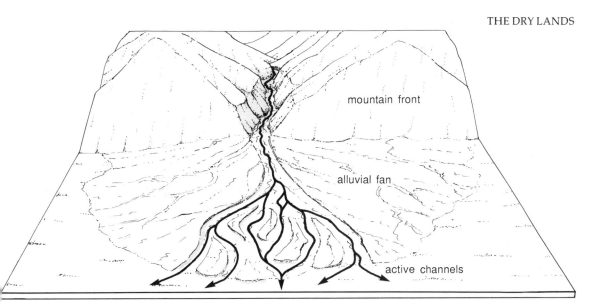

Figure 8.9 *Alluvial fans and distributaries*

The water hazard

The major hazard people face is the unpredict-ability of water flow both in time and space. Because the channel material is coarse and non-cohesive, channels will continually form and reform during the passage of a flood wave. The presence of a channel cannot therefore be used to assess the safety of an area nearby unless it is deeply incised. Thus, for example, the least hazard on an alluvial fan occurs near the apex where the channel is usually deeply incised, while the flood hazard increases towards the base of the fan where channels are little more than surface features (Fig. 8.9).

Because rivers are ephemeral, and there may not be any water in channels for several years, it is common for people to underestimate the danger of flooding and build in areas of potential danger (Fig. 8.10). This is especially true in areas newly developed as tourist resorts where the residents may have little experience of flooding in a dry lands environment and the developers may be unaware of the true extent of the potential hazards.

Many settlements have been built on alluvial fans and even in canyon bottoms. When a flash flood does arrive, there is little chance for people so located. One such flash flood was experienced in Eldorado canyon, a small canyon that gives access to the beaches around Lake Mead

(a)

Figure 8.10 (a) *potential hazard of sand encroachment*
(b) *Large channels to protect against flash floods, Los Angeles*

(b)

157

near Las Vegas, Nevada, USA. The arrival of the flash flood was described by one onlooker fortunate enough to be away from the direct flood wave:

> 'When I got around the small nose (spur) which was behind the block-ice machine and started walking towards the coffee shop, I looked up for a second. I became disoriented because I thought the mountain had moved. Then I realised what we were seeing was a wall of water about 20' – 25' high stacked with cars, trailers, etc., smash into the coffee shop, post office and they exploded like there was dynamite inside.'

This flood wave moved at about 4 km/hr and killed nine people. Since 1974 when this happened, the canyon has been redeveloped as a resort, with new buildings located away from the direct impact of a flood wave. The new car park has been fashioned on top of the 1974 debris flow that fills the lower part of the canyon where it enters Lake Mead.

The debris flow hazard has long been recognised as important by many dry land planners. In Los Angeles, for example, debris flows are amongst the most costly natural hazards to be coped with (Fig. 8.10(b)).

Playas can be of importance for their mineral resources. Borax, for example, used to be hauled by mule team from the hot arid lands of Death Valley in California. Many playas (such as in northern Chile) are exploited today. They also provide flat surfaces which may appear suitable for urban development, air strips, and even as test tracks for cars (e.g. the Salt Flats of Utah, USA). Nonetheless, playas can rapidly flood, and their surfaces may also crack as they dry up, thus representing a considerable hazard which must be planned for.

Wind in dry lands

People commonly think of dry lands as regions covered with sand dunes. Actually no more than a quarter of dry lands are sand covered, and in many environments sand occupies less than 1 per cent of the land surface.

The movement of sand and dust depends on the velocity and turbulence of the wind (the **erosivity** of the processes) and the roughness, cohesion and grain size of the material that may be blown (the **erodibility** of the environment). The removal of sand and dust by wind from dry land surfaces is called **deflation**.

Sand (material with diameters of 2mm to 0.06mm) moves largely by the near-surface hopping, bouncing process called **saltation**. The movement of sand produces what is known as a **saltation curtain**, an abrasive curtain of sand usually no more than a few tens of centimetres high. Material finer than sand, dust, is only disturbed by high winds and is non-erosive. It may, however, be transported by the wind over considerable distances.

The interaction of deflating sediment with the wind produces a variety of bedforms in much the same ways as bedforms develop in a river or near the coast. Most of the bedforms are made of sand and they vary in size from the common **ripple**, through **dunes**, to large sand swales called **draa** and sometime to sand mountains several hundred metres high called **rhourds** (Fig. 8.11). A large area of sand is called an **erg** or **sand sea**. Such areas may have many types of bedforms on them, reflecting the complex pattern of wind both locally and regionally. In general, bedforms of dune size and larger have two characteristic slopes: a concave/convex **ramp slope** that faces into the wind and up which sand is transported, and a straight threshold **lee slope** down which the sand falls. Some areas have linear dunes known as **seifs**, while others are patterned with individual crescentic dunes known as **barchans**. Of all the dune systems, barchans are usually the most mobile and present the greatest problem to settlements.

Wind hazard

As wind blows over non-cohesive sediments it causes deflation. Under natural conditions deflation leads to a naturally stable **armoured** surface called a **reg** (Fig. 8.12), as larger stones within the sediment are left behind and gradually produce a protective cover. Sometimes saline crusts will achieve the same result. Thus, deflation is only a continuing hazard where, as in sand bedforms, the material does not contain large particles.

Figure 8.11 (a) *Sand dunes*

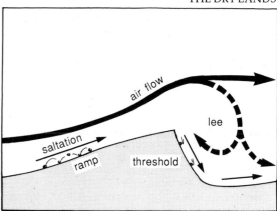

Figure 8.11 (b) *Aerodynamics near a dune*

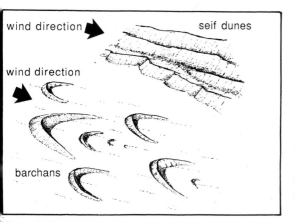

Figure 8.11 (c) *Major dune systems*

Figure 8.12 *A stony armoured desert in Morocco*

Deflation can be initiated by people if they disrupt a naturally armoured surface during construction or for agriculture. During subsequent deflation the abrasive effects of the sand may scour the base of houses, posts and other structures, frost the windscreens and even strip the paintwork from cars. Deflation may also undermine structures such as railway tracks, roads or even telegraph posts.

Dust is a hazard largely through reduction of visibility and the blocking of air filters on mechanical equipment. It can cause airports to be unusable and even stop traffic on roads (Fig. 8.13). In extreme cases it can cause animals to suffocate. The dust hazard is thus a prime cause of insurance claims.

A good dry lands rule is: 'disturb the land or air flow as little as possible'. Thus it is always wise to consider the possibility of relocation away from hazard areas; it may be cheaper in the long term than continuous preventive measures. If it is found imperative to build in a hazardous area, then sediment stabilisation should always be tried first because sand and dust deflated from one region are inevitably deposited somewhere else. The most significant problem results from the movement of bed forms such as sand dunes, which may be driven towards urban areas. Thus the advance of a sand sea can threaten farmland, settlements and airports (Fig. 8.14). The only solution to this problem is to plant vegetation or build structures that will arrest the advance of the sand, or to build in areas away from this form of hazard. There are many oases near to sand seas that have had to be abandoned because people have been unable to stop the advance of sand and even the massive planting of vegetation may not succeed unless carefully executed (see article 'Sand trickles' on page 160).

Sand trickles through China's other great wall

Jasper Becker, Beijing

China's plans to plant a "green great wall" 7000 kilometres long is failing to prevent vast areas of northern China from becoming desert. The desert is expanding by 1560 square kilometres a year and threatens to overwhelm an area twice the size of Taiwan – about the same as Wales and Northern Ireland combined – by the year 2000.

The tide of sand is endangering 328 000 square kilometres, or 3.4 per cent of China's total land area, affecting 35 million people in 12 provinces and autonomous regions. So warns Zhu Zenda, director of China's Institute of Desert Research.

Zhu blames overcultivation, overgrazing, misuse of forest and water resources, and poorly planned construction of mines, mills and communication lines. Poor land management in these areas has been accompanied by an increase in population density from 14.4 persons per square kilometre in 1949, to 59.3 in 1981. *New Scientist* 24 October 1985

Figure 8.13 *Sandstorm in northern Sudan*

Figure 8.14 *Barchan dunes engulf fields and irrigation canals at Hofuf in Saudi Arabia*

There are many techniques for stabilising sand dunes:

a) grow vegetation to bind sand grains together and restrict dune movement. This can be an effective system but it is a long term measure;

b) spread gravel on the surface in order to form a protective armour coating. In some places gravel may be difficult to obtain;

c) spray the surface with oil. This is cheap and effective, but it is unpleasant and needs repeated treatment;

d) spread chemical adhesive on the surface to bind the particles together;

e) erect fences and walls to divert the wind, or protect structures.

Some other possible schemes are shown in figure 8.15. Probably the most widespread methods involve fences and vegetation. Notice that flattening dunes is not amongst the list. This is because sand dunes are a naturally stable form – any flattened dunes would soon reform. Removal of dunes may be attempted in certain restricted cases such as near to airport runways, but the volume of material that needs to be shifted is very large and mostly uneconomic.

To gain some idea of the size of some sand dune problems consider the difficulty in protecting the houses and warehouses of the port of Nouadhibou on the Atlantic coast of Mauritania. Here the buildings were in danger from up to 1.6 million cubic metres of sand per kilometre width. Clearly there is no possibility of preventing such large scale movements; all that is possible is to design protective structures that would allow the sand to pass round, over or under them freely. Thus even modern technology can sometimes do no more than accept the natural situation in rather the same way as desert people have done for centuries. As their fields become buried by moving dunes they treat this as a fallow period; when the dune passes by and the field is again exposed the land is used again.

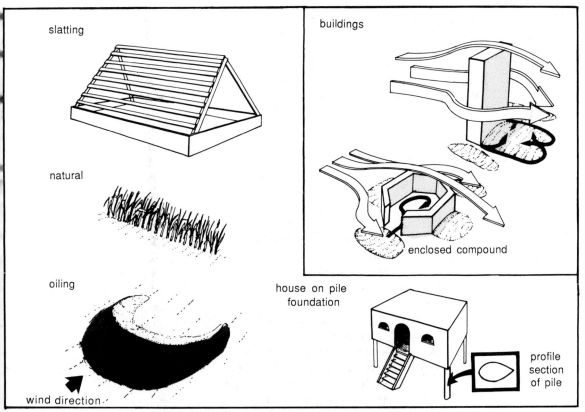

Figure 8.15 *Systems for protection against drifting sand*

Student enquiry 8B:
Making use of landform knowledge for urban planning

Enquiry 8B shows the geomorphology and present human activities of a coastal area. It is planned to expand the city in a sub-radial fashion as shown on the map. The overview perspective of the location is shown in B1.

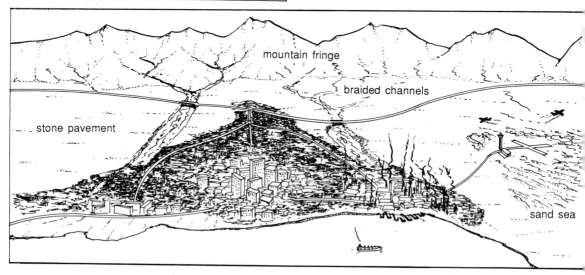

B1

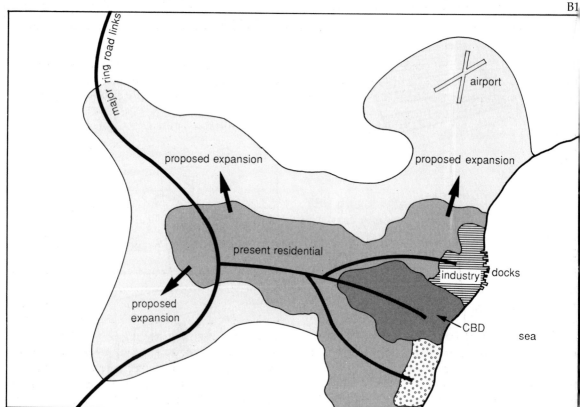

B2

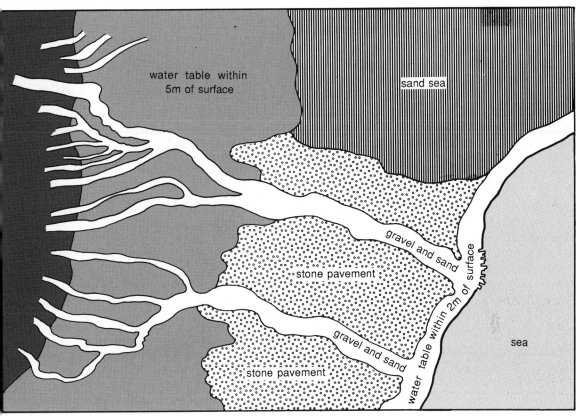

water table within
5m of surface

sand sea

gravel and sand

stone pavement

gravel and sand

stone pavement

water table within 2m of surface

sea

B3

1. Trace a copy of B2 and place it over B3. From this identify and mark on to a futher tracing the present geomorphological problems faced by the city. Mark on the additional problems that would probably arise if the planned expansion goes ahead.

2. Now produce a further overlay, marking on a suggested revised town plan that would pay close regard to geomorphological hazards, yet would still allow the functions (a) CBD; (b) residential expansion; (c) industry; and (d) tourism to go ahead relatively unhindered.

Man-made deserts

Desertisation is an expression used to denote the degradation of land by inappropriate land uses such that once cultivable or grazing land takes on the appearance of true desert. (**Desertification** is a more general term relating to the severe degradation of land in a wide variety of climates.) Desertisation is a particular problem in densely inhabited regions of the dry lands.

The Mediterranean dry lands have a population density of 45 inhabitants/km², a density which is a four-fold increase this century. The result of this population increase has been:

(a) rapidly increased cultivation and clearing of natural vegetation;

(b) increased numbers of livestock and over-grazing;

(c) the destruction of forests and woody vegetation for firewood and charcoal; and

(d) salinisation of large areas as a result of faulty irrigation projects. For example, wheat and barley are now being grown extensively in North African areas receiving only 150–200 mm of rain per year. Here crop expectancy is extremely low, being between one crop to five or ten cultivations. The land is left barren for much of the time and is thus open to wind and water losses (see Chapter 14). At the same time the use of prime grazing land for arable cultivation forces livestock on to poor land which they rapidly overgraze.

During periodically recurring droughts and famines the tendency to encroach on the desert becomes much faster. Each time the encroachment is repeated, the degradation becomes more and more severe and the time needed for recovery progressively longer. Indeed there is considerable evidence that desertisation following poor land use is irreversible in areas with thin topsoil because, once the top permeable soil has been eroded away, the skeletal bedrock does not have enough water holding capacity to allow most plants to regrow.

Desertisation can have further, even more significant consequences, for it can irreversibly alter the pattern of rainfall over an entire region. This is because cultivated or overgrazed land reflects the sun's rays more strongly than the darker surface provided by a natural vegetation cover. A light-coloured area will not store up heat as well as a dark-coloured surface and thus there will be less heat to generate the thermals that form convective cumulus clouds. When a computer model of the global circulation was run with a natural vegetation ('dark') Sahara and then re-run with an overgrazed (light) Sahara the rainfall in the rainy season dropped by a dramatic 40 per cent.

Key terms

Barchan: a crescent-shaped dune.

Deflation: the removal of sediment by wind.

Desertisation: the degradation of land by inappropriate land uses such that once cultivable or grazing land takes on the appearance of a true desert.

Dry lands: semi-arid and arid regions of the world.

Dune: an aerodynamically shaped mound of sand, some tens to hundreds of metres across.

Efflorescence: a white surface coating produced by the migration of salts as water evaporates.

Ephemeral: occurs only occasionally.

Erg: a large body of sand, at least several hundred square kilometres in area and usually made of dunes and rhourds.

Exotic river: has a source region in wetter areas beyond the regions of the dry lands.

Playa: a lake that forms in a closed depression in dry lands after occasional storms.

Reg: a stone and pebble-covered desert plain.

Rhourd: a large aerodynamically shaped sand feature hundreds of metres to tens of kilometres across.

Sabkha: a coastal region underlain by saline ground water.

Saltation: the bouncing of sediment too heavy to be carried in suspension.

Seif dune: a linear feature made of many dunes arranged in a continuous line. They may be tens of kilometres in length.

Weathering: a mechanical process involving the growth of salt crystals within the pores of rocks as water evaporates. After many evaporation cycles the crystals grow big enough to split the rock apart.

Theme:
Water resources management

Chapter 9
Water resources

Introduction

An adequate supply of water is fundamental to any society. Everyone *needs* water to drink, for cleaning, washing and cooking, and if a society is to flourish and expand water is also needed for industry and irrigation. A supply of water is also *desirable* for recreational purposes such as filling swimming pools and watering gardens.

In the early stages of river basin development people solve their water supply problems in a piecemeal fashion, satisfying their requirements without taking into account the possible impact on societies or water users in other parts of the basin (Fig. 9.1). In the same way that upstream regions pay little regard to those downstream so, in larger basins, upstream countries solve their water problems ignoring, for the most part, their impact on those downstream.

Water supply also has an important influence on the development of a country. For example, water-rich countries solve their processing and lifestyle problems by means different from those that are water-poor. Much of the waste treatment in Britain, for example, uses very large quantities of water at all stages from flushing the loo to treating the sewage and flushing it out to sea. The same methods of treatment could never be employed in the arid regions of Australia, despite an equivalent standard of living, and of course, they would be quite impossible in countries such as Mali which does not have a sophisticated water supply infrastructure. Similarly, the methods of processing food are often wasteful on water as the American Thanksgiving menu on this page shows.

Differences in water resources have far-reaching implications. Examine, for example, the statements made to a UN Water Conference:
(a) by the water-rich countries:
'in a number of countries, by the year 2000 the available water will not be adequate to meet the demands'. This implies that new water resources will have to be made available.

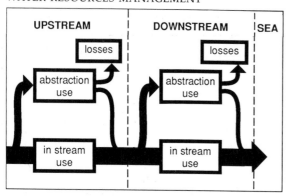

Figure 9.1 *Part of the water abstracted by upstream users may be lost to the atmosphere through evaporation; the rest returns to the river but is often polluted. Upstream users thereby deprive downstream users of water, both qualitatively and quantitatively. The situation is aggravated in arid regions where the natural losses may be large*

(b) by the water-poor countries:
'in a number of countries by the year 2000 the demands for water will have to be adapted to match the available resources'. This implies the technology and lifestyle will have to be made available to match the water supply.

Most of the world's developed countries are, or have been, water-rich. As a result people are used to thinking that water is limitless. They do not think of dry processing methods in industry or more efficient methods of irrigation. Water goes to swimming pools and to water flowers in gardens without a second thought. In this chapter we shall try to follow through some of the implications of such strategies.

The water cycle

The basic constraints enforced by nature on the interaction between water and people are determined by the global **water cycle (hydrological cycle)** (Fig. 9.2).
People interact with this cycle in many ways (Fig. 9.3):
(a) abstracting water for domestic use, for industry and agriculture;
(b) altering flow systems to allow fisheries, navigation, power production and recreation.
Also through land-based activities people modify the hydrological cycle further:
(c) by changing the vegetation cover and therefore the rate of evapotranspiration;
(d) by increasing the built environment with its impermeable surfaces, drains and sewers.

Notice that these water uses change with the stage of a country's development. In early stages water supply for people, livestock and irrigation are most important. Mostly these are organised on a local scale to meet local needs. By contrast, in late stages a very complex interaction between human drinking, recreation, transport, power production, irrigation and industrial uses develops. This often requires a high level of manipulation of the natural environment including the construction of large reservoirs and water grids (main water supply pipes or aqueducts). Furthermore, as intensity of use grows the amounts of waste water also increase, leading to ecological disturbance, and possibly to increased health risk. The main global water-related problem areas are also shown in Fig. 9.3.

The water budget

The **water budget** is a book-keeping system based on quantifying each of the components of the hydrological cycle.

At its simplest level the water budget is:

$$P - E +/- S = R$$

where:

P = precipitation;
E = evapotranspiration from vegetation and land surfaces;
S = changes in moisture stored in the soil and rocks; and
R = runoff via rivers to the ocean.
Studying the hydrological cycle and obtaining water budgets allows us to understand the

water resources of an area. It is thus a vital first step to many management schemes. It is also important in decisions concerning water supply, agricultural practices, flood control and many more.

We can view a water budget on several different scales:

(a) on a **macroscale**, where we look at the hydrologic cycle and the annual balance of water in the oceans, atmosphere and earth for a climatic region or the world as a whole;

(b) on a **mesoscale**, where we look at the water flows in a drainage basin; and

(c) on a **microscale**, where we look at a forest, a field or even the area around a single plant. However, whichever scale we choose, a water budget must take the modifying effects of people into account (Fig. 9.4). The water entering a region consists of:

(a) precipitation;

(b) natural surface inflow; and

(c) imports (man-made *transfers* of water into the basin from another basin).

Figure 9.2 *The global water cycle*

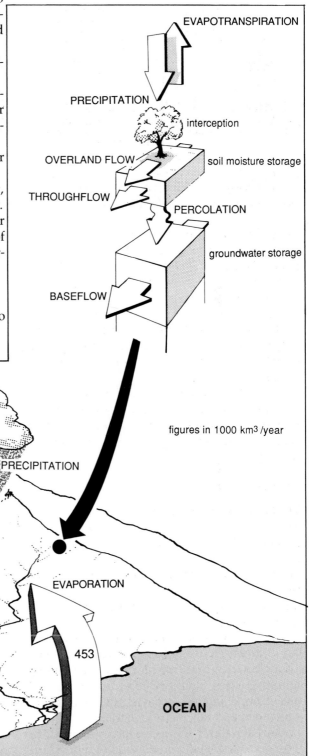

figures in 1000 km³/year

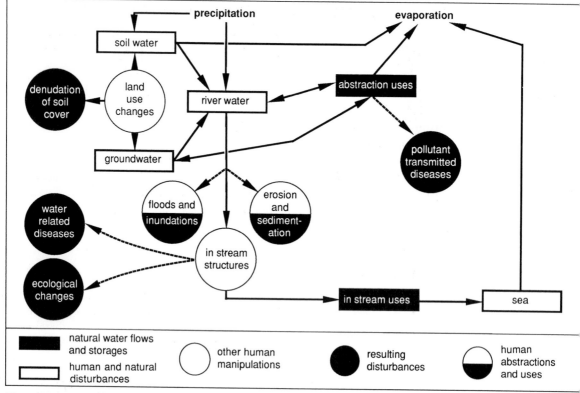

Figure 9.3 *Simplified scheme illustrating interaction between people and water*

The water leaving the region consists of:
(a) natural evapotranspiration;
(b) exports (man-made *transfers* to other basins);
(c) consumptive use (for irrigation, industry and domestic use); and
(d) natural surface-water outflow.

Making the most of the resource

In a water budget, the difference between the sum of the inflows and the sum of the outflows represents the change in storage within the region. These changes can either be due to filling or emptying **reservoirs**, or filling or depleting **aquifers** (water-bearing rocks). However, the only water that can be relied on for consumptive use is the renewable supply, i.e. the total natural inflow. Even so, in many cases governments have placed restrictions on the amount of water that must be left or returned to the river for, say, effluent dilution, downstream users, fisheries, or hydro-electric power plants,

and so the real amount that can be relied on for consumptive use is an ever smaller amount. In practical terms the best way of using the water is a combination of natural inflows, supplemented by inter-basin transfers, reservoir releases and aquifer pumping. This multiple source technique is called **the conjunctive use** of water.

One common method of making water go further is to use it more than once. Much water used in the developed world is used, treated and then returned to rivers for abstraction elsewhere. This means that we do not have to consider the **gross** demand on water, but rather the much smaller **net** demand; that is, the amount of the used water that we do not put back in rivers due to evaporative loss. We can make the resource go further by using river water only where essential; sea water can be used for power station cooling, for example. Yet, despite all of these attempts to conserve water, problems in supply are still commonplace.

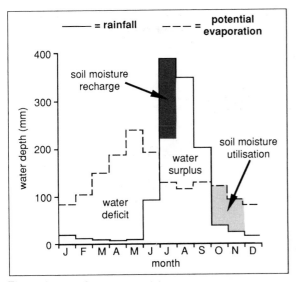

Figure 9.4 (a) *Components of the water budget arranged to show how changes in precipitation and potential evapotranspiration lead to surpluses and deficits on a seasonal basis*

Table 9.1 *Average annual water balances of the world*

Volume of water (thousands of cubic kilometers) Baumgartner, 1975			
Region	P^d	E^d	R^d
Europe	6.6	3.8	2.8
Asia	30.7	18.5	12.2
Africa	20.7	17.3	3.4
Australia	7.1	4.7	2.4
North America	15.6	9.7	5.9
South America	28.0	16.9	11.1
Antarctica	2.4	0.4	2.0
Land areas	111	71	40
Oceans	385	425	−40
World	496	496	0
Depth of water (continent-wide average) (millimeters)			
Europe	657	375	282
Asia	696	420	276
Africa	696	582	114
Australia	803	534	269
North America	645	403	242
South America	1564	946	618
Antarctica	169	28	141
World	973	973	0

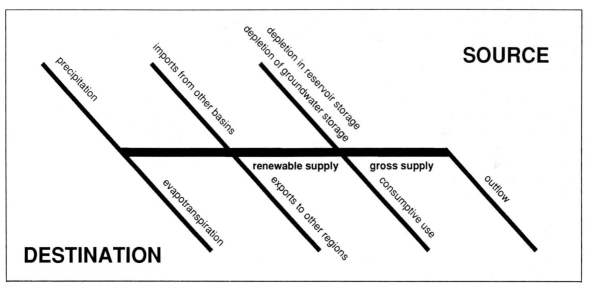

Figure 9.4 (b) *A simplified regional water budget*

World water resources

Although water is continually cycling between ocean, atmosphere and land, and in total there is no shortage for any human activity, fresh water is not evenly distributed either in space or time. This means that some areas of the globe experience a water surplus over need, while others have a deficit (Fig. 9.5; Table 9.1).

When natural supply is coupled with national population we find this imbalance accentuated: some countries have a considerable surplus (e.g. Brazil with 38 000 m³/person/year) while others have a very serious problem indeed (e.g. Egypt with 1200 m³/person/year, and this almost entirely from the River Nile) (Fig. 9.6).

Rainfall variability (Fig. 9.7) may further accentuate the problem. For example, many

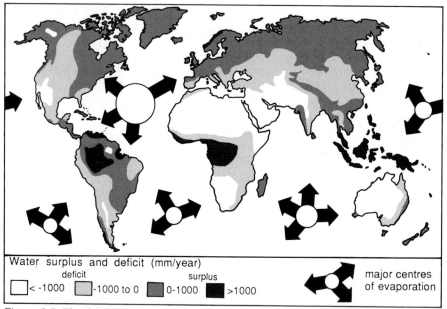

Water surplus and deficit (mm/year)

deficit   surplus

☐ < -1000   ▨ -1000 to 0   ▨ 0-1000   ■ >1000

major centres of evaporation

Figure 9.5 *The global pattern of water surplus and deficit*

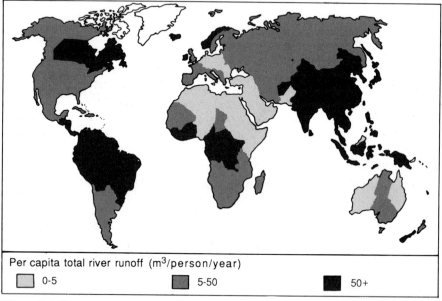

Per capita total river runoff (m³/person/year)

▨ 0-5   ▨ 5-50   ■ 50+

Figure 9.6 *Per capita total river runoff*

countries experience rainfall at only one season of the year; and very few are as fortunate as Britain with an evenly distributed rainfall. In some parts of the world rainfall varies considerably from one year to the next as Fig. 9.7 shows. This unreliability is a major problem not only for domestic and industrial consumption: it also makes agricultural yields extremely uncertain. In countries where agricultural output represents a large part of GNP such variability can lead to economic disaster and starvation. In an effort to control the water availability, many countries adopt large and often expensive water storage projects.

Renewable supply provides a rough measure of the abundance of the water resource, and when compared to the existing rate of consumptive use, it provides an index of the degree to which the resource has already been developed. Consumption in any region can increase by no

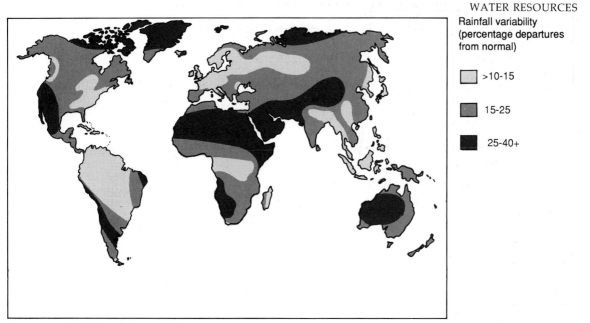

Figure 9.7 *Global rainfall variability*

more than the difference between renewable supply and existing consumption unless imports are increased or some sort of supply enhancement is achieved, e.g. by managing vegetation (change land use from forest to crops) or lowering groundwater levels to control or reduce evapotranspiration.

A useful index for comparing regions is consumptive use as a percentage of renewable supply (Table 9.2). Notice that in the Colorado Valley – one of the world's great river basins – it is 105 per cent. A percentage greater than 100 can occur only where there is a depletion of groundwater in storage. These depletions cannot continue indefinitely. As groundwater in storage is progressively depleted, becoming increasingly costly to obtain, one of the following will happen: (a) a decrease in consumption, exports or stream outflow; or (b) an increase in supply by vegetation management or by imports.

Human factors controlling water supply

The factors controlling water availability are often unrelated to the constraints imposed by the total renewable supply (i.e. the natural environment); rather they are related to the limi-

tations of the existing local or regional supply system – the reservoirs, wells, pipelines, canals and their operating policies, as well as the suitability of the water for its intended use (e.g. is it too saline for use in irrigation?).

The usual case is that many water-rich nations find that overall they have no water shortage. However, it is often not available when and where needed. In many cases problems can arise that require considerable **water transfer strategies**. This can be seen both in the UK (Fig. 9.8) and the USA.

One obvious response to water shortage is to build more reservoirs. This is both a costly and long term strategy, fraught with potential problems. Kielder Water, the largest man-made lake in Europe, was built on a predicted water demand curve that turned out to be wide of the mark (Fig. 9.9). In this case a number of factors were involved, mostly unforeseen during the planning period. They included changes in industrial processes and a global industrial recession that lowered the demand of the Teesside industry, the largest user in the region. However, it highlights the need for water managers to have a flexible policy and one in which high capital expenditure/long planning period strategies come low down on the list of priorities.

Water managers and water users have available to them a wide range of possible actions for coping with water scarcity:

(a) Impose financial or other constraints on supply

Most water users have considerable flexibility when it comes to their use. For example, an increase in the price of water will reduce consumption, as will putting meters on previously unregulated supplies. However, a 'blanket' increase in charges, such as increasing the water rates, has much less impact than a selective increase that may occur due to water meter charges.

(b) Step up educational efforts

For example, some farmers using irrigation water feel they must use all the water they can or it will be lost to other farmers. If the actual situation (i.e. groundwater depletion, or river depletion) can be explained this often results in a decrease in use. Also domestic users can be made more aware of water as a limited resource.

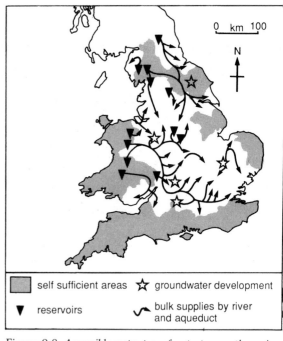

0 km 100

self sufficient areas ☆ groundwater development

▼ reservoirs bulk supplies by river and aqueduct

Figure 9.8 *A possible water transfer strategy as the main supply areas are in the north and west, but the main demand centres are in the centre and east*

Table 9.2 *Simplified water-resources budget for 1980, by water-resources region*

[Units are in billion gallons per day except where indicated]

Water-resources region	Stream outflow	Depletion of groundwater storage	Consumptive use	Renewable supply	Consumptive use as a percentage of renewable supply
New England	77.8	0.0	0.60	78.4	1
Mid-Atlantic	78.9	0.0	1.80	80.7	2
South Atlantic-Gulf	227.9	0.0	5.60	233.5	2
Great Lakes	72.7	0.0	1.60	74.3	2
Ohio (exclusive of Tennessee Region)	137.5	0.0	2.10	139.6	2
Tennessee	40.8	0.0	0.40	41.2	1
Upper Mississippi (exclusive of Missouri Region)	75.1	0.0	2.10	77.2	3
Mississippi (entire basin)	428.3	5.8	42.30	464.8	9
Souris-Red-Rainy	6.0	0.0	0.50	6.5	8
Missouri	45.8	2.2	19.30	62.9	31
Arkansas-White-Red	61.3	3.6	11.00	68.7	16
Texas-Gulf	27.9	3.1	8.30	33.1	25
Rio Grande	2.2	0.0	3.20	5.4	59
Upper Colorado	9.9	0.0	4.00	13.9	29
Colorado (entire basin)	1.6	2.1	10.80	10.3	105
Great Basin	5.9	0.0	4.10	10.0	41
Pacific north-west	263.6	0.0	12.60	276.2	5
California	50.5	1.4	25.50	74.6	34
Alaska	975.5	0.0	0.04	975.5	0
Hawaii	6.7	0.0	0.70	7.4	9
Caribbean	4.8	0.0	0.30	5.1	6

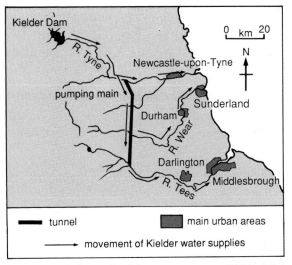

Figure 9.9 *An example of the water strategy – Kielder Water*

(c) Develop further surface water storage sites

The unregulated flow of many rivers is highly variable. Even when the rate of water withdrawal from a river is small in comparison with the average flow rate of the river (say one tenth) there will still be many days when the required abstraction cannot be achieved. Thus reliance on surface waters usually requires a dam creating a reservoir to store water from wet periods for use in dry ones.

If the reservoir is located upstream from the location where the water is to be used, the water stored during the wet periods may be released to the channel during dry periods to augment the flow and can be withdrawn at the point of use. Otherwise water has to be pumped (expensively) to the point of use through pipes or carried in canals.

Reservoirs are normally designed with a certain **'safe yield'**, that is the amount of water that can be withdrawn or released on an ongoing basis with an acceptably small risk of supply interruption. The volume that needs to be stored is the product of the flow deficiency (demand minus flow) and the length of the dry period.

Water control by storage follows a law of diminishing returns, such that each successive increment of control (safe yield) requires a

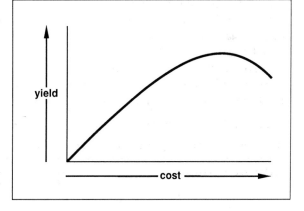

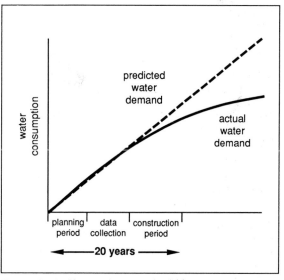

Figure 9.10 *Changes in reservoir yield*

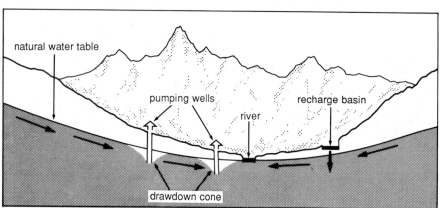

Figure 9.11
Groundwater abstraction systems

Figure 9.12 *Centre-pivot irrigation, Alberta, Canada*

larger amount of reservoir because the surface area grows and so does the evaporative loss. Alternatively less suitable sites have to be used and the construction costs are therefore high. Eventually a point is reached where net yield of a reservoir actually decreases with increasing size (Fig. 9.10). Furthermore, large surface sites tend now to be strongly opposed by conservation groups, especially as such sites tend to be in National Parks and other conservation areas.

It is possible to put an upper limit on reservoir capacity. For the 48 conterminous United States, for example, this is 1200 million acre-feet of which 450 million has been developed. The remainder can only be developed at increasingly higher cost. The same situation is true of most countries, including the UK.

The result of an increasing demand and a reduction in the rate of capacity construction has been a decrease in the safe yield from reservoirs. *Thus we are moving into a less assured supply situation, a situation that can only be rectified by a change in the demand pattern.*

Reservoirs should not just be seen in the context of water supply, for many also help protect settlements against flood, provide recreation and yield hydro-electric power. All these other considerations help determine the final size of the reservoir.

(d) Develop the groundwater resources more thoroughly

Under natural conditions an equilibrium exists between the rate of recharge from precipitation and rivers and the natural discharge via springs and seepage. Water can be extracted from such

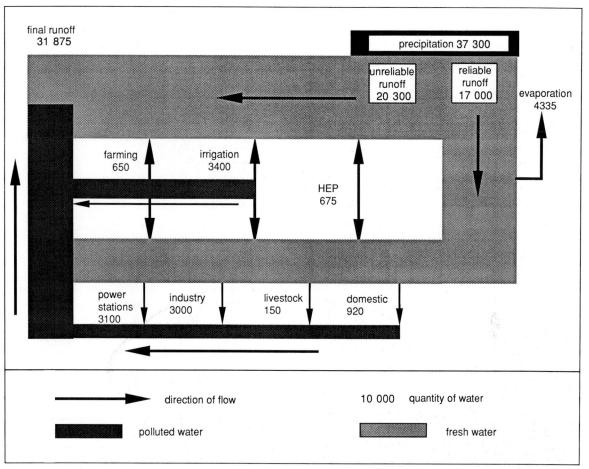

Figure 9.13 *The pattern of water use*

storage either from surface 'unconfined' reservoirs, where the water table rises and falls as abstraction varies (Fig. 9.11); or from artesian supplies where the pressure varies. Sometimes water is withdrawn from storage in conjunction with the irreversible compaction of certain fine-grained sediments as pressure is reduced. This process is always accompanied by subsidence of the land surface.

When aquifers are pumped the natural flow of groundwater is disrupted and the flow directed from natural discharge points towards the pumped location. There is no 'safe yield' in the case of an aquifer, it is simply the amount of pumping that can occur at equilibrium without significantly further lowering the regional water table. However, water pumping can be greater than this value, in which case **water mining** takes place. There is nothing wrong with water

mining, it just has to be accepted that this is what is occurring and the water supply then has a finite life. Even 'safe yield' pumping has other effects on the environment because pumping from the aquifer takes out water that would otherwise have flowed into streams elsewhere. Groundwater pumping is always accompanied by streamflow reductions and this may eventually be regarded as an unacceptable trade-off.

The largest single use for much groundwater is irrigation, because it removes the necessity for the installation of major pipe or canal systems. The typical US centre-pivot irrigation systems require only a well, a pump and a mechanised boom to spread the water (Fig. 9.12).

Finally, it is useful to assess the future results of water uses in a global context. Estimates of the future show a frightening situation, where the uses of water lead to extensive pollution unless strategies are adopted for isolating consumed but untreated waters from those naturally in circulation (Fig. 9.13). This is a further consideration which must be addressed by all water managers.

The following examples show the varied way in which water resources can be managed.

California, USA

California has most of its water supply in the north and most of its demand in the south (Fig. 9.14). For the most part early attempts to provide water to the parched, but potentially fertile areas of the south were met by groundwater pumping. California still has a groundwater withdrawal larger than most countries and the highest in the USA (about 57 billion litre days). Much of the groundwater pumpage is concentrated in the Central Valley and of this 85 per cent is used for irrigating 1.5 million hectares during the 4–5 month summer season. Furthermore, most cities in the San Joaquin valley are supplied entirely by groundwater (Fig. 9.15). But the continued pumping has had severe environmental side-effects. The magnitude of the problem that faced people in the San Joaquin valley is shown graphically by Fig. 9.15. Subsidence caused irregular changes in land level and gave great difficulties to many structures, not least of which was the California aqueduct which takes water south to Los Angeles. For an aqueduct to work properly there must be an even gradient from source to supply, but by the 1960s the California aqueduct had developed a sag in the middle! Because of the severe effects of ground subsidence associated with overpumping, surface water from the Sierra Nevada mountains was made available in the 1960s via long distance aqueducts, although at considerable cost. Indeed, moving water the long distances across California has resulted in aqueducts ranking among the longest of the State's waterways. California now has 200 major dams and although most generate HEP, the requirements of the water supply industry are far greater than the HEP capacity. For example, the waters of the California aqueduct have to be pumped up 600 m over the

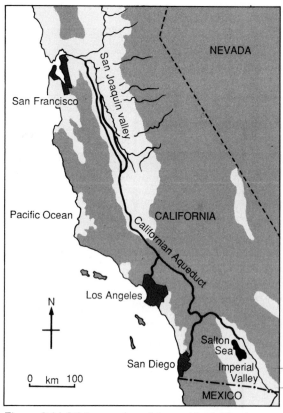

Figure 9.14 *Water supply and demand in California*

Tehachapi mountains in order to reach the Los Angeles region and pumping water in the supply system is the single largest consumer of electricity in the state (about the same amount as is needed to power a million homes!).

One reason for the large scale use of water is the Central Valley Project which covers the valleys of the Sacramento and San Joaquin either side of San Francisco. Established in the 1930s its sole purpose was to provide irrigation water. It is a federal scheme and the users only have to pay 10 per cent of the cost of the projects; the rest is paid out of Federal funds with national taxes. By way of an extreme example, the real cost of delivering water from the newest dam in the project – the New Malones dam on the Stanislaus River – is almost $200 for each 1200 cubic metres (1 acre foot). Instead the Project charges just $3.50. This unrealistically low cost of water encourages people to retain the system of flooding irrigation (Fig. 9.15(b)). In

Figure 9.15 (a) *Pumpage of groundwater in the San Joaquin valley caused widespread subsidence of the land surface elevation near Mendito, western Fresno County, California*

Figure 9.15 (b) *Irrigating with cheap water encourages waste. These Californian fruit trees are being irrigated by flooding. This is 30 per cent more wasteful of water than using sprinklers*

Britain it would make sense to help cut the water consumption by putting meters on domestic and industrial supplies, but in California these consumers are dwarfed by the requirements of irrigation.

Clearly California still has a major problem to tackle. So far, it has coped with groundwater induced subsidence by bringing in vast amounts of subsidised surface water. In many ways it has replaced one problem with another and now Californians look to their northern neighbours and even Canada as suppliers of further water. The potential disruption of these northern areas would be large if California's needs are to be met without any restraint on the part of its farmers. No wonder it is commonplace to see bumper stickers in Oregon, California's northern neighbour that read 'Don't Californicate Oregon'.

Lake Volta, Ghana

The construction of a dam across a river and the resultant man-made lake generate such harsh and adverse ecological effects that, in spite of the benefits that might otherwise accrue, the proliferation of dams continues to be a controversial subject. Indeed, there have been many instances of downright condemnation of dams. They have been described as costly to develop, of limited life and sometimes unreliable, environmentally and socially disruptive. There are now more than 10 000 large dams in the world. In Africa, the four giant reservoirs, Lakes Kariba, Volta, Nasser and Kainji, cover an area of 20 000 km^2; in the USSR sixteen lakes have an area in excess of 50 000 km^2. At the other end of the scale the N'cema dam project in the Limpopo basin in Africa brought into being 464 dams in an area of 209 km^2.

Created in 1964 the Volta Lake is the largest single freshwater impoundment in the world (Fig. 9.16). The lake is 85 km long with a shoreline of 4800 km and a surface area of 8500 km^2. Its main purpose was to provide power to allow the smelting of local deposits of bauxite and thus the production of aluminium. However, it was conceived as a multipurpose lake. The lake required the displacement and resettling of 80 000 people.

With the dam over 20 years old the overall

177

WATER RESOURCES MANAGEMENT

economic assessment is good. Electricity production has been a success (4 Gw hr/yr; enough for the smelter and an electricity grid for the country and even some export), new fisheries have been opened (allowing a quadrupling of the 'river' catch) and water has been made available for irrigation. The waterway also now allows a greater degree of north-south communication.

There have been costs: the lives of 80 000 people have been disrupted and the people resettled from farmland into 52 new towns. It has been difficult for people to adapt and no social or economic stability has yet redeveloped. There has been an increase in schistosomiasis (bilharzia), a slow killing disease introduced by snails. The larval stage prefers quiet waters of lakes rather than the faster waters of rivers. As people are drawn to the water's edge for fishing and trade, the spread of the disease has been dramatic. It is extremely difficult to set such social costs against the easily quantifiable economic gains.

Sweden

Sweden is a water-rich country, with about 9000 m^3 per person per year of supply. Although there is relatively little groundwater (because the rocks are mostly crystalline and therefore impermeable) there are about 100 000 natural lakes which provide considerable storage.

Most of the Swedish population lies in the south of the country whereas most of the water resources are in the north. The dominant water-related interests in the south are water supply, waste water disposal, fishing, and recreational use. Irrigation is a minor concern in this country. In the north, interests in river regulation for water power production are opposed by those whose concern is for environmental conservation and fishing.

The water consumption forecasts made in the mid-1960s (the time of planning the Kielder

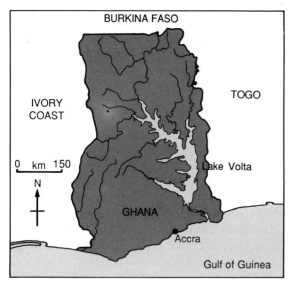

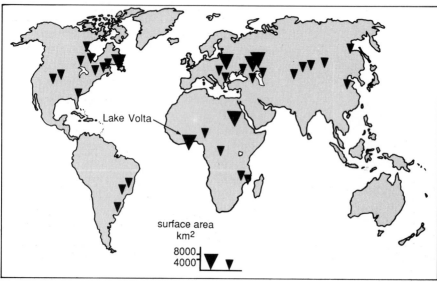

Figure 9.16 (a) *Lake Volta*; (b) *the world's major reservoirs*

178

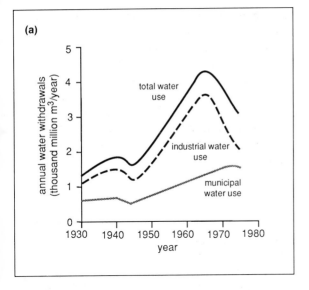

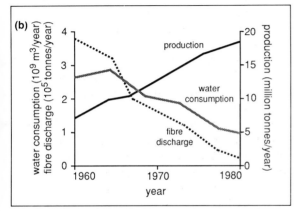

dam in the UK) showed that Sweden would face greater and greater problems of water supply during the remainder of the century (Fig. 9.17), demand perhaps reaching 450 litres/head/day by the end of the century for domestic uses while there might also be a trebling of industrial demand.

As it happened the spur to water conservation, rather than the British strategy of increased reservoir planning, came not from the prospect of a water shortage but from the increasing levels of pollution that were building up in Swedish lakes. This was brought into sharp focus in the mid-1960s by the poisoning of many lakes and the death of fish stocks.

Popular opinion on this readily perceived danger allowed the government to introduce strict water quality requirements and a careful monitoring system. However, this action also made the public more aware of water supply in general. As a result the domestic consumption began to drop. At the same time water became metered. In itself this has caused a reduction to 200 litre/head/day. The rate of increase for industrial use has also declined with metering: both because of better water management and because of new, more water-efficient processes in modern plants. Thus decreases have occurred despite an increase in production. The savings have been achieved by means of recycling and recirculating water rather than by external means of treatment.

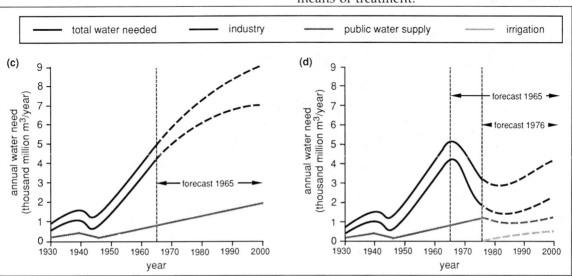

Figure 9.17 *Sweden's changing pattern of water use*

Student enquiry 9A:
Should dams be built?

1. Read A1 entitled 'How large dams have become fashionable'. Then, as a group try to assess the advantages and disadvantages of dams and reservoirs under the headings of:
(a) cost;
(b) ease of construction using local supplies and indigenous labour;
(c) power generation;
(d) reliability of water supply;
(e) social impact;
(f) ecological impact; length of useful life before complete sedimentation;
(g) disease;
(h) recreation.
You should try to gather information on many dam projects (as well as using those presented here) for comparative purposes. Dams from the developed and developing world should be chosen.

2. A2 shows the pattern of water consumption in various types of household. A3 shows the growth in irrigated areas and A4 shows the present water use. Suggest and justify a multi-purpose scheme for:
(a) a developed country in humid temperate areas; and
(b) a developing world country in the semi-arid zone with unreliable seasonal rainfall and largely level terrain, whose people are determined to raise their quality of life. Use maps to help you suggest possible sites for development. You should consider making use of all forms of water supply.

How large dams have become fashionable

ONLY three countries, the US, the Soviet Union and Canada, have more large dams than the state of California, which has 9.5 per cent of the world's total. Large dams are those more than 150 metres high, or with a volume greater than 12 million cubic metres or a reservoir bigger than 24.6 billion cubic metres. They are a relatively new and untested technology.

More than half the world's large dams did not exist 12 years ago. The first one was the Hoover Dam, built in 1936 on the Colorado River near Las Vegas. Since then 175 large dams have been built, and at least another 38 are under construction. The high dam represents half of all existing large dams and two-thirds of those now planned or under construction. These thin concrete shells are the most radical development in dam technology and are still virtually in the experimental stage. The total operating experience for nuclear power plants—outside the Soviet Bloc—is 2000 reactor-years. The comparable figure for high dams is less than 1200 dam-years.

Large dams can cause earthquakes because of the weight of water they collect in one place. The first dam-related earthquake occurred in 1936 when the reservoir of the Hoover Dam was filling. In the next 30 years, major earthquakes occurred at four large reservoirs.

But a more immediate and, in the long term, more serious, problem is the environmental impact of the massive water schemes that large dams make possible. These problems, so dramatically presaged in California, are likely to be even more severe in develop-

Big dams: white hopes or white elephants?

ing countries. The Third World now has more than one third of the world's large dams. In 1980 there were only 10 dams over 150 metres high in developing countries. By the end of this decade there will be three times that many, a rate of growth 12 times that of the rest of the world.

Large dams are powerful symbols of tech-

nological achievement and, to many people, sources of national pride. Development funds are readily available for large dams, with irrigation and hydro schemes. Brazil has already begun an ambitious scheme that will turn the Amazon Basin into a giant hydro-electric plant. The first stage, which will turn one of the country's biggest rivers into a 1700 km long chain of lakes has already begun, with the construction of Tucurui, now the seventh largest dam in the world. Seven more large dams and 19 smaller ones are planned for the Tocantins and 12 tributaries. Another nine or ten dams are planned for the Xingu River, the floodplains of which are home to many thousands of Indians and peasants.

India is embarking on a plan to equalise water flow throughout the country by linking separate catchments to one another and to canals for distribution to dry areas thousands of kilometres away. The Soviet Union's $41 billion Siberian Diversion scheme involves stopping the flow of the fourth largest river in the world, pumping its water 2500 km south through a canal, and pumping it over mountains into another watershed to irrigate the "desert republics", such as Kazakhstan.

In Sri Lanka, as *New Scientist* reported last week (p. 14), the complex Mahaweli hydro-electric and irrigation scheme has saddled the country with a heavy foreign debt. High oil prices had depressed the country's economy, so it seemed reasonable not only to generate electricity but also to provide water for irrigation. The short-term cost is high and, if California's example is any guide, the pay-off is uncertain. *New Scientist* □

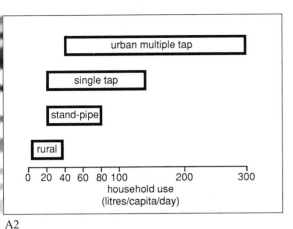

A2

A3 *Growth in irrigated area by continent, 1950–85*

Region	Total irrigated area (million hectares)	Growth in irrigated area[a] (per cent)		
	1985	1950–60	1960–70	1970–80
Africa	13	25	80	33
Asia[b]	184	52	32	34
Europe[c]	29	50	67	40
North America	34	42	71	17
South America	9	67	20	33
Oceania	2	0	100	0
World	271	49	41	32

Notes: a Percentage increase between 1970 and 1982 prorated to 1970–80 to maintain comparison by decade.
b Includes the Asian portion of the USSR.
c Includes the European portion of the USSR.

A4 *Average annual water use in selected countries, total and per capita*

Country	Water withdrawal		Share withdrawn by sector (per cent)			
	Total (km³)	Per capita (m³)	Public	Industry	Electric cooling	Agriculture/irrigation
United States	472.000	1986	10	11	38	41
Canada	30.000	1172	13	39	39	10
Egypt	45.000	962	1	0	0	98
Finland	4.610	946	7	85	0	8
Belgium	8.260	836	6	37	47	10
USSR	226.000	812	8	15	14	63
Panama	1.300	596	12	11	0	77
India	380.000	499	3	1	3	93
China	460.000	460	6	7	0	87
Poland	15.900	423	14	21	40	25
Libya[p]	1.470	408	17	0	0	83
Oman	0.043	350	2	0	0	98
South Africa[p]	9.200	284	17	0	0	83
Nicaragua[i]	0.890	272	18	45	0	37
Barbados	0.027	102	45	35	0	20
Malta	0.023	60	100	0	0	0

Notes: p Public and Industry i Industry and Electric Cooling

Key terms

Aquifer: water-bearing rock with an economically useful yield.

Conjunctive use: the method of planning the use of surface and groundwater supplies together for maximum benefit.

Drainage basin: an area from which runoff collects. It is usually taken as the area drained by a river about the river measurement point.

Evapotranspiration (e/t): is the water loss to the atmosphere from plant and ground surfaces. For a vegetated area transpiration is normally the most important. **Potential e/t** is the loss when there is no shortage of soil mosture; **actual e/t** will be lower than the potential e/t when the soil begins to dry out (in summer or a dry season).

Groundwater: is the water that reaches water bearing rocks (aquifers) and is transmitted through rocks to rivers. Groundwater reserves normally provide the water that maintains streams in a dry season.

Hydrological cycle: or water cycle for short, de-

scribes the pattern of paths followed by water over all or part of the earth's surface. Conventionally the water cycle is traced on a global scale from ocean evaporation through precipitation and back to oceans, and from precipitation to river flow on the scale of a drainage basin.

Precipitation: normally rainfall, but snow is a significant component in some climates, while even dew can be important in deserts.

Runoff: the surplus water that is not held in rocks and soil or lost by evapotranspiration. It flows over and through the ground to rivers and then the sea.

Soil moisture: the amount of water held in the pores of the soil. Some pores are large and cannot hold water against gravity; others are small and are called capillary pores. When surplus water has drained but all the capillary pores are full, the moisture content is called **field capacity**.

Water budget: a daily, monthly or annual *accounting* of moisture inflows, outflows and storages at a particular place or over a geographic area. It is sometimes referred to as a **water balance**.

181

Chapter 10
River management

Introduction

Rivers are the clearest demonstration of the working of the hydrological cycle as they carry water from the basin back to the oceans. However, the flowing water does not move passively in its channel. Rather the energy of the water erodes the channel, moulding it to the dimensions which reflect both the amount of surface water that needs to be transferred from the basin and the nature of the flow. In some circumstances, the flow changes so quickly and occurs so briefly that the channel is poorly adjusted to the flow regime. Thus an ephemeral river in a semi-arid area will flow for so short a time and have such a rapidly varying amount of water to cope with that a channel adequate to contain all the flows can never be created. Instead the peak flow almost always spills over the banks, causing widespread flooding.

River channels formed by perennial streams in regions with rainfall distributed evenly through the year come more closely into equilibrium with the flows they have to carry. But even in these cases the larger flows do not occur sufficiently frequently to erode the channel significantly. As a result channels are balanced to the more frequent flows, and flooding occurs periodically when there is much water to remove from the basin.

The increasingly intensive use of floodplains means that flooding is an expensive hazard. Today the real challenge is to curb the impact of rivers on people's lives. To achieve this people need to understand the reasons for fluctuating river flows.

The same pressures that cause progressively greater demand for river regulation also put increasing stress on the river system. For centuries people have dumped their wastes into rivers as a convenient means of disposal. The situation became so bad in industrial Britain that polluted rivers became a danger to health, while in the USA a river near Chicago became so polluted it actually caught fire! Today rivers of the developed world are still under threat and those of the developing world remain a danger to health. Thus the relationship between river regimes and their ability to transport wastes clearly also needs close study.

Rivers are invaluable for:
(a) recreation;
(b) commercial transport;
(c) water power; and
(d) provide irrigation, industrial and domestic water.

But they often:
(a) flood land causing homelessness and sometimes death;
(b) obstruct land-based communications; and
(c) erode their banks and threaten homes and other structures.

And people abuse them by:
(a) using rivers to dilute chemical wastes and other industrial effluents; and
(b) using them to dilute human effluent thereby causing pollution and health hazards and destroying the natural aquatic ecosystem.

The flood hydrograph

Water flowing in a natural channel can be thought of as having two components:
(a) **baseflow**, a more or less continuous supply of water that derives from slow seepage through

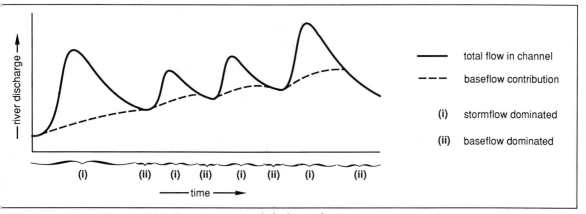

Figure 10.1 *Typical storm and baseflow components of a hydrograph*

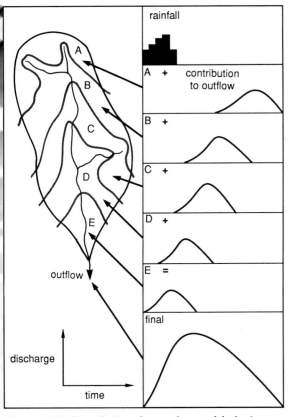

Figure 10.2 *Contributions from each part of the basin depend on the lag time needed to reach the outlet*

A hydrograph shape is only partly a reflection of the pattern of rainfall or snowmelt; it is also influenced by the time lag experienced by water flowing from different parts of the drainage basin (Fig. 10.2). Water falling on all parts of a drainage basin at the same time has different distances to flow to the outfall point, and this will cause varying amounts of lag. Water travels thousands of times faster over land and in channels than it does in the soil. Hence any surface water (overland flow) tends to correspond with the stormflow, whereas water moving as throughflow in the soil or as groundwater flow in permeable rocks (aquifers) will arrive at channels very much later.

The hydrograph pattern depends on:

(a) the amount of permeable rock to provide extended baseflow;

(b) the nature of the storm event;

(c) the amount of moisture stored up in the basin before the storm; and also landscape features such as:

(d) the size and shape of the drainage basin (Fig. 10.3);

(e) the balance between overland flow, channel flow and throughflow (more streams); thicker soil; varying soil properties, especially the soil's ability to absorb water (**infiltration capacity**) (Fig. 10.4).

Factors influencing base flows

In a period without rainfall all regions of the basin drain slowly, the rate of movement being related to the hydraulic gradients on and within individual hillslopes. Thus, during rainless

soil and through permeable rock; and

(b) stormflow, an irregular surging of water produced by storm rainfall or snowmelt travelling rapidly overland or through soil pipes.

The resultant complex pattern of flow in a channel is shown by a **hydrograph** (Fig. 10.1).

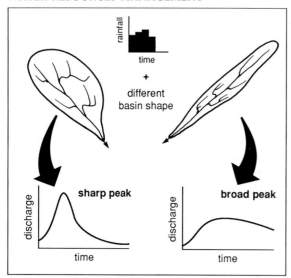

Figure 10.3 *Basin shape influences lag and thus hydrograph shape*

Figure 10.4 (a) *Flow chart showing interaction of components that affect (flood) basin hydrographs*

periods streams are largely fed with soil moisture that migrates downslope by unsaturated throughflow or groundwater flow (Fig. 10.5). Eventually this leaves a gradient of moisture on the hillslopes, the wettest soils being at the slope base, the driest at the ridge crests. The wet footslope soils thus provide a zone that is already 'primed' for quick response at the onset of further rain. But it is also the zone that carries on delivering water, albeit progressively slowly.

A drainage basin that has only throughflow to sustain the channel during periods of drought will have a very small baseflow. Only groundwater reserves can provide a sufficiently large reservoir of water to maintain a good volume of water in all but the shortest rainless periods.

Factors influencing flooding potential

Flooding mainly occurs when surface runoff from one or more source regions (Fig. 10.4) exceeds the capacity of river channels.

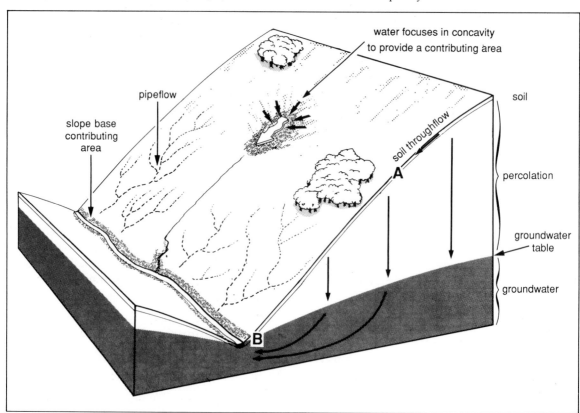

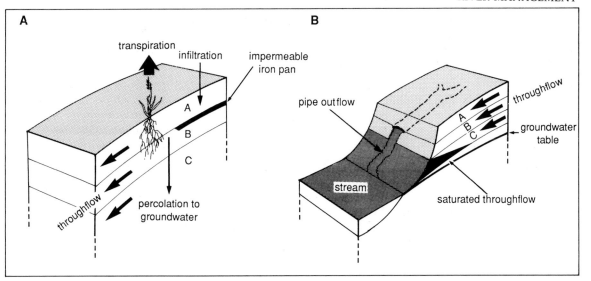

Figure 10.4(b)

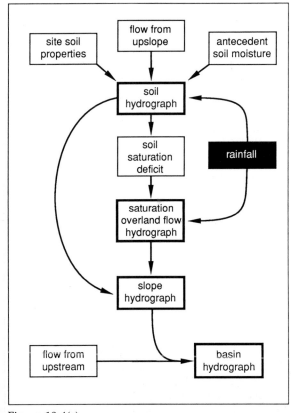

Figure 10.4(c)

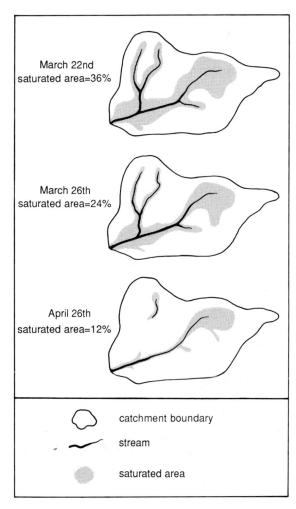

Figure 10.5 *Seasonal variation in saturated zones for a catchment at Rondboro, Quebec, Canada*

Overland flow can be caused by two different processes:

(a) By the rainfall intensity exceeding the infiltration capacity of the soils. It is called **infiltration excess overland flow**. This is very common in semi-arid and tropical regions where large convective storms produce intense downpours. Flooding is more common in such regions than in temperate zones where rainfall intensity is low.

The risk of exceeding the infiltration capacity also depends on soil and rock properties. Clay soils with small, poorly connected pores have a low infiltration capacity and are more prone to overland flow. Also, because wet soils have a lower infiltration capacity than dry soils, infiltration excess overland flow will more commonly be found during a prolonged storm.

(b) By the water table building up in the soil so that the amount of infiltration is restricted. This is called **saturation overland flow**.

Soil moisture varies considerably across a drainage basin. There are two regions in particular where soil moisture may be higher than elsewhere at the start of a storm. They are:

(a) In hillslope hollows (concavities) where soil moisture increases because water flow lines converge (Fig. 10.4).

(b) At the base of a slope because flow from the soil into the channel can only occur when the soil water table rises above the stream level and creates a head of water (hydraulic gradient).

These regions of naturally high soil moisture will quickly saturate and the water table will rise to the ground surface. Thin soils are further places where the soil moisture may be quickly replenished and soils readily saturated. These are, therefore, preferred regions for saturation overland flow and the places where floods may be generated. They are called **contributing areas** to stormflow. The soils will be the first to become saturated and cause overland flow even though the local infiltration capacity of the soil has not been exceeded. Clearly as more and more soil becomes saturated a greater proportion of runoff flows over the surface quickly to streams and increases the chance of flooding.

Soils often develop distinctive layers with sharp reductions in permeability. Under these conditions apparently thick soils can behave as

though they were only thin, and may rapidly saturate. Such soils as iron podzols or soils with heavy clay subsoils are particularly liable to cause saturation of the topsoil.

Water flowing through soils on steep slopes can build up velocities which can wash out pores, root channels and the like, and form them into a distinctive subsurface network of **soil pipes** (Fig. 10.4). Such pipes transfer water down a slope at rates comparable to open channels. They can, therefore, connect upper slopes to the main channel and allow these regions also to contribute to stormflow.

Thus runoff can be expected from lower parts of slopes, concavities and other special regions while infiltration is still occurring elsewhere. Stormflow could be expected to be generated by expansion and contraction of the contributing areas consisting, in many cases, of somewhere between 5 and 30 per cent of the basin area.

Case study

The East Twinn brook is a 159 ha basin in the Mendip hills, Somerset (Fig. 10.6). The upper half of the basin is the headwater region, with gentle slopes producing a number of concavities and seepage zones into which the brook extends during storms. The area is mantled by thin, peaty, gleyed podzol soils. The lower basin has steep uniform hillslopes with a mantle of deep brown earth soils. The lower basin has no concavities.

The hydrographs were produced by a 25 mm storm lasting 8 hours (average intensity 3.1 mm/hr). Notice how the upper basin responds with a sharp peak, showing that much of the contribution was from overland flow over shallow soils. By contrast the deep soils of the lower basin produced only throughflow and this is shown by a broader hydrograph.

This example shows the dynamic changes of the saturated zones that make up the contributing area, and that soil thickness and permeability are very important factors in determining the nature of the runoff. This observation has extremely important lessons for the management of floods. Furthermore, during a storm, the saturated contributing area advances more

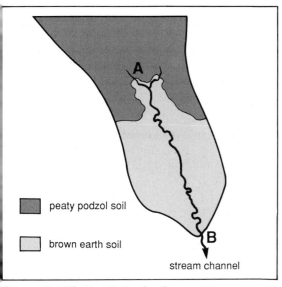

Figure 10.6 *The East Twinn brook*

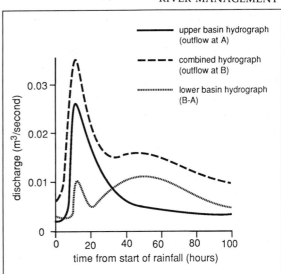

Figure 10.7 *Hydrographs generated by a storm*

rapidly up the slope with thin soil, allowing considerable stream extension and therefore faster responses from ever greater areas (Fig. 10.7). The dynamic nature of the contributing area is further shown to be seasonal in character, being greatest during the winter when the soil moisture is naturally higher and the soil can absorb less new storm water.

Land management and basin response

As people manage the land they have considerable ability to alter the response of a drainage basin. One of the clearest examples is provided by the urbanisation of a drainage basin.

When people begin to build on 'green field' land they alter it in a number of ways (Fig. 10.8):

(a) first the site contractors arrive and remove the natural vegetation and topsoil, heaping it into great mounds and exposing the more dense and less permeable subsoil. At the same time the weight of the contractors' vehicles compacts the soil and make it still less permeable. The result of this is an increase in overland flow (and also an increase in sediment transport to natural channels which may well become silted up and able to carry less water);

(b) next, the site is laid out with drainage services and the roads built. Thus the site is provided with impermeable surfaces (roads) and the means for fast transport of water to natural channels (drains). Such action can halve the time lag from onset of rain to peak river flow in nearby channels and double the peak discharge (Fig. 10.9). At this stage the channel, which previously may have overtopped its banks about once every two years, overtops its banks every year or even more frequently;

(c) providing the site infrastructure changes channel response very dramatically even though, at this stage, no houses may have been built. But as housing progresses the proportion of impermeable surface in the basin increases and the network of drains becomes more sophisticated. All these factors simply make an already difficult situation worse;

(d) the natural meandering pattern of a channel can get in the way of urban planning and many rivers are straightened and their channels lined with concrete. Both factors lead to yet faster delivery of water to natural reaches of the channels and enhance the chance of flooding.

Urban planning is not solely responsible for increasing the flood hazard. Many changes that are taking place in rural areas have as important and sometimes even more severe impact on river response. Most land management improvements, for example, involve some form of drainage which speeds the arrival of water into streamways. Most spectacular perhaps is the drainage of the peat uplands by rows and rows

187

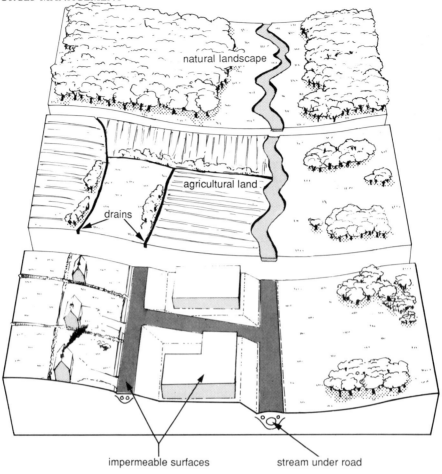

natural landscape

agricultural land

drains

impermeable surfaces

stream under road

Figure 10.8 *Changes in stream response as land uses are altered*

of open ditches. Such ditches are provided either for the gradual afforestation of the area, or for the conversion of such land to pasture for sheep grazing (Fig. 10.10). The effects can be horrendous.

Less easy to see, but even more widespread, has been the introduction of land drains as either mole or tile drainage systems buried about half a metre below the soil surface. These pipes (now usually perforated flexible plastic) intersect the rising water table in many heavy clay soils and again deliver water more quickly to channels.

Other land use changes that affect runoff include the replacement of forest with pasture or pasture with cultivated land, especially when land is ploughed up and down a slope.

Plough furrows provide ready channels for surface runoff (see also Chapter 14, on soil erosion, for further consequences).

There are also many ways in which people actively reduce the ability of the natural system to carry water away; these also make flooding more likely (Fig. 10.11):

(a) building on the floodplain reduces its storage capacity; floodplains act as temporary reservoirs of surplus water;

(b) building into the river reduces its width and therefore its capacity;

(c) building bridges and embankments for roads, railways and aqueducts puts further obstacles in the way of floodwaters. Hedges act in much the same way, although they offer less obstruction.

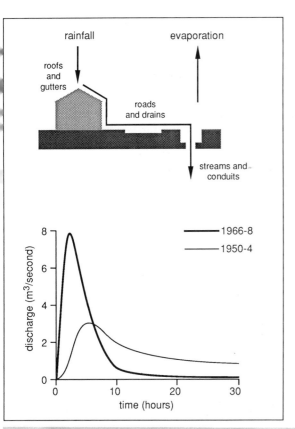

Figure 10.9 *The effects of urbanisation on hydrographs*

Figure 10.10 *Land drainage is one of the most significant means of speeding runoff. This picture shows dragline drainage of wetland habitat in Orkney, north-west Scotland*

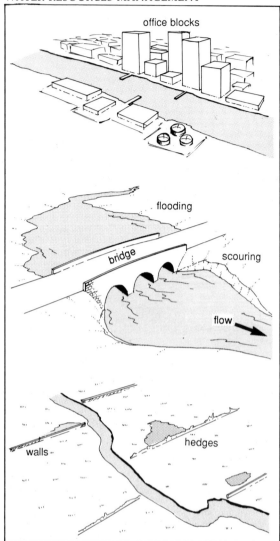

Figure 10.11 *Human-made structures that increase the flood risk*

Managing a river for flood control

Flooding is one of the major hazards that most river authorities have to face. Flooding is expensive and can cause loss of life, but it is an inevitable consequence of people changing their lifestyle and demanding 'improvements' to the land on which they live and higher yields from the land they farm.

The most sensible management approach begins by identifying the most critical sources of flooding, that is the areas primarily responsible for the sharpness of the flood peak. Look back, for example, to Fig. 10.5. In this basin the

contributing areas primarily responsible for stormflow are a narrow zone beside the stream and a much broader headwater zone. The headwater zone expands sharply during a storm and much of a flood could therefore be expected to be generated in this region. A dam just below this region would be preferable to one, for example, at the far left because it could be smaller and thus less costly (there is less water to contain); and it would allow some water to flow naturally. Thus the cost-effective 'trick' is to 'clip' the top from the potential flood hydrograph, rather than to contain all the flow. Similarly, it should be easy for you to decide whether to put a dam at the outlet of the basin or at the podzol/brown earth junction.

Figure 10.3 also shows that basin shape can be critical in influencing hydrograph shape. Thus it would be more advantageous to dam the outflow from a roughly circular basin than to dam an elongated catchment whose contribution to the peak discharge would be minor.

Using this approach there are several ways in which river authorities deal with the flood hazard, depending on whether the area is urban or rural (Fig. 10.12, Table 10.1). They:

(a) Try to contain the flood in the headwaters by putting check dams across major tributaries and thus collecting rapid runoff from contributing areas. This water is released later when the danger of flooding has passed.

(b) Ensure that the contributing areas have a land use which promotes water infiltration rather than overland flow. Thus forests are more suitable than cultivated land; undrained fields better than those with artificial drainage systems connected directly to natural channels; car parks with permeable surfaces better than tarmac, etc.

(c) Reduce the speed of water movement by maintaining channel roughness, i.e. not making any channel improvements such as dredging which would speed water on its way; not straightening river segments and not removing bank or bed vegetation.

(d) Dredge rivers to a size that will handle all possible flows (impractical and in any case it has all sorts of dire consequences, see next chapter).

(e) Embank the channel by building dykes

(a) *Urban areas*

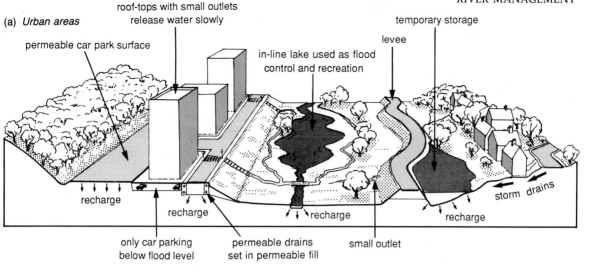

Figure 10.12 *Water regulation reservoir*

(b) *Rural areas*

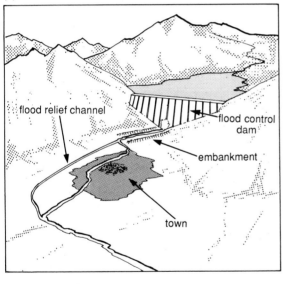

(also called embankments, levees, etc.) and thus make the channel deeper when floods would otherwise occur.

(f) Provide flood relief channels which come into operation when natural channel levels reach critical heights. These may be parallel to the natural channel or cut off at some angle to take the water well away from urban areas.

(g) Try to contain water at all contributing points by designing small runoff pipes from gutters, roofs, roadways, car-parks and other urban structures that would deliver water rapidly from impermeable areas. This can include 'in-line' urban reservoirs that act as recreation lakes during normal flows.

(h) Try to work with the local urban planning authorities to zone the natural floodplain for non-urban uses, keeping it as a natural reservoir in times of flood and and also reducing losses by floodwater damage (Fig. 10.13). Such land can be zoned as urban parks and perform other vital functions for the quality of life.

(i) Try to arrange for the demolition of urban structures that have crowded on to and constricted the natural river width. These included small arched bridges, railway and road embankments, factories in riverside locations and homes.

(j) Plan for a hazard warning system so that people can take the necessary precautions in times of danger and move themselves and their property to safer ground.

How to determine the design size of a flood

If discharge is plotted against frequency of occurrence for a river draining a non-urbanised basin without land drains in humid temperate regions (Fig. 10.14) the frequency of flooding is about 2.33 years, that is, about every 2.33 years *on average*, some form of flooding will occur

191

Table 10.1 *An overview of floodplain management techniques*

Tool	Purpose	Approach to flooding threat	Incidence of costs	Advantages	Limitations
Land use regulations	1. Foster health and safety 2. Prevent nuisances 3. Prevent fraud 4. Promote wisest use of lands throughout a community	1. Require individual adjustment of uses to the flooding threat	1. Landowner must bear cost of adjustment; community bears cost of adoption and administration of regulations	1. Low costs 2. Promote economic and social well-being 3. Promote most suitable use of lands 4. Can be put into effect immediately 5. May remain effective for long periods if adequately enforced	1. Must not violate state and federal constitutional provision 2. Can't prevent all losses 3. Generally do not apply to governmental uses 4. Limited application to existing uses
Dams, reservoirs, levees	1. Reduce flood losses, protect safety, promote economic well-being 2. Protect existing uses 3. Promote navigation, water recreation 4. Make new sites available for development, increase tax base	1. Adjust flooding threat to land use needs	1. Generally public at large pays for benefits which accrue to landowners, local communities	1. Reduce wide range of flood losses 2. Protect existing uses 3. Promote navigation and recreation 4. Permit regional approach to problems	1. Federal subsidy leads to private gains 2. High costs 3. Construction may take many years 4. May not be consistent with community plans, environmental quality 5. Maintenance required 6. Sedimentation may reduce effectiveness 7. Catastrophic losses may result from failure of dam or levee 8. No site may be available for dam, or levee; geology wrong
Land treatment (to retain precipitation)	1. Prevent future increases in flood heights; reduce existing levels 2. Promote water and soil conservation	1. Reduce existing flood conditions; prevent future increases in flood heights in frequent floods	1. Expense largely public; however, landowners may bear portion of costs	1. Limited cost 2. Attack flood problem where it begins 3. May be consistent with broad community needs	1. Not applicable in many instances 2. Effectiveness limited to relatively frequent, small floods
Public open space acquisition for parks, wildlife areas, floodways	1. Reduce flood losses 2. Achieve broader community recreation and conservation goals	1. Adjust use to threat	1. Public pays but receives multiple benefits	1. Multiple benefits 2. No problem of constitutionality 3. Permanent 4. Active public use of lands possible 5. BOR and other federal grants may be available for open space acquisition 6. Particularly attractive in urban areas	1. Acquisition costly 2. Flood losses to open space uses (e.g. campgrounds) remain 3. Sites not always suitable for recreation or wildlife 4. May create shortage of land needed for businesses, industry, etc. 5. Creates public land management requirements
Flood insurance (National Flood Insurance **Programme**)	1. Promote flood regulations 2. Promote long-term cost-bearing by individual occupant	1. Require individual cost-bearing 2. Adjust use to threat	1. Public pays, in part, for subsidised insurance 2. Private landowner pays for unsubsidised insurance	1. Spread cost of flood losses 2. Promote regulation 3. Encourage consideration of flood costs in private decision making	1. Subsidised insurance may promote continued use at primarily public rather than private expense 2. May undercut floodway regulations to abate existing uses
Warning systems	1. Warn property owners of impending threats 2. Permit advance evacuation, installation of temporary flood abatement measures	1. Adjust use to threat	1. Public bears costs (usually)	1. Can permit adjustment to threat 2. Useful in combination with regulations	1. Of no use unless floodplain occupants are willing and able to take necessary protection measures 2. Systems must be adequately operated and maintained

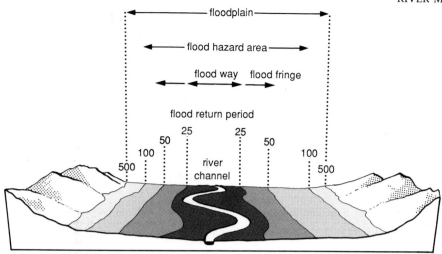

Figure 10.13 *Hazard zones on the floodplain*

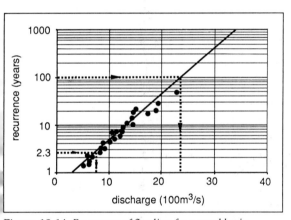

Figure 10.14 *Frequency of flooding for a rural basin*

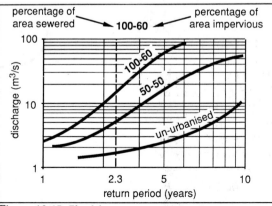

Figure 10.15 *Flood frequency curves for a basin in various states of urbanisation*

which brings the floodplain into use. Some years the degree of flooding will be small, others it will be great. It is common practice to take protective measures that would cope with a relatively large flood such as would occur every 50, 100 or 200 years. This is then the **design flood**. In Fig. 10.14 the 100 year design flood is three times bigger than the smallest flow needed to cause flooding.

The design flood is calculated by extrapolating discharge records as shown on Fig. 10.14. Once this has been done, the discharge can be used to find out the area and depth of flooding that would be caused. With this information land can be protected at the most economical cost.

Figure 10.15 shows the impact of various land uses on the design flood. If the river records are for a 'natural' basin, then the design flood will have to be changed radically as urbanisation proceeds. The increased magnitude of **the design flood means a proportional increase** in the cost of protection. This should put pressure on local authorities to implement some form of land zoning rather than pay the huge expenses of land protection by dykes, etc.

As you will see, the choices lie between dealing with the causes or the symptoms of the problem. In too many cases people try to deal merely with the symptoms. This can lead to the disastrous situation illustrated by the River Ouse floods in the following student activity.

Student enquiry 10A:
Flooding on the Ouse:
causes and effects

The objective of this activity is to examine the nature of the 1982 floods in Yorkshire, to determine the causes and to consider what could be done to alleviate the problem on future occasions.

The following questions are designed to give some structure to the way you approach this problem. You do not have to write answers to them all, but you should make sure you use the conclusions in your final statement.

1. Explain the main functions of a floodplain;
2. What basin characteristics saved people along the River Ure from more severe flooding?
3. What characteristics initially saved people in the Nidd Valley from flooding?
4. Suggest reasons for the changing width of inundation in the vicinity of Selby.
5. Define the terms **attenuation of flow** and **lag**. Show how these terms can be used to explain the hydrograph patterns in A3.
6. There seem to be many cases of 'defences under construction'. What might these be? Suggest reasons why they took on an urgency just before the 1982 floods.
7. Present an analysis of the flooding problem, areas of greatest risk and some of the corrective solutions that could be employed in this situation.
8. What might have happened if the January floods had coincided with North Sea spring tides?
9. Describe some solutions for areas upstream that would give greater problems to others downstream.
10. Now write an illustrated summary article on the problems and solutions in a style suitable for serious magazines such as *New Scientist*.

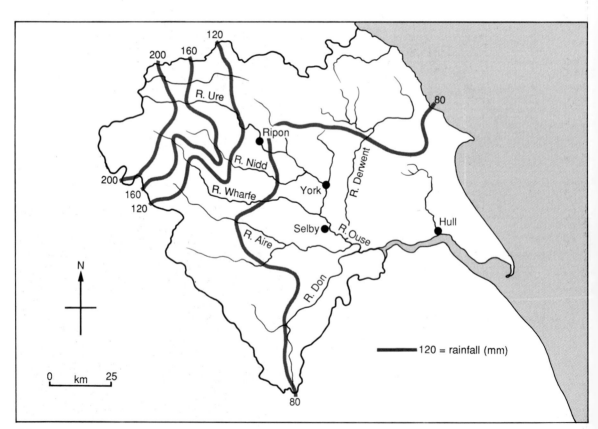

A1

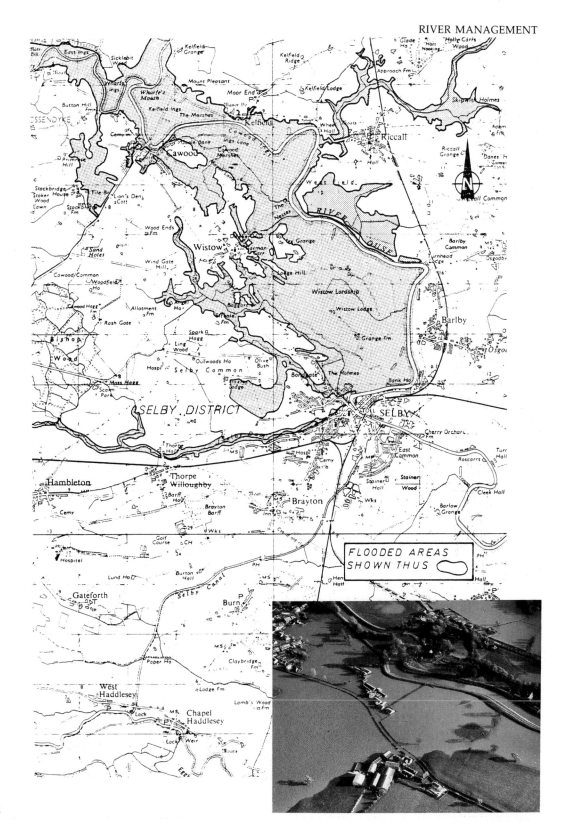

FLOODED AREAS
SHOWN THUS

A2

195

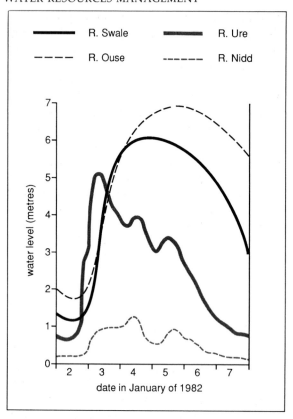

A3

A4
Extract of report by the Water Authority

During the first few days of January 1982, Yorkshire suffered the most severe floods since March 1947 with over 800 properties and 19 000 hectares of agricultural land inundated. Areas most severely affected adjoin the River Ouse between York and Selby and the River Ure at Boroughbridge. In addition, the natural floodplains of many smaller rivers and tributary watercourses were inundated. In York, Selby and Boroughbridge, it was necessary for the District Councils to call for military assistance to convery personnel and food, evacuate residents and sandbag premises.

In mid-to late December a series of deep low pressure systems brought snow to all parts of Yorkshire. On 2nd January a depression with a marked warm front began to move across the area, bringing periods of heavy rain and a rapid rise in temperature. Thus rain and melting snow were too much for the infiltration capacities of the soil and considerable over-

land flow resulted.

Following the onset of heavy rain or high riv levels, a network of rainfall and river level stations monitored. At predetermined levels, and after con sideration of the prevailing meteorological cond tions, progressive flood warnings were issued by th police on the advice of the Water Authority. Th only problems that arose concerned areas not covere on the maps of recorded flood events.

The River Swale, with a basin extending up on t the Hambleton Hills, provided the largest and mo extended contribution of floodwater to the Riv Ouse. The River Ure has a long, narrow basin an although the river rose on average more than 5 n the highest levels were of short duration. The Riv Nidd initially responded less severely due to th storage of a small component of the floodwater i the Gouthwaite reservoir. Overflow in the reservo commenced on 3rd January, following which th lower floodplain was inundated.

The total basin of the River Ouse above York 3315 km^2. The river commenced to rise at abou midnight on 2nd January and reached its peak lev of 5 m above normal, just over three days later. Th represents the highest recorded rise in level sinc 1947. On this occasion the floodwater discharge an duration was 50 per cent greater than in 1982, but th peak level in York was 125 mm lower.

Several areas flooded in York, affecting over 3 houses and commercial premises with water depth up to 1 m for three days. On the 5th and 6th January the police advised motorists against trave ling to the city and recommended the early closu of commercial premises in the city centre. The con pleted defences prevented flooding of about 3 houses.

In the areas of Selby 118 houses suffered floodin to depths of up to 1 m and several commercial an industrial premises were severely affected. The hig river discharge fortunately coincided with a perio of neap tides and the defences at and downstrea from Selby were not threatened.

A5

Draining the land means drains to the towns

Ever since the EEC support funds became available for land improvements, farmers in the Pennines and Hambleton Hills have been busily applying for the money. With this support they can upgrade their rough pastures and make the land suitable for more intensive grazing. The first step is to install a herringbone pattern of mole and tile drains, then plough over the land and plant improved grass seed. Further support through the guaranteed prices for upland sheep will make it possible to add fertiliser to the land and maintain the pH at a level suitable for the new grasses to thrive. But while housewives in lowland Yorkshire may have more prime English lamb on their Sunday luncheon tables, they may have to use life rafts to eat it on, because the increased speed of upland drainage is threatening to inundate the lowland town. Rivers, swollen by water pouring out of the land drains, have already caused water levels to rise to worrying levels and this is forcing the water authorities to spend millions of extra pounds on raising the dyke levels. No-one seems quite able to tell this reporter whether the cost of protection is less than or greater than the cost of drainage subsidy and extra lamb productivity. But with meat mountains ever heightening, the wisdom of the whole exercise seems questionable.

Student enquiry 10B:
Decision-making for small towns

Towns with the largest and most varied experimentation with non-conventional protection might be expected to be those where major protection is lacking. Numerous towns have been investigated for engineering protection which has not been found to be economically feasible. Others have rejected authorised protection by refusing to make local contributions in the form of costs of land, damages, and rights of way. It appears that places which are already partially protected show the most interest in alternative schemes. These are places where neither the complete confidence of large-scale protection nor the complete detachment of ignorance reigns. One such is La Follette, Tennessee, USA.

La Follette (present population about 8000) was laid out in the 1890s on a flood plain of the Big Creek that flows out of the Cumberland Mountains (B1). Within the rectangular street grid, the commercial and manufacturing uses are concentrated on the flood plain. The railway and main road come in beside the river and residential land uses spread up the flanks of adjoining hills. Flooding occurs ever few years and the response to this has been deepening of the Big Creek in the 1940s and again in the 1950s especially in the town centre where the bridge piles cause a constriction in the channel.

With growth of population there has been some further building on the floodplain. At several points buildings encroach on the previous channel and further reduce its cross-section. The bridge, washed out in a 1950 flood, was replaced with one having a clearance slightly less than the 1950 flood level! A new bridge built to ease traffic problems was built just to clear that flow. The city has built new offices with the floor level above the 1950 flood peak and several merchants altered the arrangement of their storage facilities to reduce flood hazard.

1. Read the article 'Whose flood plain? (B2) and then examine the plan and location of La Follette and suggest measures which could be introduced to reduce the flood hazard. Draw these on to a plan of the town.

Desert Hot Springs is a fast growing resort town in California on the desert south flank of the Little San Bernadino Mountains (B3). This town is off the main road and has not attracted commercial functions. The activities are linked almost wholly to the servicing of a population consisting of senior citizens (over 50 per cent)

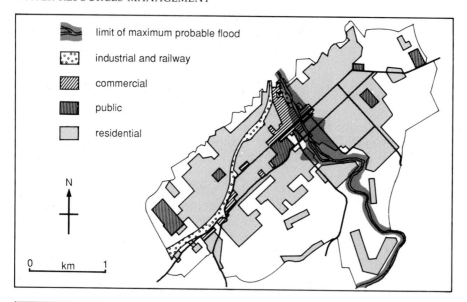

limit of maximum probable flood

industrial and railway

commercial

public

residential

N

0 km 1

B1

WHOSE FLOOD PLAIN?

The public as well as local officials have difficulties accepting the validity of a flood insurance study, the accuracy of the flood plain maps, and the existence of a genuine flood hazard because of differing perceptions of what a flood plain is.

Whereas the geomorphological flood plain is a fact and can generally be identified in the field by landform, vegetation, or alluvial soils, the "engineered" flood plain in a flood insurance study is a statistical probability and may bear little resemblance to the features mentioned above. Engineered flood plains derived by discharge-frequency curves, step-back-water models, synthetic regression equations, or other technical means are usually much more extensive than the coincident geomorphic channel and overbank area usually assumed to be flood plain. Regularly or intermittently sodden ground is usually recognized by the local populace as being floodprone to some degree, but when the ";100-year" flood plain is presented to them for the first time, many people do not accept the possibility the map may indeed be accurate (or at least represent the area having a reasonable chance of being flooded). This incredulity, however, does not usually result from lack of perception of a genuine flood hazard in the community.

Most people *will* acknowledge the existence of a flood hazard along unregulated streams where no flood control work or other structural "improvement" is present. The extent of the possible flooding is usually the controversial issue. "If it floods way up where I am, the whole town will be under water," is a common rejoinder to the flood insurance study's results. Unfamiliarity with the sophisticated methods involved in a flood insurance study, lack of confidence in engineering (or engineers), or a misunderstanding of the term "100-year flood" are more responsible for the failure to accept a flood plain map than outright refusal to admit there is a flood hazard.

However, individual and collective perceptions are influenced by memory, and that plays tricks. The "100-year" flood elevation or other significant flooding events may occur with the same or even lower discharges than were experienced in the past. Upstream watershed development, flood plain encroachments, increased friction in the channel and perichannel area during high flows, and blockage of hydraulic structures may yield higher stages than were achieved by floods-of-record having greater discharges. The community may have experienced a "100-year" or greater *storm*, and the area inundated by the resultant flood was smaller than that shown on the flood insurance study maps.

Sometimes, only the intervention of nature or luck enables the map to be accepted. Once in a great while, meterology, topography, soil moisture balance, existing development, hydrology, and hydraulics all combine in just the right prescription to generate a condition that matches the results of the engineer's and cartographer's efforts. However, vindication is not sweet when property and perhaps lives are at risk.

David L. Schein, Floodplain Management Specialist

B2

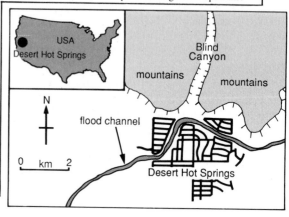

USA
Desert Hot Springs

Blind
Canyon

mountains

mountains

N

flood channel

0 km 2

Desert Hot Springs

B3

Slow flow of warnings on river of death

by Gareth Huw Davies

THE greatest ecological disaster to hit the river Rhine in modern times had a slow, almost casual beginning. Yesterday, anti-pollution experts in many parts of Europe were still trying to come to grips with the scale of the catastrophe and the lessons it presents for the future.

Early on Saturday, November 1, firemen began fighting a blaze at the Sandoz chemicals factory near Basel, Switzerland. There was no immediate air of impending crisis.

But the first and only line of defence against an environmental accident was breached within minutes. A basin to collect waste water was built to hold only 50 cubic metres. During the blaze firemen sprayed at least 25,000 cubic metres of water on to the building. Every minute more than 25 cubic metres of water polluted with chemcials from exploding drums poured into the Rhine and began its unstoppable 740-mile progress to the sea.

For almost two days none of the governments of countries along the Rhine knew the true nature of the cocktail of 34 chemicals which were passing along Europe's greatest waterway in a slick 50 miles long. By the time the Swiss authorities put out their first urgent telex to river monitoring stations downstream, 7.30 pm on November 2, the disaster was beyond human intervention.

The chemicals were so lethal to river life that parts of the Rhine may never recover, says Walter Wallmann, West Germany's environment minister.

Even on November 3, the Swiss could not tell the countries downstream exactly what had been stored in the stricken plant or even the amount of chemicals involved.

Neelie Smit-Kroes, the Netherlands' minister responsible for water resources, has warned that the full extent of the damage to river life and agriculture will take up to a year to assess. The Dutch are particularly concerned that their Zeeland oyster beds may have been ruined.

Hank Kersten, of Greenpeace in the Netherlands, says it could take 30 years to restore to life the upper section of the Rhine.

After an accident at a chemical plant in Seveso, Italy, in 1976 caused a leak of dioxin, the EEC introduced laws laying down special safety rules for chemical storage and manufacture. Stanley Clinton Davis, the EEC commissioner responsible for environmental safety, told The Sunday Times that the Rhine at Basel might not have been poisoned if Switzerland had applied similar legislation.

The Sandoz accident has brought to a head EEC commission fears that its own safety requirements may not be adequate. When EEC environment ministers meet in Brussels next week, Clinton Davis will propose that the four-year-old Seveso directive on chemical industry safeguards be tightened further.

Last week, West Germany's Wallmann called a meeting of the Rhine countries' environment ministers in Zurich to agree immediate steps to check and overhaul safety standards at their chemical plants.

The West German, Dutch and French ministers will hold further talks in Rotterdam on December 19 to examine ways to repair the damage done to the Rhine. They will also consider methods of financing a new Rhine protection pact.

Wallman also persuaded the Swiss government to agree to consider with 'good-will' the question of compensation for people living along the Rhine and other river users. Claims totalling millions of dollars are expected.

Sandoz admits that the possible consequences of a fire were 'seriously underestimated'. Five years ago the company transferred its business from its Swiss insurer, the Zurich Insurance company, partly because it had recommended additional safety measures, including larger containment basins.

In Switzerland, a country where cleanliness is almost a national obsession, there is a sense of self-reproach bordering on shame. 'Have you heard, they're twinning Basel and Chernobyl?' is one bitter quip going the rounds.

Crucially, they did not know that the 1246 tonnes of agricultural chemicals flushed into the river included 12 tonnes

of organic compounds containing mercury, one of the most harmful non-radioactive substances which can be introduced into the environment. Mercury becomes more concentrated as it passes through the food chain to accumulate in highly lethal doses in animals such as otters. And it lingers – to devastating long-term effect – in river silt.

By the time the Swiss authorities sent full details of the Sandoz chemicals to Bonn on Tuesday, November 4, the stretch of Rhine from Mannheim to Basel was ecologically dead – from micro-organisms to fish and river birds. Near Strasbourg, two sheep were reported to have died after drinking from the river.

Riverside communities in West Germany were put on high alert. The governments ordered children, animals and dogs to be kept away from the river. Villages such as Unkel, 15 miles from Bonn, which would normally receive water pumped from the Rhine, were sent emergency supplies. This weekend they were still without mains water.

By midnight on November 8, the toxic waters had begun to reach the small Dutch border town of Lobith. But water engineers, with the few days of warning, had initiated emergency procedures. They used centuries-old flood defences to ensure that the pollution did not spread through the Netherlands' network of inland waterways.

Using sluice gates and pumping stations, engineers were able to direct the main flow of the Rhine along the most direct of four possible outlets, straight into the sea and by-passing the canals.

By last Wednesday most of the poisonous slick had reached the North Sea near Rotterdam, but the crisis has not passed. The consequences are likely to be felt throughout Europe and the states bordering the North Sea for a long time.

Environmentalists believe the Rhine's ecological clock has been put back more than 20 years to the time when the river was known as the longest open sewer in the world.

The Sunday Times, 16 November 1986

together with short term visitors to the motels. There are retail service shops, but not a single wholesale commercial or industrial establishment. The arrangement of land use largely follows a grid-iron pattern, reflecting the way the land has been sold off since it was founded in the 1940s. In essence it consists of low density suburban sprawl.

The town not only lacks records of flood frequency, but also suffers uncertainty as to where the flood plain is at any given time. This is because of its location on an alluvial fan, with an average slope of 5 per cent over which two tributaries are actively moving. There are no satisfactory records of streamflow. Moreover the characteristically short tenure of all the residents means that they tend to be unaware of events that occurred more than a few years past (B4).

In this area floods are flash events created by unpredictable convective storms, rising to a crest in less than an hour and rushing out of the hills to spread over the alluvial fan. Velocities and sediment loads are high, and often boulders are carried.

2. Sketch out the plan of Desert Hot Springs (B3). Suggest ways in which the residents might act for their own protection.

B4 *A new desert settlement built near the shores of Lake Mead (Nevada, USA). This aerial view shows the hazard that cannot be readily identified from the ground. The residents are all vacationers*

River pollution

The article 'Slow flow of warnings...' shows the disaster that occurred on the River Rhine in November 1986. It highlights the way rivers are often abused. We can measure the quality of water in a number of ways: the amount of suspended matter; the acidity (pH), the parts per million of toxic substances such as heavy metals, and the Biological Oxygen Demand (BOD) which is the amount of oxygen needed to allow normal bacterial decomposition of organic wastes such as domestic sewage. In all too many cases these indicators show a marked deterioration of river quality from any acceptable standard.

For many decades, and in some cases centuries, rivers flowing near large urban areas have suffered poor water quality. Most such rivers are still unsafe to use and cannot economically be treated for use as drinking water. This fouling has caused much expense. For example, water supplies to the Midlands have to come from Wales because much of the River Trent is unusable; and water to the Rhine towns and cities often has to come hundreds of kilometres from unpolluted upland areas. Rivers are not designed to cope with excessive quantities of wastes. Such wastes are often of constant volume and thus cause particular problems during times of low natural river flow. These problems can only be solved through political initiatives.

Key terms

Exponential decay: a pattern of change characterised by initially rapid decrease in flow, but progressive slowing down such that the flow never reaches, but trends closer and closer to zero.

Groundwater flow: water passing laterally through aquifers.

Hydrograph: a plot of channel discharge against time.

Infiltration capacity: the maximum rate at which water can enter the soil.

Percolation: water passing vertically through soil or rock.

Throughflow: water passing laterally through soil.

Chapter 11
Changing channels

Introduction

River channels are essentially dynamic and it is this dynamism that may create problems of management. Study Fig. 11.1, which shows the changing pattern of the Wabash River in Indiana, USA. The meandering channel has changed course considerably since 1806, when the first survey was made. One result of this shifting course has been the formation of an oxbow lake. At present the river is causing considerable stress to the people of New Harmony as a meander is heading their way at a rate of

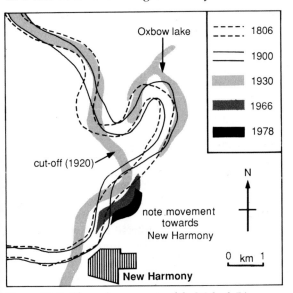

Figure 11.1 *Channel movements of the Wabash River, USA*

60 m a year! It would be possible to re-route the river or to strengthen its banks, but the costs would be huge and the implications for downstream users severe. Just to divert the current away from the eroding bank would cost half a million dollars.

Clearly changing river channels can cause management problems. To understand how serious a potential problem may be and how best to react to it, it is necessary to comprehend fully the internal and external influences upon river channel dynamics.

The changing geometry of river channels

Changes in channel geometry result from the interaction of channel materials and flowing water.

Channel materials

Alluvial channels are formed in material that has been eroded or weathered. It can be:

(a) coarse and non-cohesive such as sand, gravel and cobbles. This coarse material commonly makes up the bed of a channel, especially in regions where the source of material is glacial till or gelifluction deposits containing considerable quantities of large fragments; or

(b) fine and cohesive with a significant proportion of clay as well as silt. This is typical of rivers flowing in regions subject to humid climates.

The contrast between cohesive and non-cohesive bed and bank materials has important consequences for the pattern of channel development, the nature of the bank shapes and their rate of erosion. For example, non-cohesive material will be unable to stand at an angle greater than the threshold for particle stability (Fig. 11.2). Under strong currents this may be considerably less than 30°. Bank collapse will be by avalanche as basal material is removed. By contrast, cohesive materials will resist bank collapse and will often stand vertically or allow overhangs to develop. Such banks are eroded by slip, slide or toppling failures, dumping material intermittently into the water (Fig. 11.3).

Figure 11.2 *Braided channel of a glacial meltwater stream, Norway*

Figure 11.3 *Bank collapse along the River Severn, a simple-channel meandering river*

Flowing water

The effect of water takes place through the force of frictional drag applied to the bed and banks. Water moving in a meander normally has the greatest drag (and therefore greatest scouring ability) near the outside bank; water moving in a straight path tends to have the greatest drag near the channel centre line (Fig. 11.4). Both types of flow induce secondary circulations across the channel which may cause increased erosion or deposition. All water movements therefore selectively erode the channel, causing a change in shape with time.

Because drag varies with discharge, at higher discharges there is greater erosion. However, the scale of any event has to be balanced against its frequency. Thus a very large flood which recurs on average once every 20 years may have less influence on the shape of a channel than a flood that just fills the channel but recurs every 2 years. In practice, flows of moderate frequency and about bankfull are found to have most influence on channel shape. The exception to this is the very large and infrequent flow which may completely disrupt the channel pattern, sometimes even making recovery irreparable. This kind of catastrophic event will be discussed later.

River channel patterns

An examination of river channel patterns confirms that they tend to fit into one of three distinct patterns (Fig. 11.5):
(a) braided;
(b) meandering; and
(c) straight.

(a) Braided streams

Braided streams are associated with steep river gradients. They transport coarse non-cohesive alluvium and have low, gently sloping banks that stand at their threshold angle of stability. There are innumerable dividing islands that are destroyed, reworked and reformed at all stages of flow, but particularly by each major storm event (Fig. 11.5(a)). The extremely mobile bed is constantly traversed with a progression of

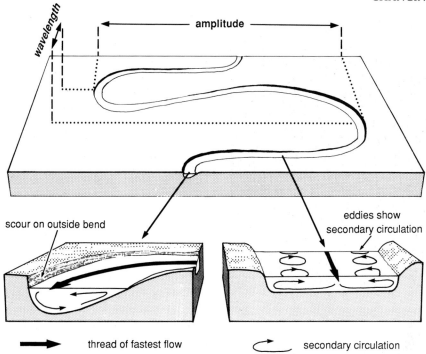

Figure 11.4 *Changing location of greatest frictional drag in a meandering channel*

small dunes. These moving dunes serve as the main means of transporting the bedload.

A braided stream system is kept in equilibrium by the growth and destruction of the dividing islands. Braided stream regimes frequently have very variable flows, with large floods that readily destroy and rework the island material. In this way the channel widens to accommodate the flood, then narrows itself by the growth of islands during the recession.

It therefore relies on continual disturbance. However, without a large disruptive flood, the fine material normally carried by the river will accumulate amongst the coarser island debris. Accumulating debris will then provide a base for vegetation growth and the islands will become stabilised. At this stage the channel would have begun an irreversible change to a new stable state.

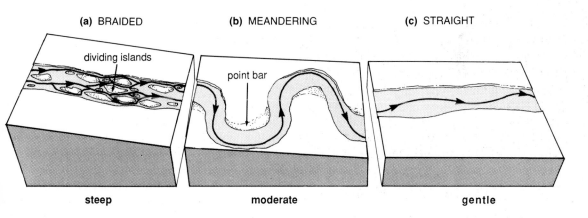

Figure 11.5 *Major river systems*

(b) Meandering streams

Meandering streams are associated with moderate gradients, have fine (silt and clay) cohesive bank sediment, non-cohesive mobile sand and gravel or cobble beds. They have steep, often vertical and sometimes overhanging banks that entrap the river into a single channel with rare, stable, dividing islands (Fig. 11.5(b)).

Meandering streams feature a sequence of bedforms that occur at a variety of scales. At 5–7 times the channel width there are regions with coarse sediment armouring called **riffles**. These features are associated with straight reaches in the stream and have markedly steeper gradients than the intervening **pool** areas. Pools frequently contain dunes and ripples of sand. In a meandering stream they are associated with curved reaches and often associated with the outside bend of a meander. The mobility of sand means that dunes can adjust rapidly to changes in flow conditions.

(c) Straight streams

Straight streams are associated with gentle gradients, have fine (silt and clay) cohesive bank sediment and non-cohesive sand beds. They have steep, often vertical banks that entrap the river in a single channel. Straight streams are relatively rare. Their low sinuosity is a reflection of their 'aimless' plan where sluggish downstream water velocity has not imposed a regular meander pattern on the system. Furthermore a straight channel does not absorb energy effectively during a flood as is the case for meandering systems.

These three forms of channel may be described as **quasi-equilibrium** states which do not grade into each other. This must mean that there are only three patterns that can be in equilibrium with the environment.

The change from one form of channel shape to another can occur in two ways:

(a) by an external change of energy (say a change in the flow regime due to a natural effect such as climatic change, or a man-induced effect such as reservoir construction);

(b) by slow internal change of the system such as when a threshold is exceeded (Fig. 11.6).

Most people live near meandering rivers. It is thus especially important to see how meandering rivers obtain their characteristic shape and the factors that affect this shape.

The 'model' meander curve is, on average, just the right shape to absorb energy evenly along its length (it is a form of sine curve). This is what makes it stable in just the same way as, for example, a curved bay is a stable form of coastline. Meander wavelength – the distance from the start of one meander to the corresponding point in the next – is closely related to the channel width, the discharge and the channel gradient. It has been found that the meandering pattern will develop from a straight channel in a series of stages until it has acquired its stable sinuosity (Fig. 11.7). This may or may not result in the creation of cutoffs and the formation of oxbow lakes.

A river channel can adjust towards a stable state in a variety of ways. In a natural state, all channel variables (width, depth, channel roughness, sinuosity, etc.) adjust to minimise the change required by any one. However, some adjustments are more readily achieved than others. For example, bed roughness can be altered speedily by the growth of dunes whereas channel width and sinuosity can only alter slowly because they require the removal of considerable quantities of bank material.

In general the steeper the gradient, the greater the degree of sinuosity and the more likely it becomes that the downslope erosion of banks will lead to meander cut-offs (Fig. 11.8). However, because the river is in equilibrium, the creation of a cut-off in one place (one consequent local steepening of the course) will automatically lead to the development of a new meander or the exaggeration of an existing meander in order to retain an overall constant gradient. This may take decades to achieve, and the river may thus never achieve a state of constant gradient in practice, but the pattern of change will always be directed toward achieving this aim.

There is no single gradient at which these changes occur because they are also related to the river discharge. Thus large rivers will begin to create 'oxbows' while at much more gentle gradients than small rivers. In fact we can use the sight of oxbows as a sign that the river is at

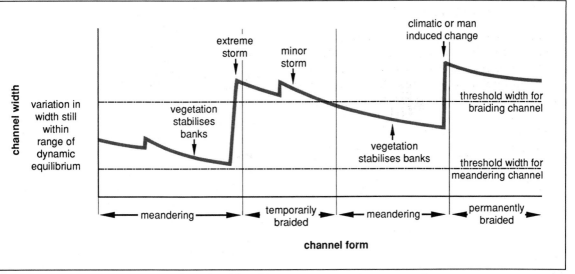

Figure 11.6 *The relationship between channel width and form*

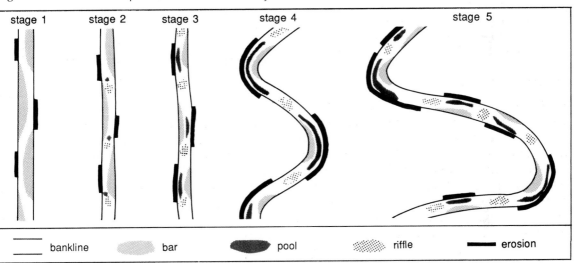

bankline	bar	pool	riffle	erosion

Characteristics of the five stages in the development of alluvial stream channels

Stage 1	Stage 2	Stage 3	Stage 4	Stage 5
No pools or riffles	Incipient pools and riffles spaced at about 3 to 5 channel widths	Well-developed pools and riffles with mean spacing 5 to 7 channel widths and mode 3 to 7 channel widths	Well-developed pools and riffles with mean spacing 5 to 7 channel widths and mode 5 to 7 channel widths	Mixture of well-developed pools and riffles with incipient pools and riffles – mean spacing is generally 5 to 7 channel widths with a mode of 3 to 7 channels widths
The dominant bed forms are asymmetrical shoals	Dominant bed forms are asymmetrical shoals	Dominant bed forms are pools, riffles, and asymmetrical shoals (mostly point bars)	Dominant bed forms are pools, riffles, and asymmetrical shoals (mostly point bars)	Dominant bed forms are pools, riffles, and asymmetrical shoals
	Pools and riffles are small			
		Pools are about 1.5 times as long as riffles	Pools are generally greater than 1.5 times as long as riffles	Pools are generally much longer than riffles

Figure 11.7 *The characteristics of a meandering stream*

205

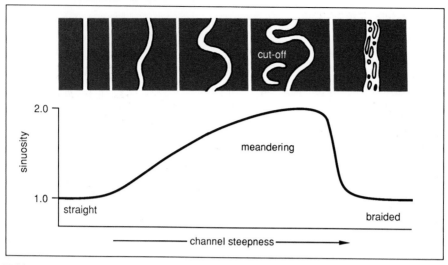

Figure 11.8 *As channels steepen and a threshold for change to braiding occurs, meandering sinuosity becomes more severe and cut-offs are more common*

Table 11.1 *The effects of lowering of river base level on a tributary stream*

Local effects	Upstream effects	Downstream effects
1. Headcutting	1. Increased velocity	1. Increased transport to main channel
2. General scour	2. Increased bed material transport	2. Aggradation
3. Local scour	3. Unstable channel	3. Increased flood stage
4. Bank instability	4. Possible change of form of river	4. Possible change of form of river
5. High velocities		

the upper limit of meandering and near the threshold that could make it 'flip' to a braided form. A further sign is provided by a high degree of bar building and bank caving; a well-vegetated river with comparably sized trees on both banks indicates a very stable river. In a sense, therefore, it is a danger signal to take care before you 'mess with the river'.

Channelisation

Changes in channels do affect people as shown by the Wabash River example on page 201. However, it is important to realise that people may also influence river channel dynamics.

Channelisation is a deliberate attempt to alter the natural geometry of a watercourse, usually a stream or river. The objectives of channelisation are:

(a) reclamation of wetlands by lowering the water table;

(b) increase the capacity of a channel to prevent flooding;

(c) provide a straighter and deeper channel for navigation;

(d) prevent bed or bank erosion;

(e) straighten rivers to make farmland more manageable; and

(f) enable bridges, highways and other structures to be built across them.

There are many methods of channelisation possible, but they usually involve some form of dredging, and often include lining the bed or banks with artificial material.

Ways to modify the channel include (Fig. 11.9):

(a) **Cut-offs:** these are dredged new channels of the same dimensions as the original channel, designed specifically to shorten meander bends.

(b) **Revetments:** these are brick, concrete, wood pile, steel sheet or rock and wire mesh structures designed to stop erosion along a particular part of the bank. They are used to prevent meander development and protect homes and farmland from erosion.

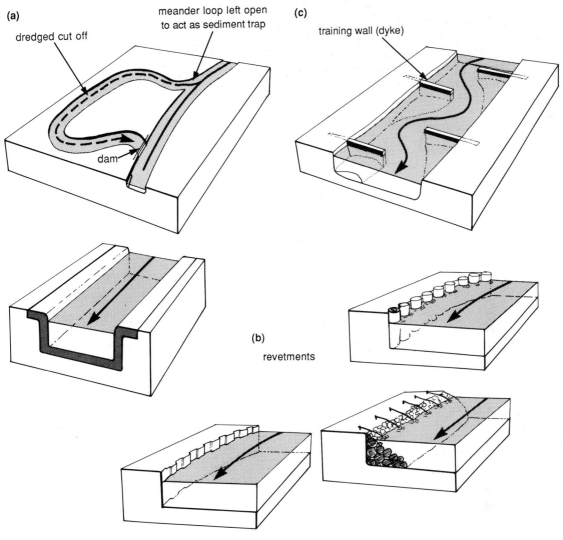

Figure 11.9 *Systems for stabilising channel banks*

(c) Dykes and training walls: these are structures built out from the banks towards the centre line of the river and designed to direct the river current away from the banks, thereby focusing it in the centre and increasing the river velocity. They are used to provide a low water navigable channel and to encourage sediment transport.

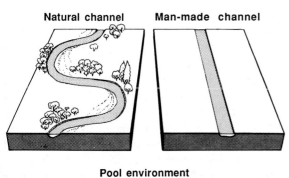

Figure 11.10 *When river channels are altered, the environment for living creatures changes. Fish, for example, use the varied habitats of pool and riffle sequences for food and protection. Straightening channels destroys much of the variety, reduces the habitats and the numbers of species that can survive*

(d) Dredging: this is the continuous activity of removing accumulating sediment from the river bed. Sediment may be dumped on the banks to form a levee or it may be dumped in the main river thread and the river used to transport it downstream. The first action quickly uses up available bank space; the second action causes severe river pollution. Dredging will also remove the 'armour plate' of coarse bed material and expose the material below to further erosion, thus giving sediment problems downstream.

The impact of channelisation on the environment is very complex and usually the desired aims are achieved only at a cost to the other parts of the environment. For example removal of natural vegetation from the banks and bed of a channel radically changes the habitat for aquatic life; straightening, which removes the pools and riffles of a meandering river, destroys yet more habitat (Fig. 11.10). Most channelised rivers are less pleasant to look at, and they will probably alter the level of the water table in the adjacent floodplain. This in turn will affect the pattern of vegetation.

Further, channelisation for one purpose may adversely affect another channel function. Thus constriction of the Mississippi by wing dykes and revetments designed to aid all year navigation have restricted the ability of the river to accommodate floods by nearly a third and, if it were not for an emergency programme of levee building, would have resulted in frequent serious flooding.

Some case study consequences of channelisation

Many rivers have been straightened and dredged to accommodate flood flows produced either by increased urban runoff or cultivation. The lower part of the Willow River (Fig. 11.11), a tributary of the Missouri in the state of Iowa, USA was bypassed by a straight, steep ditch in the 1920s. However, this lower portion has proved to be 'overdeep' with respect to the natural long profile and is now too gentle to transport the sediment delivered from upstream. As a result frequent dredging is required to maintain the design depth. Furthermore, it now backs up with

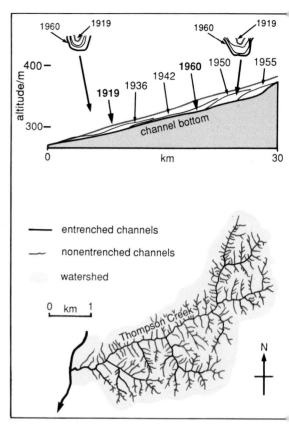

Figure 11.11 *The effects of lowering of river base level on a tributary stream*

water whenever there is a flood in the Missouri.

As the river regrades to this altered long profile it trenches into its upper channel, creating small waterfall steps or **'knickpoints'**, each of which retreats progressively upstream. Erosion of the upstream channel thus has led to even more sediment being delivered downstream, and yet more dredging. But entrenchment has also caused the tributary stream channels to be left 'hanging' above the main channel. Adjustment by these tributaries has produced downcutting by as much as 13 m into the former bed. The lower river levels have also lowered soil water tables, making drought failure of crops more likely and requiring wells to be sunk deeper. Furthermore, the trenching has oversteepened the banks causing widespread bank caving. The banks are now in the process of widening out to a stable shape – a process that will consume much valuable farmland and is virtually unstoppable.

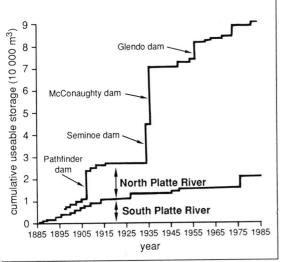

Figure 11.12 *The River Platte system progressively modified by people*

Ascalmore Creek, Mississippi was a meandering stream that was straightened in the 1940s. During the 1950s and 1960s the US Soil Conservation Service established the banks by planting vegetation. They also controlled the arrival of sediment from tributaries through the use of check dams. In this way they prevented a disastrous development sequence like that of Willow River. However, the creek has still changed, developing a meandering path in the straight channel, with alternating sand bars and a sequence of pools and riffles and so trying to move back to a meandering course.

Channelisation has particularly important effects upstream and downstream of urban areas. Many urban areas have concrete-lined and narrowed channels. The frictional drag of such channels is often less than half that in a natural channel. Because of this the energy dissipation in the urban reach is substantially reduced and flood waves carried unchanged to downstream areas (see also Chapter 10). Higher flows on the downstream channels result in considerable channel widening in areas not protected by revetments.

Student enquiry 11A: Working with meanders

1. A1 shows part of the River Severn near Newtown in mid-Wales. Investigations of the floodplain sediments have located former channels. The remains of the older channels have been used to reconstruct the former course of the river. Describe the sequence of changes that occurred.

2. Measure the sinuosity for each period of time. This is the actual channel length as measured on a map by, say, laying a piece of string along the channel course, compared with the straight line length between the two end points as measured with a ruler. Comment on the change in sinuosity during the period 1847 to 1975.

3. A stretch of the Mississippi near Willow Bend in Mississippi State is shown in A2. Set out separately on tracing paper the river channel positions for each of the dates shown and measure the sinuosity. Compare and contrast the values and patterns of the Severn and the Mississippi.

4. The object of the next section is to examine the river behaviour after the Greenville reach of the Mississippi was artificially straightened in the 1930s to make a shorter course for commercial navigation. For this you will need the remaining information in the enquiry.

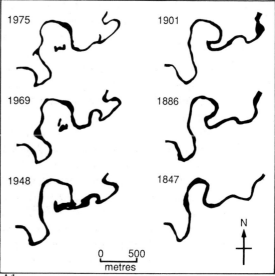

A1

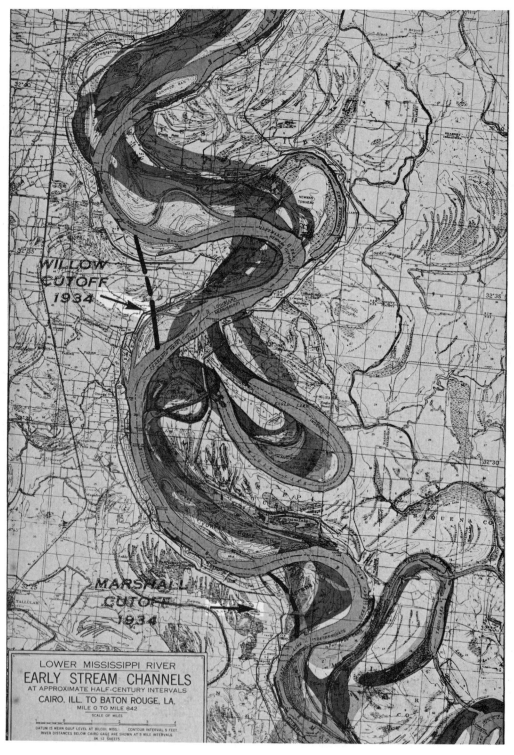

A2 *Historic development of the Willow Point and Marshall Point reaches*

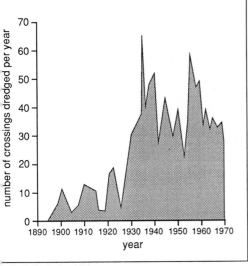

A3 *Mississippi River*

A5 *The effects of straightening a reach by cut-offs*

Local effects	Upstream effects	Downstream effects
1. Steeper slope	1. See local effects	1. Deposition downstream of straightened ended channel
2. Higher velocity		2. Increased flood stage
3. Increased transport		3. Loss of channel capacity
4. Degradation and possible headcutting		
5. Banks unstable		
6. River may braid		
7. Degradation in tributary		

Extract from a report of 1945

'A dredged channel which does not maintain itself is a very precarious foundation for trade. There is probably no place in the world where a dredged channel will have a briefer existence than in the uncontrolled part of the Mississippi River below the Missouri.... Dredging has what seems to me the fatal defect of being dependent upon never-ending effort. It is a temporary improvement adopted from compulsion and not from choice....

'...Plan the work (if it must be done) in such a manner as to obtain the assistance of the river's natural action, if possible. It has been found that much of the desired results can be obtained without directing operations contrary to a desired action. It appears that the river can be gradually trained to a desired course much more easily than it can be pushed bodily.

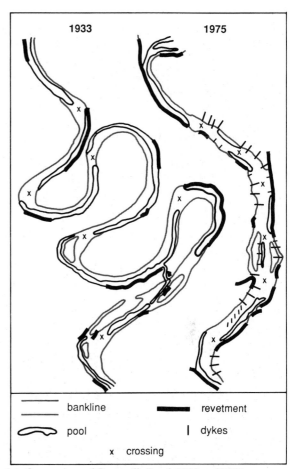

A4 *Comparison of Greenville Reach 1933 and 1976*

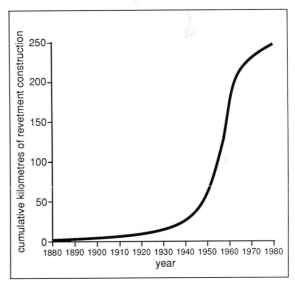

A6 *Mississippi River*

'...Since the earliest days of settlement in the valley the reach of river from Arkansas city to Greenville had been noted for its extreme sinuosity containing five great bends in a river distance of 47 miles. For decades much effort and money were spent preventing natural cut-offs across the necks between bendways. Revetments and training walls had been constructed in an effort to prevent cut-offs at any price.'

(a) Suggest some reasons why people were so afraid of natural cut-offs.

(b) In 1933 policy was changed and the river straightened. Consider the pattern in 1933 just after the cut-offs and in 1975. On a copy of the map mark on evidence of the river trying to re-build a natural channel.

(c) Describe some of the consequences of straightening, paying particular regard to the amount of effort required to maintain the system.

(d) On your map mark the location of further structures that might be needed. Use Fig. 11.7 as a guide to how the river would normally develop.

(e) Summarise the nature and magnitude of the problems that will confront the river authorities in the future.

The effects of changing the river regime

Because rivers are in dynamic equilibrium with their environments, any change in the environment induced by people will result in a corresponding change in the river. Thus if people alter the flow regime, say to abstract water for irrigation, or to add water from urban areas during a storm, then the bed geometry will also change, albeit slowly. Added stormflow water will increase peak discharges of a river and the increased energy will provide a powerful agent of erosion. River meander wavelength and width will attempt to change to match the new regime and, in urban areas, the only way to prevent this natural change may be expensive revetment programmes. If rivers cannot widen to accommodate the increased flow, then they will

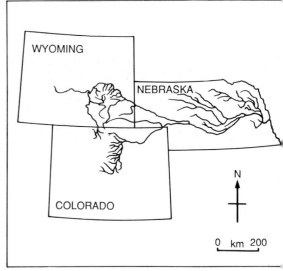

Figure 11.13 *Platte River basin*

become deeper. The result will be frequent bank overtopping. To prevent the consequent flooding, levees or other forms of embankment will be required.

The River Platte flows from the eastern slopes of the Rocky Mountains in Colorado, across extensive, thick deposits of alluvium to join the Missouri (Fig. 11.13). Most of the water in the Platte comes from spring snowmelt in the Rockies. This is supplemented by isolated summer thunderstorms. The water is mainly used for irrigation of cereal crops, being diverted directly into canals and also stored in 'on line' and 'off line' reservoirs. In the upper reaches the river is also used to generate electricity. Despite the full use of surface water, demand for irrigation has required extensive additional pumping from groundwater reservoirs and the diversion of water from the Colorado River drainage basin (see Chapter 9).

Development occurred in several distinct phases:

(a) The earliest phase of irrigation. Small ditches were dug to irrigate irregular patches of land on the floodplain.

(b) Larger and more sophisticated canals and ditches were built to irrigate lands on terraces above the floodplain. These canals used all the summer flow of the river and people downstream were unable to irrigate. Many downstream canals were abandoned.

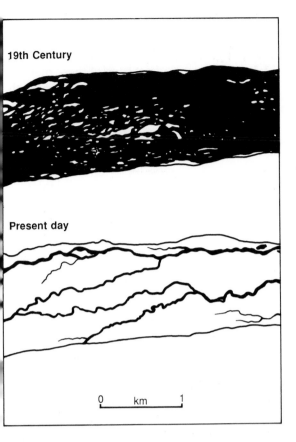

19th Century

Present day

0   km   1

Figure 11.14 *Detail of the River Platte channel*

rangeland for cattle grazing until the 1880s, when the advantage of irrigating the range was first appreciated.

Many people on the wagon trains kept reliable records of the river as they passed along the Oregon Trail in the years before development. Their descriptions show that the channel was typically braided, with many dividing islands that reformed after each spring flood. The bed was made of mobile gravel and cobbles that made distinctive bed forms. Thus:

'Looking out upon the long stretch of river either way were islands and islands of every size whatever, from three feet in diameter to those which contained miles of area, resting here and there in the most artistic disregard of position and relation to each other.

'In the same place where the day before it reached to our armpits, it did not now reach to our waists, although the river level had not fallen. Such changes in the bottom of this river were very frequent as it is composed of moving gravel.

'[The Platte] is a mile in width. Where cut up by islands, as is often the case, it extends to double or treble (that distance), and in one place is seven miles wide from shore to shore.

'The usual height of the [Platte] banks above the surface of the sand which forms its bed (does not) exceed six or eight feet.'

From descriptions such as this it is not only possible to gain a vivid picture of the river and its channel, but it is also possible to produce estimates of its size so that changes can be compared with today. In the 1800s the Platte River was braided and averaged 2 km in width. Flow depth varied between 0.3 m and 1.3 m for most of the year, with a bankfull depth of between 1.8 and 2.4 m. Large sand deposits were common in the channel whose bed was very active. High water and floods occurred in spring but the river had virtually dried up above the junction with the Loup by late summer.

Between 1860 and 1979 the channel width narrowed and today almost the entire channel of 1860 is covered with vegetation (Fig. 11.14). Only two or three meandering channels are present in the stretch above the Loup. In contrast the reach below the Loup has hardly changed.

(c) Construction of reservoirs to store water from snowmelt. Many of the canals previously abandoned were reopened, new canals dug and existing canals enlarged. Soon summer demand again exceeded supply.
(d) Canal construction ended and dam building slowed, most 'new' water being used for public supply, flood prevention and power generation. New demands for irrigation water were satisfied with groundwater for the first time.
(e) Water was diverted from the Colorado through a tunnel dug deep into the Rockies.

There are two headwaters to the Platte system and each has a different history of exploitation. Irrigation began first on the South Platte River in 1838, but a gold rush near Denver in 1858 caused a great influx in the population and a corresponding increase in the demand for locally produced food. By contrast, the North Platte remained undeveloped and was used as

Student enquiry 11B:
Measuring the channel changes of the River Platte

Changes in the upper reach of the Platte can be illustrated by two indices:

(a) **braiding index:** the sum of the length of the islands in a reach divided by the length of the reach; and

(b) **sinuosity index:** the length of a reach of existing channel in 1979 divided by the length of the channel in the same reach in 1860.

Table 11.1

North Platte

width (m)		ratio 65–65	braiding index/sinuosity index	
1865	790	0.11	3.44	1.06
1938	520		1.76	1.11
1965	90			

South Platte

width (m)		ratio 67–77	braiding index/sinuosity index	
1867	535	0.24	2.18	1.02
1952	60		1.78	1.12
1977	91			

1. Describe the changes in the braiding and sinuosity indices. What do they suggest about the evolution of the river channels? Explain how this is reflected in the channel patterns of Fig. 11.14.

2. Suggest some of the factors of management that might have led to this change.

3. The South Platte reservoirs are 'on stream', while those of the North Platte are 'off stream'. Why should the South Platte regime be more affected than the North Platte?

4. In general groundwater pumping lowers groundwater levels but it also reduces the loss from transpiration by plants. In the upper Platte floodplain there has been a 6 m fall in the groundwater level due to abstractions, whereas in the lower Platte floodplain there has been a rise of up to 3 m in the groundwater level as irrigation water seeps back to the river. People have used both reservoirs and groundwater to irrigate their crops. By drawing out a suggested yearly hydrograph for the river (as in Fig. 11.10), show what effect each of these methods has on the river flow regime and thus on the channel shape.

Key terms

Bankfull: the state of the river when the channel is fully filled with water and before overbank spillage (flooding) occurs.

Channel: the part of the landscape occupied and eroded by flowing water. It is distinguished from a gully by the presence of sorted alluvium on the bed.

Entrainment: the gathering and transport of loose particulate material from the channel banks and bed. Entrained material moves as **suspended** particles (clay and silt); **saltated** particles (sand) that are bounced along the bed or **traction load** particles which are rolled along the bed.

Hydraulic geometry: the shape of the channel in cross-section and downstream slope.

Knickpoint: a discontinuity in the channel, perhaps a direct step as extreme as a waterfall, but often just a steepened reach of channel in which there is considerable energy for erosion. Knickpoints are usually the most active regions of a channel long profile.

Negative feedback: the in-built mechanisms in a channel (such as meander cut-offs) that prevent the channel developing too far from its most stable pattern.

Point bar: a lobe-shaped ridge of sand, gravel or pebbles that occupies the inside bend of a meander, stretching downstream towards the river centre line. It is normally covered at times of high water, but exposed during dry weather flow.

Reach: a stretch of water on a river, either defined by two natural features such as waterfalls or defined arbitrarily. A reach normally refers to a distance of a few kilometres.

Shear stress: the frictional drag imposed by flowing water on the bank and loose debris on the bed. It increases with water velocity and therefore with river discharge.

Sinuosity: the degree of river channel meandering. It is normally measured as the ratio of the actual channel length to the straight line length between two points along the talweg of a channel. Straight or braided rivers have sinuosities of 1.0.

Spring sapping: the headward growth of a channel by bank collapse at the place where water first converges to form the source spring or seepage.

Theme:
Ecosystems and human activity

Chapter 12
Ecosystems

Introduction

The natural environment is under increasing pressure from human activities. Farmers across the world are intent upon producing higher and higher yields, mostly with scant regard for maintaining the balance of nature. Chemicals are widely used to boost profits. Herbicides, pesticides and fertilisers are added to the soil to maximise production and artificially maintain soil nutrients. Much of this kind of activity is unnecessarily harmful, not only to the soil, but to the wild flowers and creatures whose natural habitats are being destroyed. It wasn't so long ago that British meadows were ablaze with colourful wild flowers – now such places are rare, so much so that many wild flowers have had to be made protected species (Fig. 12.1).

Figure 12.1 *Fields of oil seed rape, a typical monoculture that has replaced natural diversity*

African violet may disappear from the wild

ONE OF the world's most popular houseplants, the African violet, is threatened with extinction in the wild.

World trade in the African violet (*Saintpaulia ionantha*) is worth an estimated $30 million per year. But all the plants are propagated in greenhouses. In the wild the species is on a list of 12 most threatened plants drawn up by the International Union for the Conservation of Nature and Natural Resources (IUCN). It has become the symbol of the IUCN's Plants Campaign.

The text of the entry for the African violet in the Conservation Monitoring Centre's database at Kew Gardens in London says: "There are few, if any, individuals left at the type locality.... The habitat is so specialised and the need for farmland so acute that the extinction of the species at this locality seems almost inevitable."

Pesticides threaten British wildlife

Michael Rands and Nick Sotherton

Unchecked and widespread use of pesticides and other agrochemicals is slowly but surely killing some of Britain's wildlife. Although existing legislation and voluntary agreements theoretically ensure that no pesticide is directly harmful to wildlife, there is no legal requirement to test for their indirect effects. The Game Conservancy and other conservation organisations cite the decline of certain species dependent on farmland, over the past 20 years, against increasing use of pesticides during the same period as evidence for the harmful effect of such agrochemicals.

The dramatic decline of the grey partridge, once Britain's most common and widespread gamebird, is a good example. Its shrinking population is matched only by the diminishing numbers of cereal-dwelling arthropods, upon which the chicks of the grey partridge, among those of many other birds, feed.

Such insects, which include plant bugs (Heteroptera), leaf-hoppers and aphids (Homoptera), caterpillars (the larvae of Tenthredinidae and Lepidoptera) and leaf-feeding beetles (Chrysomelidae and Curculionidae), thrive on the weeds that grow among cereal crops, as well as on the crops themselves. With the exception of aphids, these insects cause little or no economic damage. Unfortunately for the grey partridge and other farmland birds, the insects are susceptible to a wide array of agrochemicals.

British farmers in the 1980s spent some £200 million every year on agrochemicals to kill cereal pests. An average field of wheat now receives two or more herbicides, two insecticides and up to four applications of fungicide during the course of one growing season. In 1960 such a field would have been sprayed once with a herbicide. Because each field may receive up to four fungicides per year, their impact on the population of arthropods may actually be greater than that of insecticides.

The effects of herbicides are more complex and involve a further link in the food chain. Few weed-killers currently used on cereals are directly toxic to invertebrates but, indirectly, these chemicals are just as damaging because they kill the insects' host plants. The Game Conservancy's monitoring programme of some 62 square kilometres of arable farmland, in Sussex, shows that weeds in cereal fields have decreased five-fold in the past 30 years.

The major indirect impact of pesticides on the bird community of farmland is on their breeding success. Some species will diminish in number because their chicks will starve. Pesticides will have killed their major source of protein, insects.

New Scientist, 4 July 1985

The countryside is under increasing pressure from land uses other than farming. People demand open space for recreation and land for industrial and housing development.

It is all too easy to destroy what is natural on the path to so-called 'development', and to do so without an understanding of the natural relationships between soil, vegetation and animal, is potentially catastrophic to life on earth (Fig. 12.2). This chapter will describe these natural relationships and will examine how people can, through ignorance, often upset the natural balance. It will show you how important it is that people fit in with what is natural rather than imposing a set of artificial and ill-thought out demands and constraints. Furthermore, in this age of 'Green' politics, this chapter will evaluate the planning implications associated with the development of our environment.

How an ecosystem works

The natural environment contains a mosaic of **species** (groups of interacting organisms). They do not live in isolation but live in **association** with one another (Fig. 12.3). It is the arrangement of a particular set of living organisms (plants, animals, bacteria, etc.) and their interaction with each other and with their environment which forms the **ecosystem**.

An ecosystem can be identified at different scales. On a large scale, the whole world can be considered an ecosystem, while on a smaller scale an ecosystem can be a pond or a wood.

The components of an ecosystem (organisms, plants, soil) are linked together by transfers of **energy** and **nutrients** (ions).

The system is made from:

(a) a **mineral pool** (the soil, rainwater);

Figure 12.2 *The last of the forests? Charcoal making in Africa*

Figure 12.3 *Bluebells in a Chiltern beachwood, a typical mosaic of plant forms all growing in association*

(b) green plants;

(c) **animals** that feed directly (herbivores) or indirectly (carnivores) on the plants; and

(d) **decomposers** (bacteria, earthworms, etc.) that convert the dead tissue into soluble components through the twin processes of **mineralisation** (the breakdown of tissue by micro-organisms into soluble acids, etc.) and **humification** (the formation of long chain molecules – humus – from some of the these acids and ions) (Fig. 12.4).

Energy is obtained from solar radiation and is lost from the ecosystem at each stage as metabolic heat; nutrients are obtained from soil weathering (small), air, volcanic and other dust, and rainwater; a small percentage of nutrients are lost by leaching. However, ecosystems are very effective at retaining the available nutrients. Indeed, nutrient **recycling** is the basis of ecosystem stability.

Because ecosystems convert minerals into tissue by photosynthesis using light energy, the total possible production of tissue is fixed by available nutrients and light: it is called the **net primary productivity (NPP)** of the system. The NPP controls the mass of animals that can depend on the green plants for long term survival.

At this point it is important to note that casual observations of *apparent* NPP can be misleading. Thus a regrowing forest can *appear* to put on much mass if measured by volume of matter (e.g. diameter of trunk). But the NPP of mature trees is mostly produced by increasing the *density* of the wood. Thus NPP is the same for climax and regrowth.

Under natural conditions ecosystems are regulated by positive and (harsh) negative **feedback processes**. This is often based on the **boom and bust** (homeostatic) principle. All species within an ecosystem attempt to reproduce at their maximum rate. This self-reinforcing (*positive feedback*) system eventually increases the consumption beyond the long term NPP of green plants by, for example, herbivores. The result is starvation and death (*negative feedback*), which in turn causes a reduction in numbers sufficiently great to allow the plant communities to recover. With abundant food relative to their population animal numbers

Figure 12.4(a)

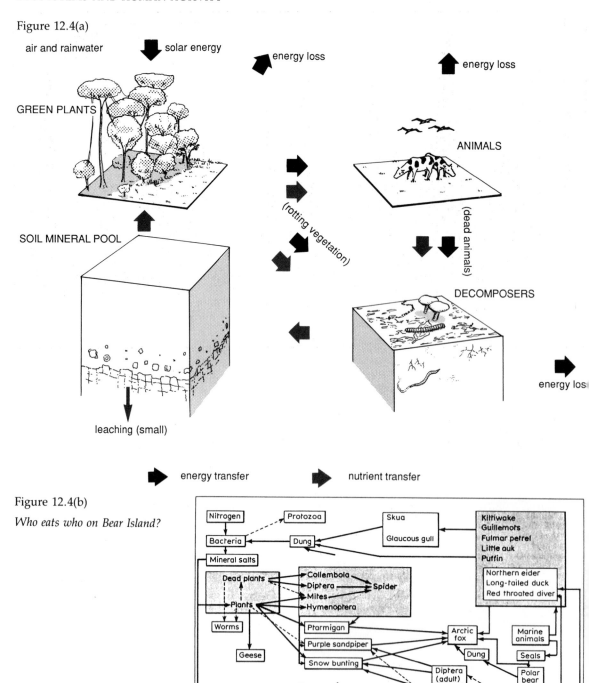

Who eats who on Bear Island?

Figure 12.4(b)

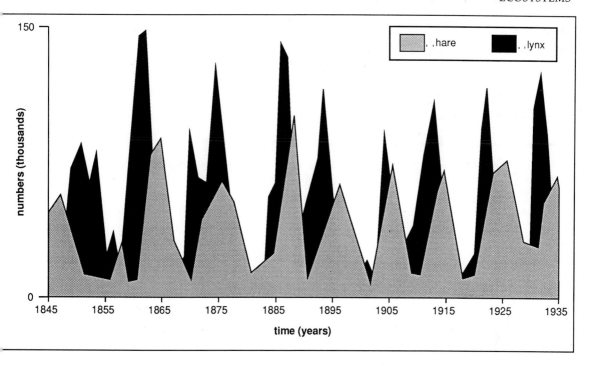

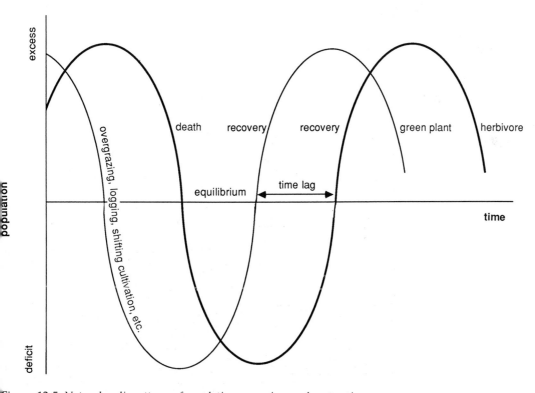

Figure 12.5 *Natural cyclic patterns of population expansions and contractions*

begin to increase again, and so on. This cyclic change in species populations is perfectly natural (Fig. 12.5) even though many people find that, on the level of an individual animal, the starvation part of the cycle is distressing. It is on the basis of preventing the long term suffering associated with starvation that many countries allow wild animals to be culled (shot) so they don't exceed the NPP. Naturally, farmers have an eye to the NPP all the time, although a complex sequence of events sometimes means that they exceed the NPP – e.g., the Sahelian countries of Africa at present.

Controls on an ecosystem

The composition of an ecosystem is determined by two sets of factors or controls:

1. Environmental controls

Each species on earth has its own preferred set of environmental conditions (i.e. light, humidity, temperature, etc.). A species will grow vigorously in such conditions but it will *tolerate* less perfect conditions, albeit less successfully. There will, however, come a point when environmental conditions are so adverse that the species will be unable to grow.

The growing of vines in Europe illustrates this principle well. Ideal environmental conditions exist throughout southern Europe. The further north, the less successful they are as temperature and sunshine values decrease. So, in England, vineyards are not common and are restricted mainly to south-facing slopes in the south-east. Further north, vineyards are not found as the environmental conditions make economic growth impossible.

2. Competitive controls

Ecosystems are almost never composed of a single species. A single species is unstable because it cannot usually fully utilise all the available energy and nutrients (see Fig. 12.3). Farmers, who try to grow just one species in a field have a constant battle with other species (that farmers call weeds) which would be able to make use of 'spare' nutrients. In this sense, farming with one crop is a wasteful system, although it is convenient for farm management and the use of machinery. Many smallholder farmers of the tropics (whose aim is long term self-sufficiency rather than cash return) have operated a much more ecologically balanced system of cultivation for centuries (Fig. 12.6).

Ecosystem composition depends on two factors:
(a) the **number of species** that could survive in the particular environment; and
(b) the ability of a species to compete with others for the available energy and nutrients.
There will usually be a large number of species that could thrive at a particular site, so the actual distribution depends on successful colonisation and competition. The stages of this process are most readily observed on a newly cleared site (Fig. 12.7).

Stage 1
The site is first colonised by species that have a great tolerance to harsh conditions. Seeds

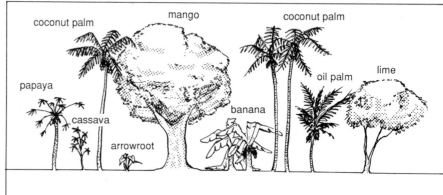

Figure 12.6 *Typical plants grown in a tropical rainforest clearing and traditional husbandry practices*

blown on to the site may have to lie exposed to direct sunshine and withstand desiccation; the germination process must therefore be particularly vigorous and rapid. The growing plant may also have to withstand beating sun or freezing cold. Relatively few species have this adaptation and so the early stages of colonisation are characterised by small numbers of species, often annuals and with good seed dispersal mechanisms.

Stage 2
In the shelter of the early colonisers less resilient seeds begin to germinate. These seeds need the shady, more moist conditions provided by a continuous plant cover, but they are able to grow in reduced light at least until they grow above the early colonisers. These plants are often more slow growing, but have a more woody structure and develop into shrubs or small trees. Eventually these plants may shade out the early colonisers, depriving them of the light levels they need and causing them to die back. As they die they leave a niche for a new species to colonise.

Figure 12.7 *Colonisation, competition and succession*

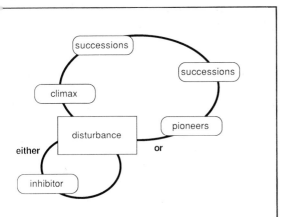

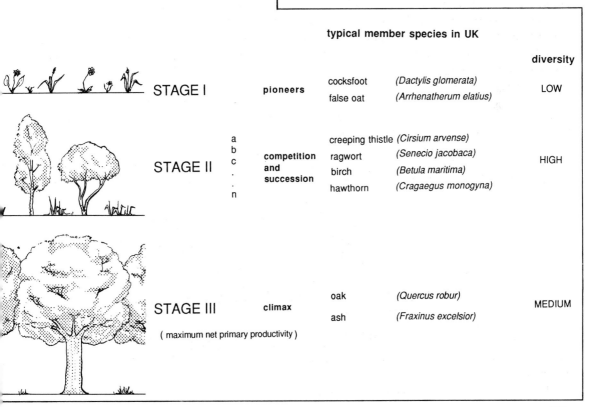

typical member species in UK

				diversity
STAGE I	pioneers	cocksfoot	(*Dactylis glomerata*)	LOW
		false oat	(*Arrhenatherum elatius*)	
STAGE II	competition and succession	creeping thistle	(*Cirsium arvense*)	HIGH
		ragwort	(*Senecio jacobaca*)	
		birch	(*Betula maritima*)	
		hawthorn	(*Cragaegus monogyna*)	
STAGE III	climax	oak	(*Quercus robur*)	MEDIUM
		ash	(*Fraxinus excelsior*)	

(maximum net primary productivity)

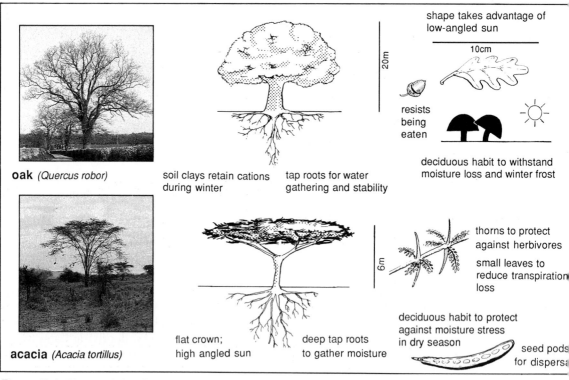

shape takes advantage of
low-angled sun

10cm

resists
being
eaten

deciduous habit to withstand
moisture loss and winter frost

oak *(Quercus robor)*

soil clays retain cations
during winter

tap roots for water
gathering and stability

thorns to protect
against herbivores

small leaves to
reduce transpiration
loss

deciduous habit to protect
against moisture stress
in dry season

seed pods
for dispersal

acacia *(Acacia tortillus)*

flat crown;
high angled sun

deep tap roots
to gather moisture

Figure 12.8 *Characteristics of two common world trees*

Stage 3

The slow growing trees begin to rise above the shrubs and quick growing small trees. They provide a closed upper canopy which shades out much light, and shrubs and small trees may die back. Again the composition changes and fewer species survive, but the final stable ecosystem – the **climax** – has been attained.

The form and diversity of species in an ecosystem

The **form** of a species refers to the size, arrangement and the shape of its leaf area; the pattern of its flowering; its root characteristics, and so on. The form of a species reflects the environment in which it lives, in particular the climate. Figure 12.9 compares the form of a deciduous woodland tree with a savanna tree. Notice the way in which both are ideally suited to their environments.

The **diversity**, or wealth of species will vary from one ecosystem to another. A frequently grazed pasture will only contain those species

able to tolerate high levels of stress. Even in a climax ecosystem some species will become dominant.

What may be good for plant diversity may be bad for animal diversity. For example, on the Calf of Man Island a cessation of grazing was thought to be the best way to create a natural habitat for birds. Instead, the long grass made it difficult for the birds to detect insects and, as a result, bird numbers decreased. Limited grazing has been reintroduced. Clearly, careful management based on a sound understanding is essential if the aim is to promote the greatest diversity of species.

Ecosystem management problems

The tropical rain forests

The natural ecosystem

The development of a tropical rain forest depends particularly on the environmental controls:

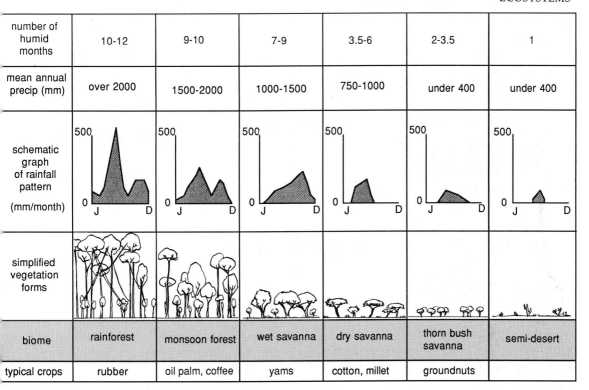

number of humid months	10-12	9-10	7-9	3.5-6	2-3.5	1
mean annual precip (mm)	over 2000	1500-2000	1000-1500	750-1000	under 400	under 400
schematic graph of rainfall pattern (mm/month)						
simplified vegetation forms						
biome	rainforest	monsoon forest	wet savanna	dry savanna	thorn bush savanna	semi-desert
typical crops	rubber	oil palm, coffee	yams	cotton, millet	groundnuts	

Figure 12.9 *Controls on West Africa's vegetation patterns*

(a) Insolation and temperature. The consistently high temperatures in lowland tropical forest areas promote rapid growth throughout the year, provided sufficient moisture and nutrients are available.

(b) Moisture. In the tropics, it is rainfall that varies seasonally – there is often a distinctive wet and a dry season. The natural vegetation thus reflects the differing lengths of the dry season. Evergreen forest (tropical rain forest) exists only where the dry season is less than two months. As the dry season increases in length, so evergreen gives way first to deciduous forest, then savanna and thorn scrub until finally, as the wet season becomes completely unreliable, the thorn scrub thins to desert. This is well illustrated by referring to the south-north vegetation transition in western Africa (Fig. 12.9).

(c) Nutrients. In an ecosystem nutrients may be stored (i) as plant tissue, or (ii) within the soil. Nutrients are generally scarce in tropical

rain forests; however, the plants have developed ways of conserving the available nutrients so enabling them to grow successfully. For example, their root systems are especially well developed near the surface so as to tap the nutrient source of decomposing plant tissue.

A vital role is played by fungi in nutrient recycling processes. The fungi in the upper soil attach themselves to decomposing leaves and wood and also to the roots of growing plants. Transfer of nutrients (as opposed to energy) through the body of another organism, in this case fungi, can be very efficient.

Nutrients are also conserved by retranslocation of nutrients from leaf to twig before the leaf falls from the plant. Furthermore, the growing leaves are often covered with mosses, lichens and algae which can fix nitrogen and scavenge nutrients from rainwater.

The two nutrients required in largest volumes are phosphorous and nitrogen. The rate of phosphorous input from the atmosphere is very low compared to other major nutrients and, for this reason, soil phosphorous takes on special importance. Phosphorous is mostly locked up in compounds of iron and aluminium in tropical soils and is only released by exuded silica from roots. Thus, to achieve the release of phosphorous, tropical plants often need to contain high levels of silica.

Nitrogen is obtained through nitrogen-fixing bacteria or algae and through breakdown of plant tissues, first by larger organisms such as termites, and then through other decomposers. Thus an effective and balanced soil animal community is essential for the production of nitrogen.

As you can see, the ecosystem of a tropical rain forest is very finely balanced in its difficult environment. Unless care is taken, this balance can easily be upset.

The impact of disturbance on tropical forest ecosystems

(a) **Natural.** Even climax forests are part of a dynamic ecosystem that is continually evolving and changes – disturbances – occur all the time. On the smallest scale are changes of a diurnal nature due to light and temperature; on a seasonal scale changes are due to rainfall regimes; on a scale of decades there are changes due to death and regrowth of plants as they complete their lifespans; and on a scale of centuries or thousands of years there are changes due to climatic change.

Natural disturbances occur when trees fall, creating an opening or gap in the canopy. It is a useful starting point with which to compare the effects of people. After a tree has fallen and the trunk and branches begin to decay a pulse of nutrients are released to the forest floor. There are several mechanisms ready to retrieve the nutrients and prevent nutrient loss. The 'emergency squad' comprises:

(i) regrowth from the stump of the broken tree – using the original tree root biomass to take up nutrients very quickly.

(ii) decomposition and storage within the bodies of the soil fauna and flora.

Later as existing saplings grow using light flooding into the gap opened up by the fallen tree they can use the nutrients stored by the fauna and flora. More nutrients are absorbed by the growth of new seedlings from seeds.

Recovery of an open space in the forest takes place by a natural succession process which we can describe as (i) gap closing; (ii) rebuilding, and (iii) climax phases. Succession depends on the nature of the disturbed site. If the site is nutrient poor then species with high nutrient use efficiency, low nutrient uptake and slow growth take over. If the site is fertile then growth of early successional species can be rapid. This imposes a drain on the nutrient reserves after a while and the early colonisers are unable to maintain the early growth. Other species then come in which can maintain growth under lower nutrient conditions and shade. This gives the late successional and climax species a competitive advantage over early successional plants and the vegetational community changes.

Thus native successional vegetation is able to increase its biomass rapidly despite the low fertility and in this time it stores nutrients in its tissues, thereby slowly restoring site fertility using nutrients that are unavailable to crop plants whose natural environment is not the rain forest.

(b) **Human disturbances of the rain forest.** There are many groups of people interested in harvesting the products of the rain forest.

(i) **Coppicing:** Tropical forests used to be managed commercially by poisoning undesirable trees and the removal of vines. Those tree species thought desirable were thus allowed to flourish. When sapling growth was well established the canopy trees of the same species were then harvested and the seedings harvested as thinnings or mature trees later on. The advantages were that the native trees were adapted to their environment and so did not suffer heavily from predators; no tree nursery needed to be kept; soil erosion was minimised because the ground was not disturbed; and soil nutrient stability was nearly maintained because harvesting only occurred on a selective basis. The system was abandoned commercially because it did not make sufficiently intensive use of the land to compete with the profit from tree crops such as cocoa and oil palm.

(ii) **Shifting cultivation:** Many people still need to earn a living from the land. Many poor peasants involved in a near subsistence economy do not have access to sophisticated husbandry techniques or machines, but they do often have the inherited wealth of generations of experience.

Ground is cleared at the end of the dry season and the cut material burned to provide important nutrients such as potash and phosphorous. Burning also kills off weeds and pests. Crops are then grown until yields decline significantly, then the land is abandoned and left to regenerate naturally (the fallow period). Figure 12.10 shows the declining yields. This form of farming uses only a few hectares at a time.

(iii) Savannaisation: When fallow is shortened by repeated cultivations within a short period or repeated burning of a forest floor and the subsequent grazing of livestock, the soil nitogen stock – which is primarily locked away in soil organic matter – becomes depleted and a serious limiting factor. Futhermore, under these conditions of great environmental stress the ability of grass rhyzomes (sub-surface 'runners') to survive fires and regenerate rapidly is far greater than the regeneration mechanisms of most tree species. Eventually, therefore, such mismanagement will turn a rain forest into grassland – savanna (Fig. 12.11).

Table 12.1 compares the nutrient stocks of fire-burned grassland and unburned forest. If forest is to become re-established, nutrient stocks will need significant rebuilding. For example, potassium extracted from rainfall alone amounts to about 5 kg/ha/yr, so over 1000 years will be needed to replenish the stocks to levels held in forests.

(iv) Tree crop plantations: Harvesting the fruits or nuts from trees removes only a small amount of biomass. Nevertheless, in order for plantations to be successful in producing large quantities of fruit, plenty of nitrogen must be fixed in the soil. This can, of course, be expensively done using fertilisers, but it can also be achieved by growing other nitrogen-fixing trees in association with the crop. Tree crop cultivation is perhaps one of the most ecologically sensitive uses of the forest, except that the trees are mostly grown as a monoculture and are thus subject to severe and ravaging diseases.

Table 12.1 *In a disturbed system in Gran Pajonal in Amazonia the fire burned grassland has developed quite different nutrient stocks to those of an equivalent unburned forest.*

Vital plant Nutrients kg/ha	Old forest	Grassland
N	15 000	8 000
P	250	5
K	6 500	150
mg	1 000	400

Nitrogen losses will be even more severe because the trees grown do little to return a supply of nitrogen to the ecosystem and stocks may well progressively decline, making nitrogen supply critical to growth. Such long cycles are about the same as harvesting logs on the Arctic Circle...and there trees are mostly left alone!

(v) Pulp plantations: The removal of forests for use in making paper is one of the most damaging uses of the rain forest as the following example shows. In 1967 billionaire industrialist Daniel Ludwig bought 1.6 million hectares of Brazilian rain forest to begin a pulpwood plantation. The 'Jari Project', as it was called, turned out to be a financial and ecological nightmare – a lesson in how important it is to fit in with the natural environment! He cleared the primary forest growth and replaced it with a rapidly growing tree that was normally very suitable for harvesting to make pulp for paper. The new (imported) trees grew unsuccessfully in comparison with their productivity elsewhere in the world, and in 1982 the forest was sold at a loss of millions of dollars. It failed because the removal of logs deprived the forest floor (and subsequently the new trees) of huge quantities of calcium and nitrogen and no-one was prepared to go to the expense of replacing these nutrients artificially.

Better management of tropical rain forests

From the examples studied above, you can see how vulnerable the rain forest ecosystem is and how easily it can be upset. Disturbance by human activity is mostly far more drastic than natural disturbance, and it can have far reach-

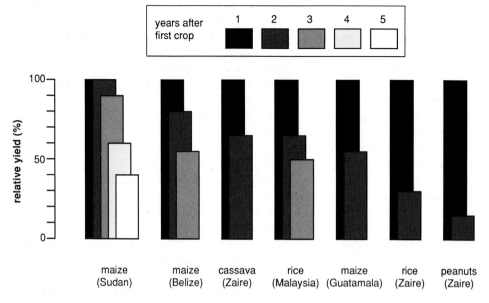

Figure 12.10 *Decline in yield with continued cropping under shifting cultivation in forest environments*

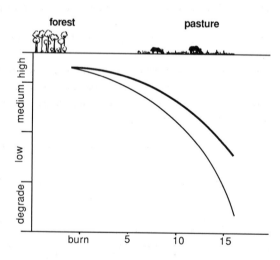

——— 'traditional' system at optimum grazing pressure

——— 'traditional' at grazing pressure above optimum

Figure 12.11 *The changing productivity of cleared forest lands*

ing – even irreversible – consequences. Some of the important effects are summarised:

1. Promotion of a single species (monoculture) presents herbivores with a uniform food source to which they can readily adapt, so becoming a harmful pest. Diversity of species in natural forests protects against one species building to pest proportions;

2. As rain forest soils have a poor nutrient store, removal of plant material (where 99 per cent of all nutrients are stored) can be potentially disastrous. If nutrient supply falls, so does forest production.

3. Some nutrients, for example potassium, are locked away in insoluble compounds. Natural forest species are able to extract these through specially developed mechanisms. Without such mechanisms plants do not grow successfully. Shortage of potassium is a major cause of poor production in previously forested areas;

4. The decomposers below ground are vital components of the nutrient cycle – they must not be destroyed either by pesticides or by changing their habitat drastically;

5. When a forest is cut the decomposers (e.g. bacteria) that release nitrogen and other nutrients remain, whereas those that fix nitrogen (e.g. lichens) are lost and the ecosystem rapidly becomes depleted of vital nutrient stocks.

Better management therefore involves:

1. Employing appropriate techniques to reduce

the amount of fertiliser that is needed, i.e. maintaining soil organic matter – keep burning to a minimum.

2. Maintaining structural diversity of crops – getting as close to the natural ecosystem as possible, e.g. some form of alley cropping or polyculture, so that plant root stocks can use nutrients from as much of the soil as possible, not just one level or one balance of nutrients. This also reduces liability to erosion. Diversity also reduces the pest hazard and utilises incoming radiation more effectively.

3. Minimising soil disturbance – keep heavy machines away and don't use heavy animal densities.

4. Trying to restrict the size of the disturbed area so that nearby undisturbed areas can take up nutrients in the leachate water that would otherwise be lost.

One of the apparent contradictions in the tropical forest areas is that over a few years crop productivity declines rapidly, whereas total net primary productivity of the natural vegetation immediately increases markedly when land is finally abandoned. Measurements have shown that in Amazonia, NPP declined from 5.6 t/ha dry weight in the first year to 4.1 t/ha by the third year, edible crop dropping from 1.4 to 0.7 t/ha in the same time. Yet when abandoned, NPP of the natural succession plants was 7.2, 11.4 and 12.4 t/ha in the next three years (control climax yielded 11.7 t/ha over the same period). Thus it is clear that native species are able to utilise soil nutrients that are unavailable to crop plants. There are several possible reasons for this:

(a) native plants can survive on lower nutrient uptakes whereas crops have been bred for high nutrient uptake and high growth rates under conditions of high fertility;

(b) native plants tend to produce a large total root biomass quickly and can thereby exploit infertile soils;

(c) the leaves of succession plants are long lived and this reduces the need for high nutrient uptake to replace shed leaves;

(d) wild plants need fewer nutrients than crops for the same production of biomass;

(e) native plants on acid soils have a high tolerance of aluminium whereas this may be toxic to crops;

(f) successions have greater species diversity than monoculture crops and are less susceptible to herbivorous predation because host plants are far apart; they also utilise insolation and nutrients more effectively.

To be ecologically and economically successful an agricultural system for the humid tropics should therefore include:

(a) zero tillage and extensive use of plant residue mulches;

(b) mixed crops to include those that are disease and pest resistant;

(c) fertilisers to replace the phosphorous and other nutrients lost during harvesting, or retain a long fallow;

(d) legumes to provide nitrogen for all crops; and

(e) control the soil pH to prevent high acidity and locking up of some nutrients like phosphorus and the release of potentially toxic nutrients like aluminium.

Student enquiry 12A:
The nature of disturbance by people

The objective of this enquiry is to establish, through selected data, the impact of various forms of land use in regions having tropical forests and some of the techniques needed to evaluate the impact.

1. In an experiment in Venezuela a plot was cleared then allowed to regenerate (A1). Its nutrient status was compared with a control, uncut plot (A2). Discuss the losses measured and the time required for regeneration, commenting especially on the relationship between plant succession and soil recovery.

2. Read the account of the Lua' ten year forest pattern (A3) and explain, in the context of nutrient cycling, why this system may be sustainable indefinitely without fertilisation.

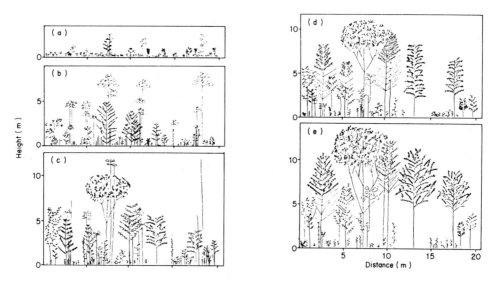

A1 *Scale drawings representing the plants present on a permanent transect during the first five years of succession followin* *cutting and burning of a rainforest plot in the Amazon Territory of Venezuela.* (a) *1 year* (b) *2 years* (c) *3 years* (d) *4 years* (e) *5 years*

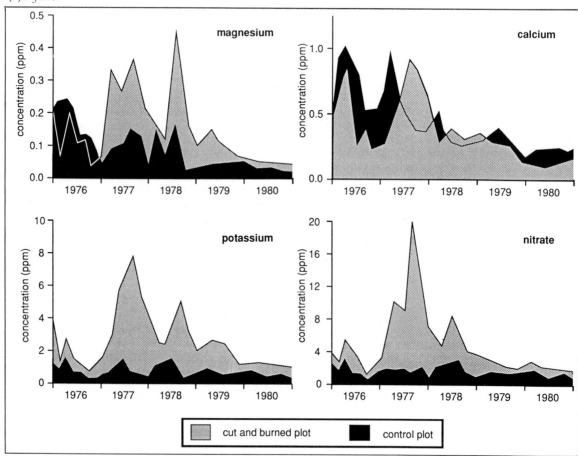

A2

Burning the Fields

The Lua's forest fallow system can be considered as a cycle lasting approximately ten years, beginning and ending in the early part of a dry season when the forest cover is cut in a previously cultivated field (see figure). The trees and other vegetation are felled to lie uniformly: they form a fuel bed which is allowed to dry for six or more weeks. Farmers fell smaller trees, leaving a one-half-meter or one-meter stump from which sprouts may later grow. These stumps show evidence of repeated cutting and coppice growth, confirming the fact that the fields have been used repeatedly. Lua' farmers leave most of the larger trees standing, but trim their branches to reduce shading of the crops.

The fields are burned a few weeks before the end of the dry season. Too late a burn may result in a fuel bed wet by thunderstorms that occur several weeks before the start of the monsoon, while too early a date may find fuel incompletely dried. The approximate date of burning is known several months in advance, and in 1968 the fields were burned on the preselected date of March 25, in coordination with the burning of fields of an adjacent village. Lua' avoid burning during a time of waning moon for fear there will be too many weeds. A leeway of several days is possible if the headman thinks the weather is unfavourable or if a neighbouring village plans to burn their fields at an earlier date.

The burn left a fairly uniform ash bed laid over the fields. Most leaves, branches, and smaller stems were burned. In the next few weeks, the villagers laid charred logs horizontally on the slopes behind stumps to form revetments which are effective in controlling soil creep. They placed as many as 100 logs per hectare, and collected the rest of the larger logs and stems for field border markers, fencing, and firewood. The remainder of unburned slash they piled and reburned in small hot fires. The ash is black over most of the area, with whiter ash where fire temperatures were higher and small regions of white ash and reddened earth where the reburn piles had been.

Villagers plant rice in the ash-covered fields after cleaning up the unburned slash. Men jab the soil with long metal-tipped bamboo poles making about 14 holes per square meter. Women, children and older men follow, casting a few seeds at each hole.

The rice begins to grow with the onset of the monsoon rains, and is harvested toward the end of the rainy reason. Even before the rains begin, soil is moist below about 5 cm, because the early cutting of the forest conserves soil moisture which would otherwise be lost by evapotranspiration in the dry season.

Despite continuous weeding throughout the rice-growing season, herbaceous species, dominated by *Eupatorium odoratum*, cover the swiddens soon after harvest. Most of the trees are not killed by cutting or the fire. They begin sprouting from stumps soon after the fire, and eventually form a coppice of sprout growth shading out most of the herbaceous plants. Thus the fallow fields are eventually dominated by tree species, with some bamboo. A high proportion of presumably nitrogen-fixing leguminous trees occur in the forest fallow vegetation, which grows for about nine years before the cycle is repeated.

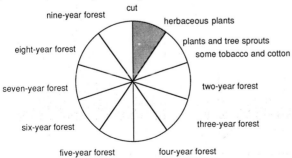

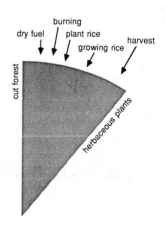

A3

Conserve or manage?

Europe and North America long ago destroyed much of their natural vegetation and wildlife under the heading of expediency. Today we think about the value of other creatures differently, yet many are still endangered, especially in tropical areas where the pressures on land for food brings people into conflict with wildlife. In this section we ask: can wild animals and undisturbed vegetation survive in a world with people?

We can begin by noting that between 1970 and 1980 about twice as many new protected areas were created as in the preceding 100 years. For a long time conservation programmes were widely seen as a restriction to economic development, especially in the developing countries. Today people see that failure to conserve natural resources makes economic nonsense. Presently, mainly due to enlightened self-interest, the conservation areas listed by the UN total 4 million square kilometres – still a tiny proportion of the land surface, but it is growing steadily.

In the same decade came the realisation that conservation could not mean putting a fence around nature and leaving it alone, but rather that the environment should be *managed* in such a way as to give the greatest sustainable benefit now and for the future.

In the previous sections of this chapter, the fundamental ideas of ecosystems have been detailed. From these ideas should develop management practices less destructive than in the past. At the very beginning it was also stressed that ecosystem management carried with it very severe political overtones. The implications of these will be seen in the following material.

Table 12.12 shows the global biome distribution. Notice that some biomes have very small global coverage. How does conservation and management work in practice? Some of the problems can be seen from the case study of the Royal Chitwan Park of Nepal (declared a National Park in 1973). This park consists of 900 km^2 of largely Sal forest (a straight-boled deciduous tree) with stretches of grassland and river marsh. The area contains important collections of rare tiger and rhinoceros (Fig. 12.12). Advantages of the park are:

(a) since 1973 the biomass of hoofed animals

Figure 12.12 *The Royal Chitwan National Park*

has nearly trebled, as poaching has nearly been eliminated. Important species near extinction have been saved;

(b) restrictions on grazing/cutting/burning have led to better water control during the monsoon and fewer landslides;

(c) the tourism revenues have become important to the national economy; and

(d) it provides some direct local employment. However, these advantages have been achieved at the price of conflict with the local people in the following ways:

(a) increases in wildlife populations have caused heavy damage to the agricultural crops, loss of domestic animals and even human injury in the areas around the parks. For example, 30 per cent of the kills by tigers near the park boundaries are of domestic animals;

(b) the park authorities have stopped collection of fuelwood from the park, shooting of any wildlife (an important source of food), collecting thatch from *Imperata cylindrica* grassland, and grazing of domestic animals in the park area; and

(c) the promised benefits from tourism have not yet materialised for the majority of the population.

In 1980 there were 320 villages around the park, housing 261 000 people. Their farming system is mainly cultivation, but they do keep domestic animals, many of which used to graze in the area now designated as park. In order to keep the frustration of the people to a minimum, 7000 villagers were resettled from the area of greatest wildlife nuisance to alternative areas with more fertile soils and no marauding animals. Even so this involved only 10 of the 320 villages around the park and further relocation is not feasible.

Most of the visitors to Chitwan are non-Nepalese and therefore the National Park 'consumers' are 'western' outsiders who have little interest in, or knowledge of, local problems. At the same time most villagers who farm a few hectares do not understand the aesthetic or intellectual arguments for preserving natural ecosystems. They are too busy trying to feed themselves. And how does one explain to the villagers that a tourist can use the National Park for recreation because he is wealthy, while the residents of the area cannot use it because they are poor and therefore in greater need of the resources?

To improve the prospects of the park's long term success and acceptance, the authorities are therefore trying:

(a) to help educate people about the purposes of the park and to talk with them and meet as many of their grievances as possible. In this way local people are beginning to believe they are involved in the park;

(b) more recently local people have been allowed to enter the park to collect grass for building materials over a 15 day period each year. Thus they can collect *Imperata* for thatch and 'elephant grass' canes for house partitions. By allowing the local people regulated access to a resource central to their livelihood, the authorities illustrate one principle of conservation in terms that villagers can understand. Thus there is a practical trade-off that relieves pressure from the local population on the park and gives the villagers part of what they want and partial compensation for wildlife damage.

Table 12.2 *Types of Biome protected throughout the world (mill ha)*

1. Tropical humid forest   47
2. Sub-tropical/temperate rain forest/woodland   11
3. Temperate coniferous forest/woodland   28
4. Tropical dry forests/wood   76
5. Temperature broad-leaved forest/woodland   14
6. Evergreen sclerophyllous (Mediterranean)   8
7. Warm deserts   60
8. Cold winter deserts   7
9. Tundra   101
10. Tropical grassland/savanna   8
11. Temperate grassland (prairie/steppe, etc.)   3
12. Mixed mountain system   28
13. Mixed island system   1
14. Lake system   0.4
Total   ~400

Student enquiry 12B:
Planning for long term management of the natural ecosystem

1. Early morning: a middle-aged woman sits at the base of a buttress-rooted tree in a tropical rain forest within Africa. She is making careful notes on the behaviour of Colobus monkeys trying to establish territories, breeding family sizes and sources of foodstuffs. She is a world-renowned expert on monkey behaviour. Explain why such expertise is an essential input to ecosystem management and suggest how you would use the results of this type of research in planning the size of effective and stable conservation areas.

2. Discuss the following objectives of living resource conservation:

(a) to maintain essential ecological processes and life-support systems;

(b) to preserve genetic diversity;

(c) to ensure that any utilisation of species and ecosystems is sustainable.

3. Draw up a list of priorities for future global planning in conservation. Why might a priority system based simply on area be a naive approach to conservation?

4. Many tropical areas have seen great reductions in the quantity of their natural forests. This creates problems both for the people directly, since they depend on wood for fuel and building, and also for the environment. Mt Kilimanjaro, the 6000 m giant volcano on the borders of Tanzania and Kenya, for example, has been virtually stripped of its tree cover in many areas. Datafile B shows a block diagram of the Himo area on the southern slopes of the volcano, together with the distribution of the natural vegetation and the pressures on each biome. Study the data of block diagrams and suggest, while remaining sympathetic to the lifestyle of nearby subsistence farmers, methods for conserving and managing the area for the long term benefit of the people and the natural ecosystem. One example from the plains is given as a means of guidance. You should consider means of preventing erosion as well as ways of upgrading the ecosystem.

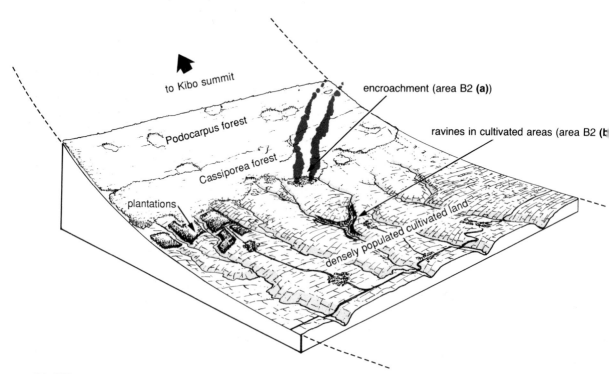

to Kibo summit

Podocarpus forest

Cassiporea forest

plantations

encroachment (area B2 **(a)**)

ravines in cultivated areas (area B2 **(b**

densely populated cultivated land

B1 *Kilimanjaro Forest Reserve*

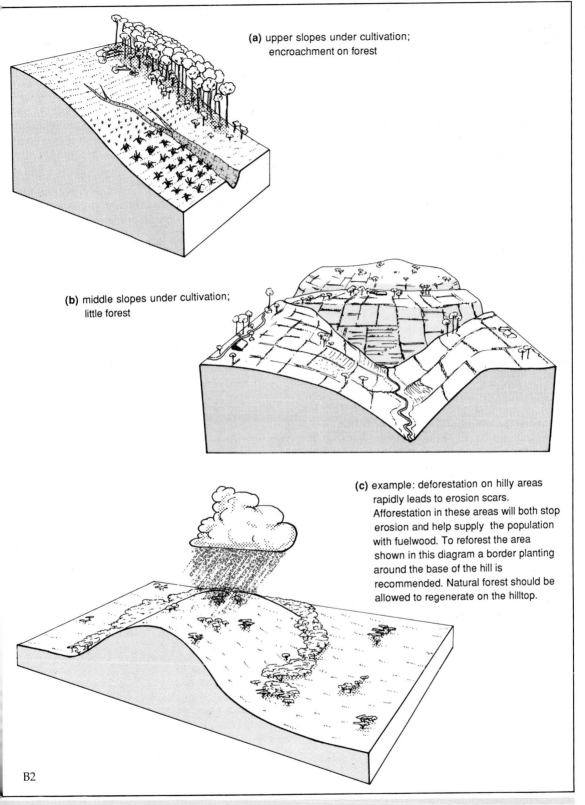

(a) upper slopes under cultivation;
encroachment on forest

(b) middle slopes under cultivation;
little forest

(c) example: deforestation on hilly areas
rapidly leads to erosion scars.
Afforestation in these areas will both stop
erosion and help supply the population
with fuelwood. To reforest the area
shown in this diagram a border planting
around the base of the hill is
recommended. Natural forest should be
allowed to regenerate on the hilltop.

B2

The temperate deciduous forest biome: does it have a future?

There are many fears and problems associated with the industrialised temperate forest zone. Much of Western Europe and the most densely populated parts of the north-east USA lie in a region that could once have reasonably been called the temperate deciduous forest biome. Here oak and elm, beech and maple, hickory and ash clothed the landscape. In woodland glades splashes of light bathed the woodland floor and allowed a great profusion of shrubs and herbs to flourish.

Perhaps this idyllic scene could still have been seen by the Romans in many lowland areas, but already the drier and less heavy soils had been put under the plough and, as the centuries progressed, so more and more land was taken into cultivation. If you stand on many hills in Britain today and look across nearby lowlands the hedgerow trees are super-imposed by the eye to give an impression of what the original forest might have looked like. But in reality the 'natural' vegetation is now confined to narrow strips, and these strips are increasingly under pressure as farmers rip them out to make fields more suitable for mechanised agriculture.

How to recycle a park

In 1930, the long strip of ridge land, some 130 km long and up to 20 km wide, now called Shenandoah National Park in Virginia, USA was entirely private property. There were some large tracts of badly eroded second-rate pasture and cut-over timberland. There were also hundreds of small subsistence farms that were the sole means of survival of 2000 people. All had to be resettled.

The park has been described as 'recycled' because it started with ruined land which, under the protection of the National Park Service, has begun its long recovery towards primitive forest, and has reached the interme-diate stage seen today.

It was acquired piecemeal by purchases of land from private landowners over a period of time, a process that is continuing. The re-

covery of this land from human abuse, and the succession of plant and animal life that goes with such recovery, will continue. Some roads will become trails and some trails will vanish. The number of visitors will increase and the park personnel must cope with the resulting pressures. The park has recently spent large sums to build new sewage treatment works; eventually it may be necessary to ration access to the park in order to protect those things the park was created to preserve. Each year the 195 000 acres are visited by 3 million people using 500 km of road and 800 km of trail. There are five campgrounds, eight picnic areas, six

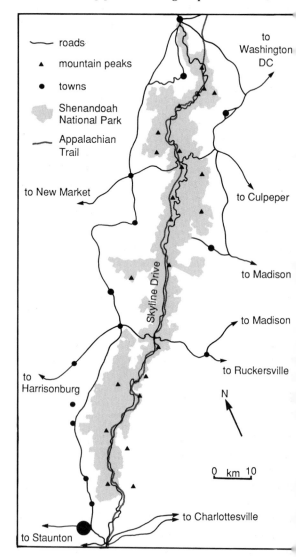

Figure 12.13 *Shenandoah National Park, USA*

restaurants and two lodges with accommodation for 911 people.

In Shenandoah the removal of the farmers and the creation of the park allowed thistles and brambles to move quickly back on to the abandoned meadows; then black locust, hazel and pine followed. In the cut-over forests young oaks and hickories grew unhindered and began slowly to replace the pioneer species in the meadows. With the return of food and cover the birds came back, the small mammals and finally the deer, the bear and the cougar. The change goes on. If the wilderness remains undisturbed it will begin, within a century or two, to approach the climax forest that the first settlers found there. But it can never return entirely to its primitive state because the area is too small, too closely hemmed in by civilisation.

The park is a living museum of nature, and to fulfil this role all remains of the former settlers must be removed and the majority of roads closed. Trails are maintained but only one person wide – and maintenance is small – a wilderness is for solitude, you don't want it spoilt by hordes of maintenance men with noisy clearing machines.

Many national parks throughout the world have been 'recycled' in various ways. Once they have been taken under the public wing people have to be shown the treasure that is preserved on their behalf. This is partly achieved through information materials. Figure 12.14 is an example of part of a nature trail guide produced for the Grand Tetons National Park. It shows one way of helping educate people in some of the benefits of a national park.

Ensuring the global ecosystem survives

The global ecosystem has undergone many changes, depending on the demands put on it by society at the time. Recently there has been much public concern over the amount of natural land still left within the industrial world. The emergence of political 'Green' parties show this only too well. The reasons for this concern are diverse. They can be summarised as:

(a) romantic ideas of what the country should look like;
(b) desire to experience recreation;
(c) concern for the natural ecosystem;
(d) reaction against the 'industrial society'.

There is, however, widespread ignorance of natural ecosystems, how the natural ecosystem works and when it is under real danger. This is shown by the following example.

The mushrooms and the berries

In Sweden the high standards of living have led to an increased use of the forests for recreation. At the same time the higher levels of technology have enabled forestry to be undertaken with greater efficiency. Forestry accounts for over a fifth of the GNP of Sweden, but although it is one of the country's major resources, there has recently been intense conflict between the public and the forestry authority over the methods used to run the forest industry. And the debate is not over dying trees or soil erosion – but over mushrooms and berries. This is because over 80 per cent of the adult population of Sweden collect forest mushrooms and berries: indeed there is unrestricted right to do so by law, on public or private land. As it happens people are not very efficient at their harvesting and they pick perhaps no more than 10 per cent of the total yield of mushrooms and berries. Nevertheless, they have objected strongly to the use of fertilisers and biocides over even small areas of the forests. The conflict is thus typical of that prevalent in the developed world. On the one hand the public expect industry to maintain an economic resource at its highest possible efficiency so that it will provide the basis of a continued high standard of living. However, at the same time they wish to put as many obstacles in its way as possible in order to improve the 'quality of life'. As we will see, many ecological debates are not really about the ecosystem, but about the conflict between those with the power to decide the fate of the resource (the owners) and those of the public who feel a sense of anxiety and helplessness in a technocratic society.

Although only 10 per cent of the mushrooms and berries are actually harvested by people, day to day experience of gathering in the forest gives them a very different impression, and many feel that the resource might run out and that berries and mushrooms contaminated with herbicides and fertilisers will be harmful as well as unpleasant to taste. They fear this because clearcutting forests destroys the environments for both berries and mushrooms, and at least ten years is required before a new tree planting will provide a suitable habitat. Yet only 1 per cent of forest is clearcut each year and areas that have been sprayed are clearly posted. Decisions about human use of ecosystems and their future are clearly not simply a matter of scientific knowledge, but require a combination of science and an understanding of human nature. The same problem comes up again over the removal of hedgerows in Britain. Most people have a 'gut feeling' that hedge removal is a bad thing for the environment, although they still want farmers to produce more. The need for a biological basis for decision-making is clearly paramount in the developed world, just as it is in the developing world. But people are only just coming up with the answers.

The importance of island biogeography

Land is subject to many pressures. Practical conservation or 'management' is concerned with deciding priorities of land use and balancing people's needs against those of other species. This conflict is clearly seen in the article 'Ecology big guns train on the army'.

Perhaps the biggest pressure is gradually to eat into undeveloped land, causing its fragmentation. You can see this particularly at the edge of suburban areas where one housing estate seems often to follow another on to 'green field' sites. One way to move forward from a sound basis is to use the concept of **island biogeography**. This treats the species composition of islands of undisturbed land as the result of a dynamic balance between extinctions and colonisations (Fig. 12.14).

Suppose a previously continuous area of woodland is broken into several fragments, as might happen due to urban encroachment or agricultural reclamation. Each fragment then becomes effectively an island. In each island there are two types of species:

(a) those susceptible to extinction because they are not good at dispersal between islands; and
(b) those that are resilient to extinction because they are good at colonising islands.

When the original habitat is in large blocks little change is first observed if those blocks are divided. However, as fragmentation proceeds the susceptible species become extinct at an increasingly rapid rate.

This model can be used to show how to manage land. Where large amounts of original habitat remain undisturbed, it is important to try to preserve its integrity. But if the area has already been fragmented and is under further pressure, the larger fragments should receive the highest priority in preservation, and the smaller areas should be sacrificed because the large areas are still likely to contain more of the susceptible species.

Some species become extinct because the islands are too small to support them. For example carnivorous birds such as the marsh harrier need tens of square kilometres of territory per breeding pair. However, there are further reasons for rapid extinction. As the islands become smaller the distance from the centre of the island to the boundary decreases. The boundary is a place of battle between colonisers from the surrounding countryside, and the place from which susceptible species are quickly driven. There comes a stage, therefore, when the island becomes so small that the boundary 'battle zone' extends to the centre. At this stage there is a rapid rise in the number of species going extinct. It is therefore vital to know the size of the buffer zone required to prevent extinctions. Any clearing is a battle zone, and thus woodland clearings can be as much of a menace to survival as losses from the outside edge.

The conclusions from this are that if a large area exists, breaking it up will increasingly threaten the number of species; such action should be resisted; if a reduction in its area must occur, nibbling at the edges is a better solution. But if the area is already fragmented, then, from the point of view of preserving species, one should sacrifice the smallest areas

Stop 3 How many animals have you seen on your trip? When we are asked such a question, most of us would immediately begin to tally up all the bear, elk, moose and bison that we might have seen. But what about the smaller animals — the birds, the rodents, and a multitude of insects?

They are animals, too, and many have far more interesting life patterns than the larger animals. Now look again for the smaller animals. They make up the basis of a food pyramid at the top of which we find ourselves, cougar, coyote, otter and others. Now close your eyes and listen. You're expanding not only your tally sheet but also your natural senses, the very senses that wild animals depend upon for survival. Now look for other evidences of wildlife. The scarred bark of aspen tells us that porcupine, elk or perhaps bear have crossed this trail. Look for the tracks of the smaller animals as we go to the next stop.

Published by the

GRAND TETON NATURAL HISTORY ASSOCIATION

A nonprofit organization pledged to aid in the preservation and interpretation of the scenic and scientific features of the park. In cooperation with

THE NATIONAL PARK SERVICE
DEPARTMENT OF THE INTERIOR

Extracts from
Park Trail leaflet

A Guide for Adults

OXBOW BEND N.E.S.A. TRAIL

Text: Robert A. Huggins/Illustrations: Ted Sharpe

Figure 12.14 *Which species can survive in fragments of forest? Population biologists are coming up with practical answers for managers*

completely rather than allow the large ones to be nibbled.

This problem has confronted many people. In Britain areas in danger of species extinction have been designated SSSIs (Sites of Special Scientific Interest). The SSSIs are a sort of conservation skeleton, preserving the minimum number of habitats needed to preserve maximum species variety in our country. But they can be put under threat by the need, for example, of a new road. Because they are protected sites they have no development value. So on a cost/benefit basis it will be cheaper to build through an SSSI than through, say, a suburbanised area. But, although it may be argued that the road takes up little space, the island theory outlined above shows that a road will introduce two new boundaries, and thus cause considerable damage to an SSSI right into its heartland, just the place that should be protected most vigorously.

Conservation and management at low cost

Pressure on the countryside requires many solutions. The theory of size has been outlined above. But we can use the theory in a positive way to encourage the preservation of low productivity areas as well as to try to defend from encroachment. Here are some examples:
(a) the inside bend of a meander, which presents difficult access for farm machinery, could be left as woodland, and an oxbow could be left as wetland;
(b) trees can be used to help stabilise eroding banks of a river; if they are planted on a south bank instead of using piles, not only will they protect the bank, but as no usefully productive land is shaded they will only provide shade over the river, where it will be vital to a diversity of aquatic life;
(c) areas near streams have a low productivity

237

due to the difficulties of drainage, but they are pleasant places for walks. If farmers made access to stream bank footpaths easy, then people would be less liable to trample over other parts of their land. Without the destructive effects of pesticides and herbicides, such linear parks would also encourage the diversity of wildlife.

One example of such imaginative action is provided by the Fermilab nuclear research facility near Chicago, Illinois, USA (Fig. 12.15). Of a potential 145 000 km² of prairie, only 10–12 km² remain intact. Clearly the situation is desperate. But inside the land occupied by the particle accelerator Fermilab have allocated 184 ha for reconstruction as a prairie. Tiny though this may be, with careful selection of native prairie species just one more patch of the environment is being actively preserved.

Figure 12.15 *Within the accelerator ring at Fermilab lies the grassland that has gradually been restored to prairie over the past decade*

Student enquiry 12C: Ecological planning in action: management and conservation

The environmental situation of many towns leaves something to be desired. In this activity you are asked to use maps of your local area to find a suitable location for a new country park. For this purpose assume you are the local planning officer.

Acquire the following base information:
(a) present and past use of the town and surrounding area;
(b) land capability map;
(c) future planning land use;
(d) geology map;
(e) topography map;
(f) flood-prone hazard map;
(g) road system.

You should decide on a bold and imaginative

plan which has the following features:

(a) a nature trail for teachers and children;
(b) maximise ecological diversity;
(c) segregate functions by zoning;
(d) provision for sailing, golf, fishing, wildlife watching, horse riding, walking;
(e) a good car park;
(f) maximise the number of managed environments;
(g) provide an area large enough for reasonably trophic levels to be maintained, e.g. deer and hawks;
(h) finance will be provided from the rates, explaining that, if people want recreation they must be prepared to pay for it;
(i) hold the option of renting or buying land from farmers, or paying farmers to conserve parts of their land. It is argued that, in a country where food surpluses are a problem, it is not necessarily best to devote all land for agricultural use at high intensity, but that any land use changes should not cause hardship to the farmers. Farmers are to be encouraged to be real custodians of the landscape.

You will also have in your mind:
(j) a report about the success of concentric land zoning, (extract attached);
(k) a report on ecosystems that stresses the demands of conservationists;
(l) projections for future land use for recreation and leisure (you could base this on a sample questionnaire survey and census data);
(m) the nature trail handout, an extract of which is in Figure 12.14;
(n) the sort of scenario that has occurred in many towns similar to yours and parodied in the example of Hayston (attached).

Activity objectives
1. From these articles establish the main pressures on the recreation and leisure department.
2. Given the remit and the information in enquiry C suggest a pattern of development that your department might put forward to the full council and which would take account of all pressure groups.
3. Make up a descriptive illustrated brochure that could be used to support the proposal when it is launched on the public.

Part of a report on concentric zoning

...Perhaps the landscape should be recognised as serving two separate functions, one protective, the other productive; with the protective area confined to the least productive parts of the landscape. But would it be possible to protect areas for amenity use in the midst of a sea of intensive farmland? The highest levels of the food chains, predators such as marsh harriers, need large territories for survival. Reserves of land thus need to be substantial before they can yield stable ecosystems. Where will further large viable units of land be found? Mainly they will include such areas as golf courses, country estates and managed forests. They will have to be wherever they may be rather than built around areas of special scientific interest which may lie in land otherwise quite unsuited to amenity development.

If sufficiently large areas can be zoned from agricultural use, they can be further zoned in a concentric way, with the outer, most visited, areas acting as buffers to the remoter central areas, which can be used as sanctuaries. Some features of the zoning concept have been adopted in Sussex, where the East Sussex County Council has bought 280ha of chalk cliffs adjacent to the Cuckmere estuary and declared it 'The Seven Sisters Country Park'. Next to it are 800 ha of Forestry Commission beech wood, National Trust and local council lands, all of which can be integrated when planning land use policy....

The establishment of a country park
Hayston is a growing town of 200 000 people. It has some formal parks laid out in Victorian times, but these are now far from the growing suburbs. The suburbs are enclosed by farmland with very limited public access. In a recent public meeting of the town council there was yet more lobbying for the town, in conjunction with surrounding district and county councils, to improve the recreation facilities for the townspeople. Some of the arguments are summarised in articles in the local *Evening Post* and *Echo*.

People slam council

The poor facilities for recreation in Hayston are now recognised as a public scandal, according to Mr A.T. Grave, the chairman of a recently established pressure group 'Sport for all'. If, he argued, a century ago the Victorians recognised the value of open space and laid out parks, why can't we also see their advantages. Since these times the percentage of recreation land per person has dropped by half. What, Mr Grave wanted to know, was the council's policy?

Mr Sowerby, speaking on behalf of the recreation and leisure department, commented on how difficult it was to get the money to buy new land. However, he assured Mr Grave that his department were actively investigating the development of a comprehensive plan.

Dr Bog then spoke for the Conservation Group, 'Heritage near Hayston', declaring that he hoped due attention would be paid to the needs of natural vegetation and hedgerows. 'After all, farmers are still grubbing up hedgerows and spraying pesticides and fungicides everywhere, to say nothing of all this land drainage which is changing the environment for wild flowers. Where is it all going to end?' Dr Bog asked, threatening to organise a lie in on a hawthorn hedge whose destruction has recently received planning permission.

Our reporter said the meeting broke up in disarray.

Daily Echo

County must find more room for development

In a recent report from the government, the county planners have been told they must find room for another 60 000 people in each of the next three 10 year periods. At 1/16 ha/family this means 20 000 families and 1500 ha of new land in each 10 year period must be grabbed in a county already described by local residents as 'overcrowded'. The county has said it will appeal and villagers faced with being overwhelmed by housing estates have already formed protest groups. 'Where will they seek recreation and leisure – by running all over our fields,' one angry farmer told me. . . .

Key terms

Biome: the largest recognisable vegetation assemblage that shows some unity (e.g. savanna).

Carrying capacity: the maximum number of any organism that can be supported by an ecosystem without degradation.

Climax: the most developed form of ecosystem in which organisms fully utilise their environment and leave no niche for further competition or colonisation.

Colonisation: the arrival and establishment of an organism at a new site.

Ecosystem: a closely interdependent system of soil, vegetation and animals.

Food chain (web): a sequence (network) of organisms each dependent on another as a source of food.

Habitat: the environment in which a species lives.

Net primary productivity (NPP): the amount of added growth each year (i.e. gross growth less leaf fall).

Prairie (steppe, pampas): a temperate grassland area of low rainfall, often showing adaptations to very hot summers and very cold winters.

Rain forest: a forest where moisture stress is not a limiting factor. This term is often loosely used as equivalent to tropical rain forest, but there are other types of rain forest (e.g. broad-leaved temperate rain forests in Europe and North America).

Savanna: a tropical mosaic of grasslands and trees showing a pronounced seasonal character because of a long dry season.

Succession: a sequence of stages during which the balance of organisms changes within an ecosystem.

Taiga: the northern coniferous forest zone of high (boreal) latitudes.

Trophic level: the position of an organism in the dependence hierarchy (e.g. plants are the first level; plant-eating animals (herbivores) are the second).

Tundra: the dwarf shrub zone of the very high latitudes where conditions are too severe for tree growth.

Chapter 13
The challenge of using soils

Introduction

Soils are an integral part of the environment (Fig. 13.1). Everyone on earth depends directly on the soil, for without it no crops would grow and life would cease.

Soils result from the breakdown of mineral matter *and* the incorporation of decomposed organic matter They are far from independent of their environment, being influenced by five fundamental natural soil forming factors:

(a) climate;

(b) the material on which they form;

(c) vegetation and soil animals;

(d) the nature of the landscape; and

(e) the length of time they have been forming.

They are also influenced by:

(f) people.

Soils vary widely both laterally and vertically. Some soils are deep and fertile, others shallow and stony, yet others can be waterlogged, or

acid and infertile. It is possible to recognise several hundred types of different soils in Britain alone, and many thousand types world wide. Such variety also makes a classification necessary.

It is common to classify soils into a hierarchy consisting of four levels. At the broadest and highest level soils are grouped according to the *dominant process* influencing their development. These are called **major soil groups** and ten of them cover Britain (see Fig. 13.5). These can then be subdivided into **soil series**. This classification is achieved using characteristics such as texture, degree of stoniness and mineral

Figure 13.1 *Dependence on soil makes it important to understand how soils work*

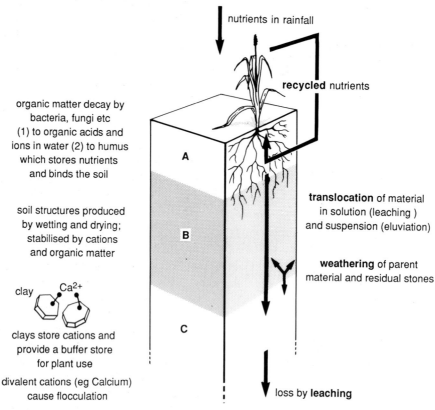

nutrients in rainfall

recycled nutrients

organic matter decay by
bacteria, fungi etc
(1) to organic acids and
ions in water (2) to humus
which stores nutrients
and binds the soil

A

translocation of material
in solution (leaching)
and suspension (eluviation)

soil structures produced
by wetting and drying;
stabilised by cations
and organic matter

B

weathering of parent
material and residual stones

clay   Ca²⁺

clays store cations and
provide a buffer store
for plant use

C

divalent cations (eg Calcium)
cause flocculation

loss by **leaching**

Figure 13.2 *Soil processes*

composition. It is widely used by farmers, planners and engineers to assess the potential uses and productivity of an area of land.

In Britain the natural process of weathering will commonly form 100 tonnes of new soil per square kilometre per year, while other natural processes such as loss in solution and soil creep remove about a tenth of this amount. Thus soils in undisturbed ecosystems in humid climates should get progressively thicker. Even at this seemingly rapid rate of weathering, soils take thousands of years to form. By contrast, they can be destroyed in a fraction of that time by the actions of people. At present rates of loss it has been calculated that by the end of the century there will be a third less topsoil throughout the world per person than there is today. Intensive farming, overgrazing and de-forestation can all cause soils to be rendered useless – management of soils is therefore essential. To do this effectively it is important to understand the processes of soil formation.

Soil formation

Soils are mostly produced from chemical weathering (Fig. 13.2). The reaction of rainwater (sometimes acidified by gases dissolved from the atmosphere) with the parent material causes the formation of new materials made of tiny plate-like crystals which we know as **clay minerals**. But the creation of these new minerals does not use all the products of weathering. These 'left-overs' remain in solution. Some are the vital nutrients needed by plants for continued growth. The five natural soil-forming factors each have a specific role:

(a) Climate

As a general rule, climate dominates soil formation. It controls the balance between percolation and transpiration in soils that drain well, and also the amount of plant matter that can grow. Thus, as the climate becomes drier the mass of plant material decreases and there is

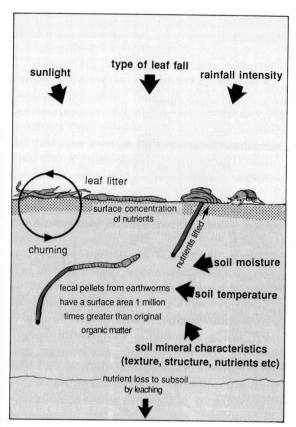

Figure 13.3 *Soil decomposers*

ing is plate-like clay minerals. Clay minerals (which carry a negative charge) are vital to a soil because they are able to retain the positively charged nutrients (cations such as calcium and potassium) released to the soil water during weathering.

The fertility of a soil is closely connected with the nature of weathering. As a general rule, soils containing a high proportion of clay minerals tend to be more **fertile** than those that do not. Clay minerals also affect the strength of a soil as they **flocculate** (group together) to form larger particles which make the soil more resistant to erosion.

(c) Vegetation and soil animals

Organic matter consists primarily of leaf litter and is vital in the formation of a soil. This material is a huge source of nutrients which are released as it decomposes (Fig. 13.3).

There are two products of organic matter decay, just as there are two products of mineral weathering. The equivalent of clay minerals is called **humus**. Humus is made of long chain molecules which are physically sticky and can bind all kinds of soil particles together. They have an especially vital role in preventing soil erosion. The other product is ions, many of which are nutrients. Humus has a negative charge and is at least as important as clay minerals in retaining nutrients in the soil.

The character of the growing vegetation sometimes influences soils. Replacement of broad-leaved forest with a coniferous forest always leads to severe leaching because conifers do not recycle nutrients as quickly as broad-leaves. Coniferous plantations often cause a fertile brown earth to degenerate into an infertile acid podzol.

(d) Nature of the landscape

Soils on slopes tend to drain well. Those on upper slopes may drain excessively and lose many ions by leaching. Soils near streams tend to become waterlogged (**gleyed**).

(e) Time of development

Soils take many thousands of years to form.

correspondingly less humus created to prevent erosion. Where it is cold plant transpiration is small and soils either experience increased leaching loss or they become totally waterlogged.

(b) Parent material

The material that is weathered to make the soil skeleton is called the **parent material**. It may be solid rock, or unconsolidated mineral particles brought by rivers, slope processes, wind or glaciers. Many of the properties of a soil are inherited from the character of its parent material. The **texture** of a soil – the proportion of sand, silt and clay sized particles – is a good example of an inherited characteristic. The parent material also plays an important role in influencing the amount of nutrients in a soil that can be used by plants for growth.

Most soils are formed by chemical weathering (Fig. 13.2). The residue of this type of weather-

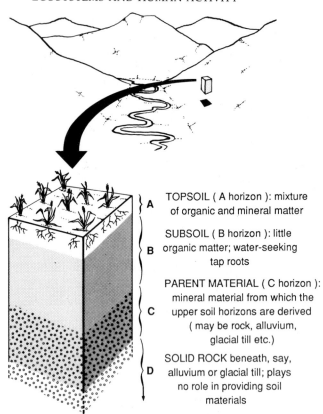

TOPSOIL (A horizon): mixture of organic and mineral matter

SUBSOIL (B horizon): little organic matter; water-seeking tap roots

PARENT MATERIAL (C horizon): mineral material from which the upper soil horizons are derived (may be rock, alluvium, glacial till etc.)

SOLID ROCK beneath, say, alluvium or glacial till; plays no role in providing soil materials

Figure 13.4 *Soil in the landscape*

Most soils in Britain are still developing and many of them are forming on glacial till or peri-glacial materials.

The soil profile

The most common way to examine the soil is to dig a pit and examine one of its faces. This gives a soil 'fingerprint' called the **soil profile** (Fig. 13.4). The profile usually shows that the soil is formed of layers – called **soil horizons**. Normally the horizons will be darker near the surface (the **topsoil** or A horizon), indicating that organic material has been decomposed into black humus and then coated over the mineral grains.

The **subsoil** (or B horizon) contains far less organic material that the topsoil and is there-fore lighter in colour. The subsoil is a kind of transition zone between the more or less com-pletely weathered topsoil and the unweathered

parent material (the C horizon). Thus frag-ments of unweathered rock (stones) would be expected to occur more frequently towards the lower part of the subsoil.

A soil dominated by weathering normally has merging boundaries between horizons because there are many organisms such as earthworms, to mix materials together. Thus it would be common to find such a soil displaying a dark brown surface, but grading to a lighter brown at depth. To indicate that the main pro-cess in the topsoil is humus creation and the main process in the subsoil is mineral weather-ing, the topsoil is designated A (top) h (humus) and the subsoil B and w (weathering). Continu-ing to use the alphabet gives the letter C for parent material (Fig. 13.4). The well drained brown soil referred to under major soil groups earlier thus has an Ah/Bw/C profile and is called a **brown earth** (Fig. 13.5). It is the best agricultural soil in Britain. The equivalent in the tropics is a red-coloured soil, but the processes and horizon sequence is the same.

It is quite normal for materials continually to be lost from the soil profile in solution. This is one way the landscape forms. If the combined effects of weathering and recycling retain suffi-cient nutrients for fertility and soil stability then a brown earth forms. However, in many circum-stances the rate of leaching exceeds the release of ions. This change in the balance of processes has several effects:

(a) the small clays in the topsoil become separ-ated and are readily washed down the soil profile, where they tend to block the subsoil pores, leading to topsoil waterlogging. This form of translocation is called **eluviation** (de-signated by E);

(b) the top soil becomes more acid and less fertile; and

(c) the number of soil organisms that can sur-vive decreases.

If this change is very pronounced then earth-worms will no longer be able to survive and there will be no mechanism for mixing topsoil materials. As a result the topsoil horizons will be seen as distinct horizons. At the same time the nature of organic material decay changes so that the strong acids released by the first stage of decay (mineralisation) are not reformed into

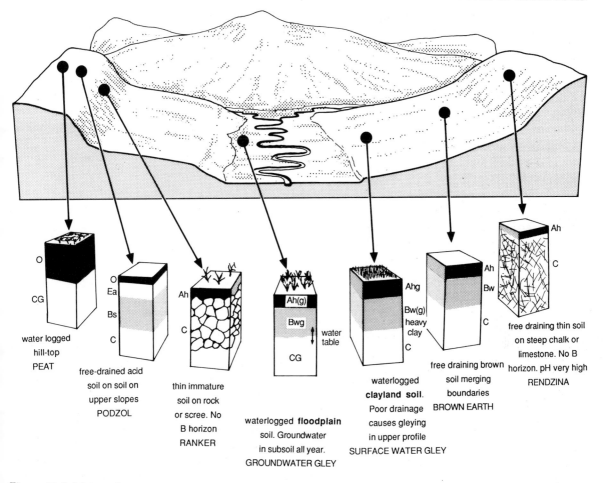

Figure 13.5 *Major soil groups in the landscape of Britain*

humus (humification). These acids are then free to combine with iron and aluminium oxides in the topsoil, dissolving them and carrying them down to the subsoil. This leaves part of the topsoil ashen coloured (now designated Ea), and imparts a striking orange stain on the subsoil (now designated Bs). Such **podzol** soils are always infertile and, with no cation or humus bonding, also readily blown or washed away if their surface cover is removed.

Making use of soil mapping and soil properties

The theory of soil formation is an essential pre-requisite to the successful interpretation of soil information. Soil maps are required to assess the usefulness of soil to the community at large

and commonly form one major element in planning proposals. For this purpose some assessment must be made of the suitability of the soil for agriculture assuming a reasonably high level of management. This economic benefit can then be weighed against the benefits that might be gained by changing the land use to, say, the site of a hypermarket or the route of a new road.

The capability of land is not really controlled by chemical problems such as acidity. These can be corrected by suitable fertilisers. But physical problems often take much more money and effort to overcome. For example, if a soil is very stony or is on very steep land mechanical cultivation will not be possible and the value of the land is thus reduced. Soils with a heavy clay texture might be 'cold' and give poor yields, and they may not stand working by heavy machinery or trampling by animals. Soils that are frequently waterlogged can be drained, but only to some degree, and thus this, too, is a significant limitation. Other soils are very liable to erosion if exposed or if they dry out rapidly and need irrigation, and this limits the range of use to which they can be put, and again decreases their value. The Soil Survey has developed a seven class scale of land capability to help evaluate soil potential (Table 13.1).

Soil surveys are also widely used by civil engineers for two purposes: (a) to help find the strength of the soil on which they may need to build; and (b) to help find out the likely drainage requirements of their construction site. The natural degree of drainage will be indicated both by the overall character of the soil profile (i.e. is it a gleyed soil?) and the degree of gleying.

Student enquiry 13A:
Using soils in planning

Table 13.1

Class	Gradient	Climate	Wetness	Soil	Erosion
1	Not above 7°, but usually below 5°	usually below 500 ft	not a limitation; soils are usually well or moderately well drained, with some imperfectly drained in areas of low rainfall (< 750 mm)	usually loams, sandy or silt loams, or humose variants deeper than 75 cm, or peat; stoneless or only slightly stony	risk should be very slight
2	not above 7°	usually below 750 ft	soils subject to this limitation are usually moderately well or imperfectly drained	soils usually have a rooting depth > 50 cm; stoneless or slightly stony; clays in wet areas and coarse sands or loamy coarse sands in areas with low summer rainfall should be excluded	wind erosion is possible in some eastern areas, affecting root crops, such as sugar beet, red beet, and carrots, growing in light peat. Otherwise risks should be slight.
3	not above 11°	usually below 1250 ft; *land over 400 ft with more than 1000 mm annual rainfall (1020 mm in western Britain) not better than class 3*	usually imperfectly or poorly drained soils where an effective drainage scheme has been, or could be, installed. There will be a continuing wetness limitation even after drainage	rooting depth is usually > 25 cm; textures range from stoneless to stony and sandy to clayey	risk should be slight
4	not above 15°	land with more than 1250 mm annual rainfall *usually not better than class 4*	poorly drained soils, with or without peat, requiring a comprehensive drainage scheme, but where piecemeal drainage has, or could, effect improvements; land may be subject to occasional damaging floods	soils sufficiently deep to allow ploughing; they may be very stony and with a wide range of texture	risk should be low; some difficulties may be encountered with sandy soils in exposed areas
5	not over 23° but usually below 20°	usually below 1750 ft; *land over 600 ft with more than 1250 mm annual rainfall not better than class 5*	very poor or poorly drained land where drainage can be improved to maintain grassland; land may be subject to floods	only rocky, boulder-strewn soils which prevent mechanized improvement are excluded from this class	mountain soils may be subject to severe erosion without expert management, and some soils are liable to be eroded by wind if the natural vegetation cover is destroyed
6	level to over 25°	usually below 2000 ft; *land over 1000 ft with more than 1500 mm annual rainfall not better than class 5*	very poorly drained peat or humose soils of the uplands, and estuarine marshes or undrained peats of the lowlands	extremely stony, rocky or boulder-strewn land, with enough vegetation to maintain grazing	severe hazard on steep slopes
7	level to over 25°	land over 2000 ft (1750 ft in the Western and Central Highlands)	usually very poorly drained soils	extremely stony, rocky or boulder strewn soils, bare rock, scree or beach sands and gravels	severe

The purpose of this activity is to show how a soil capability map can be used as one means of coming to objective planning decisions. These decisions will then be weighed with other social and political issues before a final decision is reached.

The Department of the Environment wishes to realign a major road and seeks to take the shortest route that avoids built-up areas. This will take it over some previously undisturbed farmland (a 'green field site'). The local farmers protest that this will involve the loss of irreplaceable land. A soil survey is commissioned with the purpose of providing a base map for more detailed planning.

1. You will need to produce two maps as tracing overlays:

(a) a land use capability map; and

(b) a map suitable for civil engineering purposes.

urban area

podzol

brown earth

surface water gley

ground water gley

rendzina

A1(a)

To produce the land capability map use the information of the survey and Table 13.1. The tracing overlay should then only show classes 1–7. Shade them in accordingly. The engineering map is produced from the strength and wetness data of the survey.

2. On each prepared map suggest a route for the road alignment, using only the information on that map; then compare the two routes and suggest a compromise. Write a short explanation of the reasons for your compromise.

SOIL GROUP	PARENT MATERIAL	SOIL BEARING STRENGTH	SOIL SERIES
RENDZINA	chalk rock	high	I
RANKER	chalk rubble	low	R
BROWN EARTH	heavy clay	moderate moderate moderate moderate	AS BR CM C
POPOL	coarse gravel	high	P_0
GROUNDWATER GLEY	alluvium (mainly clay)	low	GWG
SURFACEWATER GLEY	heavy clay	low moderate	S SWG
PEAT		low	

A1(b)

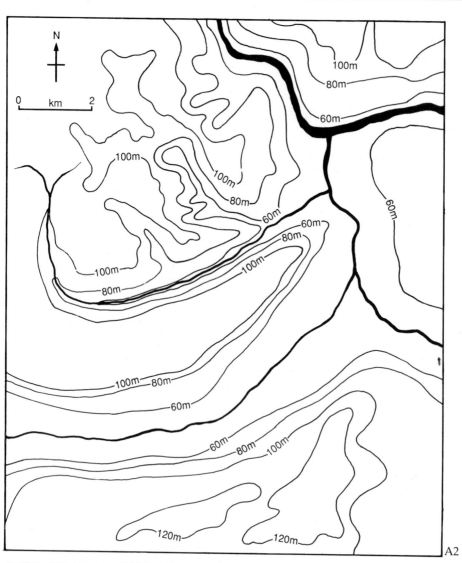

A2

Key terms

Acidity: is a measure of the hydrogen ion concentration in the soil. Measurements use the pH scale where 7 is neutral (10^{-7} gm/H+/litre of solution); values smaller than 7 are acid; larger than 7 alkaline.

Cellulose: the 'fleshy' part of tissue containing simple chain sugars; it readily decomposes.

Divalent cation: positively charged ions with sufficient charge to link together two clay particles (e.g. calcium, Ca^{2+}). Vital for stable soil structure and prevention of erosion.

Eluviation: the physical washing from the A horizon of small suspended soil particles downward with percolating water.

Flocculation: the grouping of clay particles using divalent cations.

Gleying: the process of oxygen depletion by bacteria in a (stagnant) waterlogged soil. Gleyed soils have their iron compounds changed from ferric browns and reds to ferrous blues and greys.

Horizon: a layer of soil that has characteristics different from adjacent layers. The **terminology** is as follows:

O surface organic horizon not incorporated into the mineral soil.

A the surface (topsoil) horizon in which there is mixing of mineral and organic matter.

E a near surface horizon showing evidence of loss.

  Eb: still retains brown colour with loss of clays and some calcium;

  Ea: an ash-coloured horizon with loss of iron and aluminium as well as clays and calcium.

B a subsurface (subsoil) horizon without organic matter.

  Bw dominated by weathering only;

  Bt containing clays washed from the topsoil;

  Bs containing iron and aluminium as well as clays (orange colour).

C little altered parent material.

  g gleyed horizon (showing evidence of waterlogging).

Humification: the production of humus from simple acids released by mineralisation.

Humus: fully decayed organic matter showing no traces of original tissue.

Ion: a charged atom (**cation:** a positively charged ion e.g. calcium Ca^{2+}, hydrogen, H^+: **anion**, a negatively charged ion e.g. nitrate, NO^{3-}). Some ions are also **nutrients**.

Illuviation: the precipitation of leached and eluvial particles in the B horizon.

Laterite: an old term for a tropical soil dominated by an iron and aluminium rich horizon that becomes rock-like when exposed to the air.

Leaching: the downward translocation of soluble ions in solution.

Lignin: the 'structural' part of tissue (bark, veins, etc.) where cellulose has been impregnated with various substances to make it more rigid; it is resistant to decay.

Litter: the surface accumulation of dead plant remains.

Major soil group: the broad grouping of similar soils based on dominant formation process (e.g. brown earths are dominated by weathering; podzols are dominated by severe translocation, including movement of iron).

Mineralisation: the breakdown of organic matter whereby simple acids and ions are released (see humification).

Mineral matter: the non-organic solid constituents of a soil.

Photosynthesis: the process of building tissue using the sun's energy.

Organic matter: for soil purposes, all dead organic tissue. Humus is vital for the storage of ions (nutrients) and (because some forms are long sticky threads) for soil stability and therefore the prevention of erosion.

Peat: accumulation of poorly decomposing plant remains in a waterlogged environment to a depth over 30 cm.

Podzol: a soil showing distinctive ash-coloured near surface horizon due to accumulation of iron from above horizons. It commonly occurs after severe leaching and especially on silica-rich parent materials.

Pores: voids (sometimes tubular, sometimes fissure-like) within a soil left because of poor packing of soil particles or the formation of soil structures. The biggest pores are between structural units.

Structure: patterns of aggregated particles within a soil (e.g. particles arranged in small, roughly spherical clusters a few mm across are said to have a **crumb** structure; clusters that form cubes, a centimeter or so across, have a **cubic** structure (also **prismatic** (elongated in vertical direction) and **platey** (platelike shape).

Texture: the proportion of various sized particles in a soil made from (a) sand ($> 60\mu m$ diameter); (b) silt ($60-2$ μm diameter); and (c) clay ($>2\mu$ diameter). Larger particles are called stones for soil purposes: loam is a textural name for roughly equal proportions of sand, silt and clay.

Translocation: the movement of soil constituents from one region of a soil to another.

Chapter 14
Soil management and the future

The disappearing planet

WHEN spring ploughing begins in north China, an air sampling station at Mauna Loa in Hawaii can detect it within days, at a distance of over 5,000 kilometres. The losses of China's prairie soils, blown so far out to sea, are a significant but still small part of an immense global problem. The world's soils are being eroded so fast that, by the end of the century, there will be one third less topsoil per person than there is now. And in case you think that this is a problem largely confined to the dustbowls of the American mid-West or to the crumbling, terraced valley slopes of Nigeria, down in Somerset substantial quantities of fertile soil are suffering a similar fate.

A recent report* by Lester Brown and Edward Wolf of the Worldwatch Institute points up the severity of soil erosion and its implications for future agricultural production worldwide. Between 1977 and 1982, 1.7 billion tonnes of soil were lost each year in the US; 44 per cent of American farmland is now losing soil faster than it is being replaced, mainly by it being washed and blown away. Crop monoculture is largely to blame, and productivity has been maintained only by massive doses of fertilisers which have so far succeeded in masking the enormity of the losses.

In the developing countries, where sustained (or increased) agricultural crop productivity is essential, the reasons for soil erosion vary. Ploughing further and further up the slopes of fertile valleys without constructing terraces to properly hold the soil can cause incredible losses, mainly by rain washing the soils out. Studies in Nigeria with cassava crops show that on a 1 per cent slope, three tonnes of soil are lost per hectare annually. on a 5 per cent slope the loss jumps to 87 tonnes per hectare and on a 15 per cent slope, an unbelievable 221 tonnes of soil per hectare are lost. In parts of the tropics where shifting cultivation is traditional, the food demands of an increasing population are reducing the time inter-vals when land is allowed to lie fallow between cultivations from 10-15 years down to 5 years. Poor tropical soils then fail to regain enough fertility to support crops, compounding the effects of soil erosion.

Where does eroded soil end up? Much of it is blown over land and out to sea, often for many thousands of kilometres, hence north China soil being detected at Mauna Loa every spring. Soil eroded by water runoff ends up in streams and rivers, eventually emptying into lakes, reservoirs and the sea. It invariably ends up in places where it does no good and may do harm.

As Brown and Wolf's report states: "Grave though the loss of topsoil may be, it is a quiet crisis, one that is not widely perceived. And unlike earthquakes, volcanic eruptions or other natural disasters, this human-made disaster is unfolding gradually. What is at stake is not merely the degradation of soil, but the degradation of life itself."

Malcolm Smith
The *Guardian*, 9 May 1985

Introduction

Soil is a vital resource in a world where an increasing population demands greater production of food and materials. Soil management concerns the techniques required to maximise agricultural productivity while causing least environmental damage. Misuse of soils, apparent in degraded, eroded and waste land, is a clear reflection of past and existing failures to understand and manage the soil adequately.

The erosion of soil as part of landscape formation is a perfectly normal part of the landscape's evolution – it has been happening for hundreds of millions of years. The term 'soil erosion', however, tends to be used to describe an *acceleration* of this natural process. The rapid removal of soil following overgrazing, intensive cultivation or de-forestation, the formation of rills and gullies and the clouds of dust whipped up by the wind; all this is 'soil erosion' (Fig. 14.1). However, soil erosion is only part of the problem, for soil degradation is a more widespread and insidious problem. Degradation concerns the overuse or misuse of a soil such that its fertility declines and thus it becomes less productive.

(a)

Figure 14.1 *Examples of soil erosion*

(b)

The problem of soil erosion

The 'disappearing planet' article on this page outlines some of the problems associated with soil erosion. Perhaps the most serious effect is the removal of considerable thickness of valuable topsoil, a problem which exists throughout the world. Once agriculturally prosperous areas have been turned into bare, infertile plains. Much in the news over the last few years has been the term desertification. This is where overgrazing of fragile soils, particularly in the sub-Saharan region of Africa called the Sahel, has rendered huge areas of land virtually useless. Here, soil is rapidly removed by wind and rain as all the protective vegetation has been destroyed.

One of the most famous examples of soil erosion which has become a lesson to all involved in land management is the case of the American 'Dust Bowl'. The dust storms of the 1930s were

(c)

Figure 14.2 *The Dust Bowl States. The contours indicate the number of days with dust storms or dusty conditions in March 1936*

the worst man-made environmental problem the United States has ever seen, whether measured in physical terms or by their human and economic impact. The dust bowl stretched across several states in the mid-west of the USA (Fig. 14.2). Its name stems from the vast clouds of dust (soil) that were whisked up into the sky from this drought-stricken and misused area and which culminated in huge clouds of soil blocking out the sun and turning the sky yellow as far away as Chicago. Its effects almost became taken for granted:

'When we reached western Oklahoma a dull fog gradually obscured the landscape, and as the wind whipped over the barren fields and swirled across the road, we realised that we were in the midst of a real "panhandle" dust storm. Furthermore, the storm continued without much abatement for seven of the eight days we spent on the ranch near Arnett' (Fig. 14.3) (reported in 1932).

'This state (Kansas) is like a big, dusty blotter, 200 by 400 miles in size. Countless tons of rain fall on it every year, but as some complain "the rains don't stick", so it has bad floods.

'All over the west you hear talk about dust

Figure 14.3 *Effects of the Dust Bowl*

storms ...the material that moves through the air is not sand, but good, honest dirt, fine soil from the fields. It all started from plowing up buffalo grass, that great natural carpet that used to spread over so much of the West... but the plowing up of that sod covering, together with improper tillage and the abandonment of large acreages has added to dust storm problems during very dry years. There is now a popular demand for restoration of grass to check these dust storms, but the natural revegetation of land in W. Kansas will take 25 years or more...' (reported in 1937).

The economic and social consequences of the dust storms were aggravated by two reinforcing problems – drought and depression – that made recovery very much more difficult. In 1937 the Soil Conservation Service estimated that 43 per cent of a 64 000 km² area in the heart of the Dust Bowl had been seriously damaged by wind erosion. In some southern plains counties more than half of all farm families were on state social aid in 1935.

For about a century, plains agriculture has followed a boom or bust pattern. Before the arrival of the first settlers – the cattlemen – the undisturbed ecosystem changed in response to variations in weather, but the alterations to the land brought by wave after wave of settlers magnified the impact of the weather cycles. The conversion of the plains from grassland to cultivated crops was accomplished by waves of optimistic farmers arriving during periods of favourable rainfall. But each period was followed by serious drought, leading to dust storms, bankruptcies, foreclosures and out-migrations. The period of the 1930s was made exceptional only by the world depression and the low prices that could be obtained for corn. Thus, farmers had so little money in the bank from crop sales that they simply couldn't survive the period of low yields that accompanied the onset of the drought; and because they hadn't the money to plant crops, the soil lay bare and vulnerable.

By 1937 the horrific dust storms of the 'dirty thirties' had struck to the hearts of the people in the US and popular opinion had already been mobilised. But from the outset the Soil Conservation Service was predicting recovery time in decades. Note also that the problem involved not just wind erosion but also water erosion, and that both were partly caused by mismanagement of land.

In its 1937 report the Great Plains Committee criticised the view that 'an owner may do with his property as he likes'. They commented that 'all too frequently what appears to be of immediate good to the individual in the long run is not good for the people of the region'. People also harboured a false philosophy of the inexhaustibility of land and soil resources.

At the time there was much controversy as to how to deal with this problem. The committee quoted above takes what could be regarded as the middle ground. But at one extreme there were those who maintained that dust storms were a purely natural phenomenon in which man was the innocent victim, while at the other extreme some people maintained that the only solution was to abandon cultivation and return the whole area to pasture. As it happens it has subsequently been demonstrated that crop production need not result in excessive erosion.

Eventually the US government saw that changes in land use practices required massive federal intervention since the problems of the Dust Bowl were regional and beyond the ability of individuals or even states to solve for themselves. (Note: this is an important lesson when thinking of how best to deal with the present desertified areas of Africa.)

In the 1970s the Dust Bowl suffered another period of crisis, although not widely reported. And this happened despite lessons learned about management because production had been stretched on to yet more fragile soil. Ironically, this time it was produced when a period of drought coincided with US farmers being urged to expand their cultivation in order to beat the 'world food crisis' caused by desertification in Africa and elsewhere. To 'feed the world' wheat prices were made premium and people dutifully (or commercially) turned every last hectare over to wheat. Support was taken away after only a few years, however, and the prices fell. By 1977 some wheat land was taken out of production as part of the price support programme. Once again, management could be profitable, at least for a while.

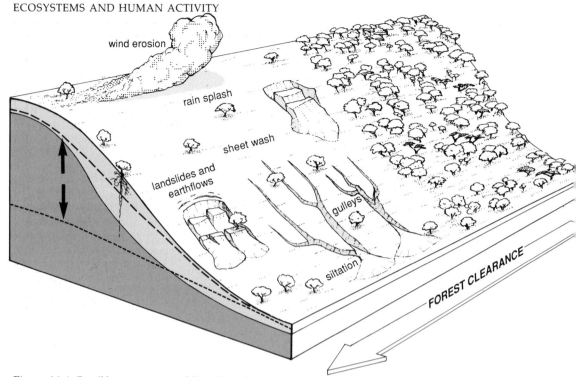

Figure 14.4 *Possible consequences of disturbing the natural ecosystem*

The causes of soil erosion

Accelerated erosion of soil will mainly result from wind and water action, although mass movement may also be important locally on steeply sloping areas. The effect of these processes is exacerbated by exposure of the soil following vegetation removal (Fig. 14.4). The removal of vegetation has a number of direct effects:

(a) soil particles will no longer be bound together by plant roots;

(b) rain will no longer be intercepted and the soil will suffer the full effects of rain splash;

(c) lack of humus (sticky, thread-like material that binds the soil) will cause the soil aggregates gradually to fall apart, thus making the individual mineral particles more liable to erosion; and

(d) there will be no protection from the wind.

Management (conservation) measures

A growing world population puts ever increasing pressure on the land to produce greater food yields. We cannot stop cultivation as a means of preventing soil erosion; instead, we need to modify our methods so that agriculture can be practised in such a way as to cause minimum environmental damage.

There are a variety of management measures employed throughout the world. These are mostly aimed at reducing the effect of wind and water erosion. Conservation systems can be either cultural and/or biological or physical (Fig. 14.5).

(a) Measures against wind loss can be achieved to a limited extent by windbreaks, and more thoroughly by cover crops, strip cropping, inter cropping or agroforestry.

(b) measures against water erosion are more diverse. They involve (i) contour farming; (ii) establishing infiltration zones; (iii) producing buffer strips; (iv) strip cropping; (v) growing trees; (vi) mulching; (vii) employing new forms of rotation that put organic matter back into the soil; (viii) adding fertilisers that contain divalent cations (e.g. Ca^{2+}) to stabilise the clays; (ix) using a cover crop rather than clean tilling; (x) agroforestry; (xi) digging cut-off drains; (xii) constructing artificial waterways; (xiii) building

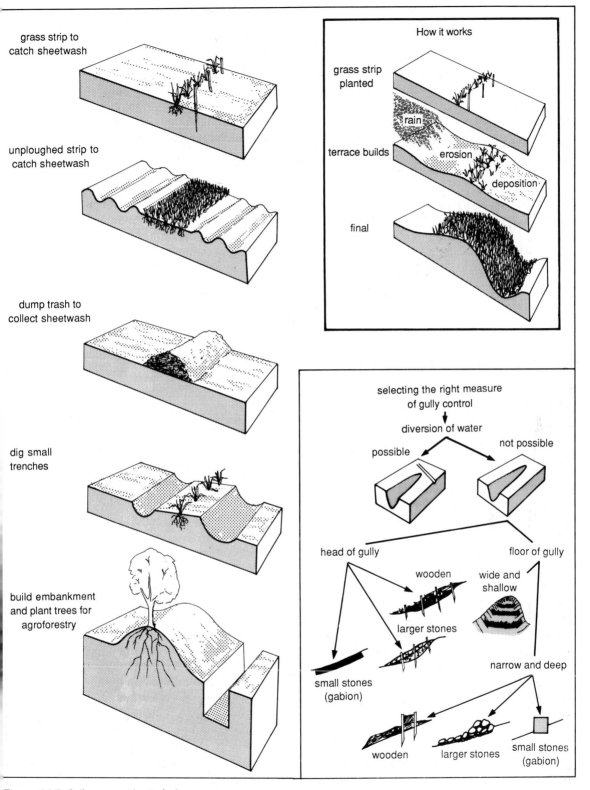

Figure 14.5 *Soil conservation techniques*

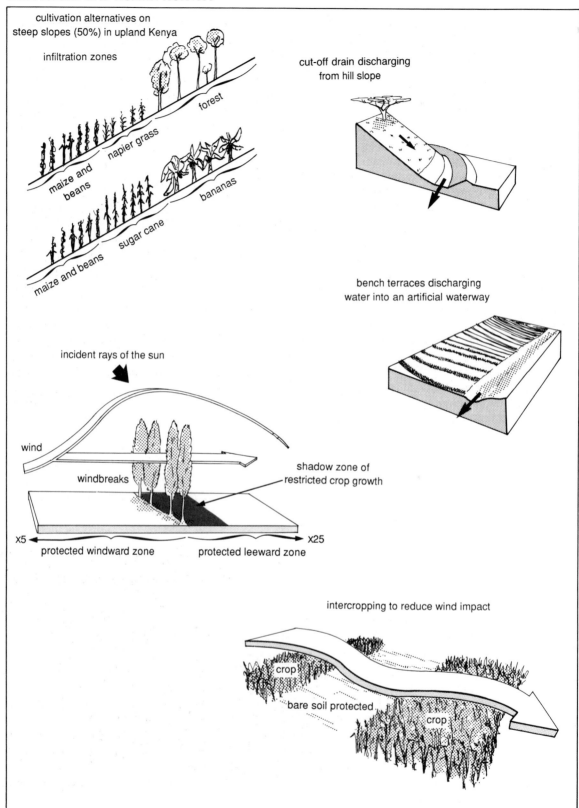

cultivation alternatives on
steep slopes (50%) in upland Kenya

infiltration zones

forest

napier grass

maize and
beans

bananas

sugar cane

maize and beans

cut-off drain discharging
from hill slope

bench terraces discharging
water into an artificial waterway

incident rays of the sun

wind

windbreaks

shadow zone of
restricted crop growth

x5

x25

protected windward zone

protected leeward zone

intercropping to reduce wind impact

crop

bare soil protected

crop

Figure 14.5 *(continued)*

Figure 14.6 *A close-up of a soil with strong structure. Notice how these large aggregates would be difficult to move by wind or water action*

water-deflecting bunds; and (xiv) constructing terraces.

The actual measures adopted depend very much on the specific characteristics of the area concerned. Climate is of great significance. To appreciate fully the application of soil management, we will study three different climatic regions.

Humid environments with low intensity (depression) rainfall (e.g. W Europe, north-east N America)

Soils produced in these environments tend to have a high clay and humus content. They are structurally quite strong and will bind together even when exposed in a cultivated field (Fig. 14.6). The frequent, but not intense, rainfall keeps the soil moist which also serves to increase the cohesion.

So, at first sight, these environments would not appear to suffer much soil erosion. How-ever, there is quite severe erosion in certain localities where, for example, the soil has a high sand content, or where there is a steeply ploughed field. The Fens of East Anglia have also suffered frequent 'Fen blows' (wind erosion) in the past, as the fertile peat soils have dried out on exposure.

Soil management measures involve maintaining a high humus content, and this is made possible by careful crop rotation. Windbreaks of trees are common especially in the arable lands of Cambridgeshire, but the area for which they provide cover is limited, and tree belts often conflict with the need for large fields on which to use machinery efficiently. Growing of winter cereals is a useful way of maintaining a vegetation cover (Fig. 14.7). For the future, farmers must continue to heed the example of the Dust Bowl if soils are to be conserved and yields maintained.

Figure 14.7 *Winter wheat. This photograph was taken in early spring, the time when soil is most vulnerable to wind erosion. Notice the additional protection from trees in the background*

Humid temperate environments with high intensity rainfall (e.g. Central Europe and southern USA)

Although soils are generally deep and loamy, the higher intensity rainfall means that sheet-wash is a major hazard even on gentle slopes (Fig. 14.8). Once exposed, these soils are not able to withstand erosion by wind and water – gullies will soon result if erosion goes unchecked. Some areas of the USA have been very seriously affected, particularly within the former cotton and tobacco belts. The following student activity will provide an insight into this environment.

Figure 14.8 *Some of the consequences of rainsplash and sheetwash are exposed tree roots. Clearly, considerable topsoil has to be lost before such exposure occurs*

Student enquiry 14A:
Management at Coon Creek Basin

Coon Creek (A1) lies in a region of dissected plateau in the state of Wisconsin. The rocks of the basin are friable sandstones and shales and the plateau has a cover of loess. The first settlers arrived in 1850, and by the time the first management measures were begun in 1933 soils had been severely depleted in fertility and eroded. (A2 top). Sediment from sheet, rill and gully erosion was more than the streams could handle and the main valleys were infilling by 2 m depth a year. The area had been managed in the way traditional to the West European colonists. The land was organised into rectangular fields even on rolling to steep slopes. This, together with poor crop rotations for the type of climate, lack of cover crops, the removal of crop residues and insufficient manuring led to nutrient depletion and very active erosion. Even pastures and woodland had become severely overgrazed as poor farmers tried ever more intensively to scrape a living off their degrading land.

Much of the erosion before about 1900 was by sheetwash and rills. It was confined to discontinuous areas on the few steep slopes then in cultivation. However, the progressive erosion of loamy topsoil exposed the heavier textured clay loam subsoil which was not only less fertile (because nutrients are generally recycled in the topsoil) but had a lower infiltration capacity. Exposure of subsoil thus further increased surface runoff. By 1930 it was stated that 'field gullies are common and a whole series from 6 inches to 3 feet deep can form in a field as the result of one hard rain if it occurs in a large field that is devoid of vegetation or in a clean tilled crop'. The result was not only field soil loss but severe deposition on the valley bottom pastures, often rendering them unusable. Cattle had to be moved from the floodplain pastures to the upland pastures and woods, an increase in land use that led to overgrazing, soil compaction and further erosion.

In about 1937 measures were begun to check the erosion and re-establish a stable environment. (A2 centre) This changing character of the land is clearly revealed in a sequence of photographs taken between 1905 and 1975 (A2).

1. Using the photographs describe the pattern of land use and evidence of erosion in 1905, in 1940 and again in 1975.

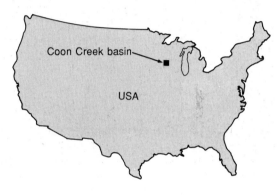

A1

A2

1905

1940

1975

A3

A. BEFORE PROGRAM
1933

ACREAGES 1933

Cropland	**57.0**
Corn	10.8
Alfalfa	5.8
Clover and timothy	9.5
Grain	28.0
Miscellaneous	2.9
Pasture	**75.7**
Open	19.5
Wooded	56.2
Farmstead, etc.	**5.3**
Total	**138.0**

B. AFTER PROGRAM
c. 1940

EXPLANATION

- ×—× Fence
- – – – Field boundary
- Waterway
- Terrace outlet
- Terraces
- Woods
- Diversion dike
- H Permanent hayland
- P Pasture
- 1, 4b Field numbers. See appendix I

Data from Coon Creek file, Soil Conservation Service State Office, Madison, Wisconsin

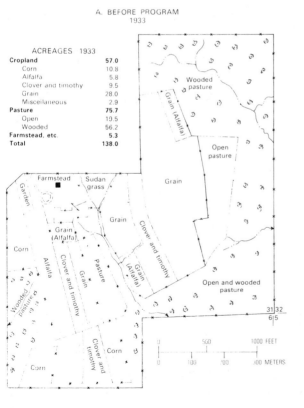
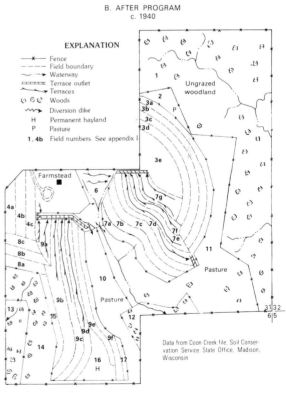

261

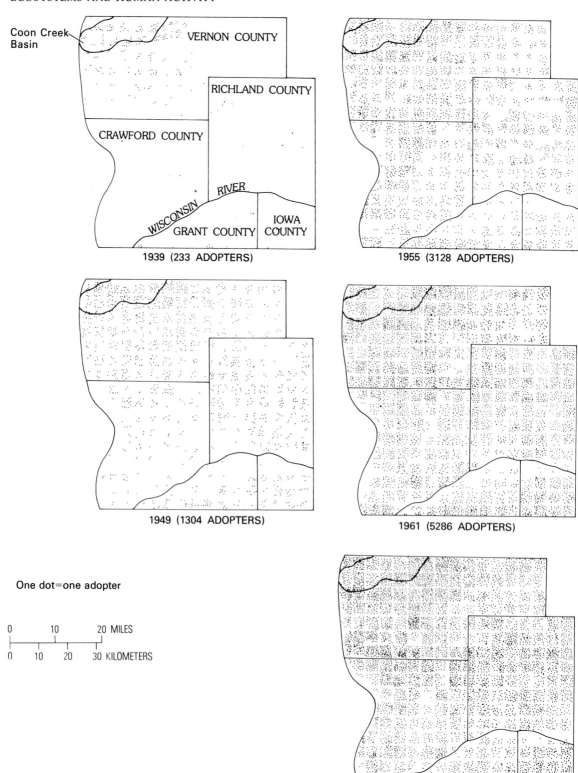

One dot=one adopter

A4 *Spread of contour-strip farming from the Coon Creek Conservation Demonstration Area, Wisconsin, 1939–67*

2. It is possible to quantify the losses of soil by the use of the universal soil loss equation (USLE) which states that:

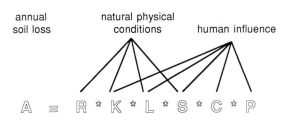

$$A = R * K * L * S * C * P$$

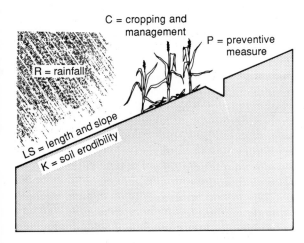

Table 14.1 gives data regarding soil loss for a variety of soils and land uses for 1934 and 1975. Copy and complete the table by calculating A (annual soil loss). Also express A in tonnes/km^2/yr.

3. Compare and contrast the rates of soil loss before and after treatment, paying special regard to the effect of each type of land use change. (Refer to A3).

4. How would such information be of assistance in planning for land use? What would be the economic restraints on implementing full management measures?

Table 14.1 Universal soil loss data for formerly eroded areas similar to Coon Creek, Wisconsin

Land use	RK	LS	CP	A
Woodland with				
no grazing	150	0.28	0.27	0.002
1934 pasture	150	0.28	0.27	0.04
1975 pasture	150	0.28	0.27	0.005
woodland with				
no grazing	150	0.37	4.97	0.002
1934 crop	150	0.37	4.97	0.45
1975 wood	150	0.37	4.97	0.003
woodland with				
no grazing	150	0.37	5.37	0.002
1934 crop	150	0.37	5.37	0.45
1975 crop	150	0.37	5.37	0.2

(Soil loss (tonne/km^2/yr) = A × 226)

A = RKLSCP
A = soil loss factor
R = rainfall factor
K = soil erodibility factor
L = slope length factor
S = slope gradient factor
C = crop management factor
P = erosion control factor (no control P = 1.0)
(units are dimensionless)

5. In recent experiments to find acceptable cultivation practices the values in Table 14.2 were obtained. Comment on the results and suggest an acceptable length of grass rotation, bearing in mind that economic yield from crops is higher than for grass.

6. On the new farms shown several management systems have been employed. Refer to (a) land use; (b) contour ploughing; and (c) terracing and describe how they work and their advantages in the situations where they have been employed.

7. In A4 you can see the pattern of adoption of the new management techniques. The spread of adoption is called an 'innovation wave'. Plot a graph of cumulative adopters against time and then describe the geographic and time pattern of the wave.

8. Drastic management measures were essential in land which was rapidly becoming a desert and have been widely adopted in vulnerable areas of the USA. However, with soil losses in the UK much less dramatic than the US, how would you expect UK farmers to react to management measures?

Tropical dry season environments (e.g. Central Africa)

Soils in these regions tend to be sandy and non-cohesive. They also have a low humus content. These characteristics make many tropical soils the most fragile in the world because, with very high intensity rainfall, sheetwash is widespread and gullies can form very easily (Fig 14.9).

These soils are at their most vulnerable at the start of the rainy season, when the vegetation has withered and the ground is dusty. On over-grazed lands, and those under cultivation that cannot be tilled until the ground is softened by rain, enormous quantities of soil can be lost in a few days. Management measures involve educating farmers in new management techniques, and trying to re-establish vegetation in those areas which have been over-cultivated. Enquiry 14B studies a Kenyan example.

Table 14.2 *Soil loss with grass in rotations for an experimental area using full management measures.*

number of years	soil loss (tonnes/km^2)
continuous grass in rotation	
1	2200
2	1300
3	800
4	700

Figure 14.9(a)

Figure 14.9(b) *Erosion near Kitui, Kenya*

**Student enquiry 14B:
The case of the Machakos-Kitui
region of Kenya**

Figure 14.9(a) and (b) show some scenes near Kitui which are typical of areas that have suffered overgrazing damage and severe erosion. In Kenya, as in the tropical world generally, rainfall intensity is higher than in temperate lands and typical USLE values are therefore startlingly high.

B1 shows the increase in annual soil loss with increase in slope and cumulative infiltration time.

B1(a)

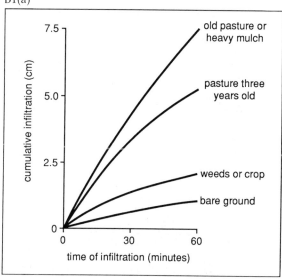

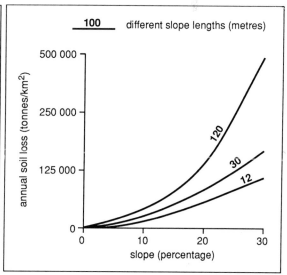

in humid tropics R = 500
in dry season tropics R = 200

K = 0.1 for sand and loamy sand (low because of high infiltration)
K = 0.4 for loam (high because of low infiltration and weak cohesion)
K = 0.1 for clay (low because of strong cohesion)

loams are typical of the savanna regions, and these are therefore the most vulnerable.

C for natural undisturbed forest and savanna	= 0.01
C for maize (sorghum, millet) and pineapple cultivation	0.7
C for cotton, tobacco	0.5
C for cover crop such as tea	0.2
C for thick straw mulch	0.001

P value for ploughing up and down slope = 1.0
for contour arming

slope degrees	contour	contour + strip cropping + rotation	contour + terracing
2–10	0.5	0.3	0.1
10–20	0.9	0.4	0.2
20+	1.0	0.5	not applicable

B1(b)

1. Using the information in Fig. 14.5, explain the advantages of the management system shown in B2.

2. Trace B3 and show how you would tackle the erosion problems indicated.

3. Suppose you have to advise a smallholder whose shamba (farm) is on a 15° slope and leads down from ridge to river for 200 m (B4). At present he has no form of management system and he plants maize, coffee, pineapples, bananas and vegetables. In this area the R value is 200, the LS value is 7.5 and the soil has a loam texture. Using the USLE from activity section 2.3, calculate the A value. Use data from Datafile B and convert this to soil loss/km^2/yr as shown in Table 14.1.

If the natural rate of topsoil formation is 1400 tonnes/km^2/yr how severe is the erosion problem faced by the farmer? How does this compare with the problems faced at Coon Creek?

4. Discuss some management systems that would help to correct the problem. Remember the farmer will need educating in management techniques; he also has to find fodder for two cows and four goats; he needs fuelwood for cooking and poles for building. His only labour is his family.

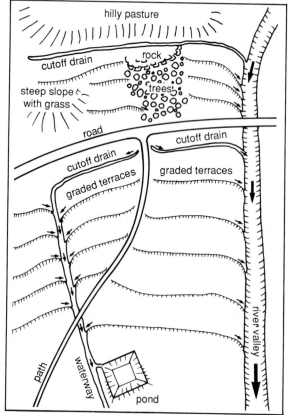

B2 *Siting of terraces or a slope*

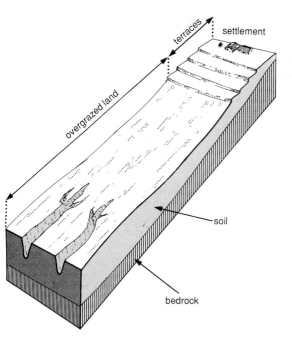

B3 *A farm with a cultivated, terraced upper slope and an overgrazed, gully eroded lower slope*

B4 *Farm near Ndarugu*

Key terms

Agroforestry: a system of planting, management and harvesting which combines agricultural crops and/or animals with trees.

Artificial waterway: is a wide and shallow drainage way down a slope, with a gradient of less than 2°. On steeper slopes check dams (sills) are required. Waterways are used at the end of cut-off drains or bench terraces to feed water to natural watercourses.

Buffer strips: are narrow strips of grass (2 m wide).

Bund: (for soil management purposes) a low earthen embankment built across a slope and designed to prevent sheetwash travelling further downslope.

Channel terrace: is created by embanking soil on the downslope side of a trench.

Conservation: the practical management techniques aimed at retaining maximum long term land productivity with minimum environmental damage.

Contour farming: is cultivating along the contour instead of up and down the slope.

Cut-off drain: an open trench dug across a slope with an embankment on the lower side.

Degrade: a general term referring to lowering the status of a soil, either by loss of fertility or by loss of soil mineral or organic constituents.

Desertification: the virtually irreparable degradation of a soil such that it is unusable for agriculture.

Developed terraces: are created when natural processes of sheetwash are controlled by trapping material on an infiltration strip or other water control structure.

Excavated bench terraces: terraces formed by extensive excavation. They are little used because they require much work and bring less fertile subsoil to the surface.

Infiltration zones: are permanent belts of grass set upslope of a cropped area.

Mulching: is using dead plant residues to cover the ground against splash.

Ridge terrace: involves moving the soil from two trenches to form an intervening ridge.

Strip cropping: is the use of alternate bands of grass and crops, forming part of a rotation.

Terrace: (for soil management purposes) is either a level piece of ground on a slope, or a hillside ditch or ridge for controlling the flow of surface water down a slope.

Index

Acknowledgements

We are grateful to the following for permission to reproduce photographs and other copyright material: Australian Overseas Information Service, London, page 46 *below*; Barnaby's Picture Library, page 75; Mr G. De Boer, page 104; Cambridge University Collection of Air Photographs, page 196 (inset); Camera Press, page 180; J. Allan Cash, pages 53 *above left*, 151 *below*, 160 *above*; John Cleare/Mountain Camera, page 145; Bruce Coleman, page 230; Fermilab Photo Department, page 238; The Fotomas Index Library, London, page 67; Grand Teton Natural History Association, National Park Service, Department of the Interior, page 237; *The Guardian*, pages 39 *below*, 250; George Hunter, page 133 *below*; Mr R Jessop T.D, MA, page 50 *above*; Frank Lane Picture Agency, pages 53 *above right* (NOAA), 53 *below* (US Dept of Commerce, Weather Bureau), 129 *centre* (Steve McCutcheon), 129 *below* (Hall Lee Canal, Zernez), 190 (Peter Reynolds); Library of Congress, page 14; Maps Alberta, Forestry, Lands & Wildlife, Bureau of Surveying & Mapping, page 174; Mount St. Helens National Volcanic Monument, page 32–33, NASA, page 84 *below*; NOAA/NESDIS/NCDC/SDSD, page 51; *Natural Hazards Observer*, pages 4 *above*, 5, 22, 64, 83 *above*, 103, 129 *above*, 151 *above*, 182, 201, 215 *above*; Peter Newarks Western Americana, page 252 *below*; *New Civil Engineer*, page 73; *New Scientist*, pages 142, 215 *below right*; Ordnance Survey, page 99 *above*; Peter Charlesworth/Panos Pictures, page 39 *above right*; Rapho, page 147; Keith Ronnholm, page 24; Science Photo Library, pages 78 *centre* (NASA), 78 *below* (NASA); Southwest Water Authority, page 64; *Sunday Times*, page 28; The Swedish NGO Secretariat on Acid Rain, page 60; The Telegraph Colour Library, page 41; Tendring District Council, pages 119, 121 *above*; Tropix Photo Library, page 50 *below* (R. Cansdale); UTGITT AV, page 4 *below*; United States Department of the Interior, Geological Survey, pages 9, 10, 16, 17, 46 *below*, 114, 177 *above*, 260, 261, 262; US Corps of Engineers, page 210; Mr Andrew Warren, Dept of Geography, University College of London, page 160 *below*; University of Dundee, page 59; The map on page 196 was based upon the Ordnance Survey map with the permission of the Controller of HMSO, Crown Copyright reserved.

We are unable to trace any information of copyright holders of the following, and would appreciate receiving any information that would enable us to do so; pages 15, 26, 35, 39 *above left*, 140, 199.

We are also grateful to the following for permission to reproduce copyright material: National Swedish Environment Protection Board for diagrams from *Acid Magazine*; diagram from T J Chandler : *The Climate of London*, publ, Century Hutchison; The Daily Telegraph Plc for articles from the *Daily Telegraph* 'Thaw today after snow battering' by Charles Nevin (14.12.81) & 'No end in sight yet' by Con Coughling (12.12.81); figures and diagrams from *Ambio* /Royal Swedish Academy of Science; IPC Magazines Ltd for articles & diagrams from *New Scientist* 'Acid rain may trigger Alpine Avalanches' by Debora MacKenzie (2.1.86. p10), 'Caicos may play host to American Sewage' by Andrew Kerr (31.7.86. p19), 'Pesticides threaten British Wildlife' by Michael Rands & Nick Sotherton (4.7.85), 'African Violet may disappear from the wild' by Martin Redfern, 'How large dams have become fashionable', 'Who will save the Caribbean?' by Stephanie MacKenzie (5.11.81), 'Tapping a World resource (1.11.84); the Author, Dr. Malcolm Smith for his article 'The disappearing planet' from *The Guardian* 9.5.85; Times Newspapers Ltd for the articles and diagrams 'How death came by night to Urirchar' by Michael Hamlyn in *The Times* 28.5.85, 'San Francisco Earthquake' in *The Times* 1906, Clues emerge on quake damage buildings' by Dan Williams in *The Times* 10.85 '20,000 feared dead after volcano erupts' by Tony Jenkins in *The Times* 14.11.85, 'How Rol turned the tide of History' by Dalbert Hallenstein in *The Sunday Times* 15.5.83, 'Slow flow warnings on the river of death' by Gareth Huw Davies in *The Sunday Times* 16.11.86; all (c) Times Newsapapers Ltd. adapted scale diagrams from Uhl & Jordan: reprinted by permission of the Ecological Society of America; *The Geographical Magazine*, London; tables and chart from *World Resources* 1986, produced by the World Resources Institute and the Institute fo International Environment and Development. We have unfortunately been unable to trace th copyright holder of the article 'Shrugging of winter's cold' by the late Donald Fields from *The Guardian* 21.2.85 and would appreciate an information which would enable us to do so.